Tom A. Steffen

Passing the Baton

Church Planting That Empowers

Passing the Baton: Church Planting that Empowers

Published by:

Center for Organizational & Ministry Development
120 East La Habra Blvd., Suite 107
La Habra, CA 90631
Phone: 562 / 697-6144; 800 / 604-2663; Fax: 562 / 691-2081
E-mail: 76344.1632@CompuServe.com

Request additional copies from the above address or:

Dr.Tom A. Steffen
Biola University, School of Intercultural Studies
13800 Biola Ave., La Mirada, CA 90639
Phone: 562 / 903-4844; Fax: 562 / 903-4851;
E-mail: tom_steffen@biola.edu

Cover design: Steve Barber

ISBN 1-882757-02-5

Printed in the United States of America

This book is dedicated to:

My dear friend, Claire Mellis
My supportive parents, Manny and Ruth Steffen
My beautiful wife and best friend, Darla
Our three lovely daughters, Dawn, Lori, and Wendy

Requests for copies should be addressed to:

Center for Organizational & Ministry Development
120 E. La Habra Blvd., Suite 107, La Habra, CA 90631
Phone: 562 / 697-6144; 800 / 604-2663; Fax: 562 / 691-2081
E-mail: 76344.1632@CompuServe.com

The Center for Organizational & Ministry Development (COMD) is a resource and support organization serving the Christian Community. The mission of the Center is to facilitate and catalyze ministries of individuals and organizations in advancing the kingdom of God throughout the world. COMD fulfills its mission through the pursuit of five objectives:

1. Identifying and equipping North American and cross-cultural church planters.
2. Assisting individuals in personal assessment, career development, and ministry enhancement.
3. Providing support service to the church growth and extension process.
4. Assisting Christian agencies and groups in organizational development.
5. Equipping and training individuals for the task of organizational and ministry development.

TABLE OF CONTENTS

PART FIVE: POSTEVANGELISM

PART SIX: CHALLENGE AND CONCLUSION

1

Introduction

Our adrenaline ran high as the jet touched down in the Philippines. At last our long-anticipated dream of planting tribal churches capable of reproducing themselves was to become a reality. To accomplish this, my wife and I, along with our two young daughters, planned to live for a time among an animistic tribe—the Antipolo/Amduntug Ifugao who numbered approximately 3,500—in the mountains of central Luzon. All our preparation had been directed toward eventually working ourselves out of a job as soon as the churches themselves could begin to assume the reproducing responsibility.

We had just completed two hard years of intensive study in the USA. Those who trained us began by teaching us how to learn a new language, conduct a cultural analysis and meet basic physical needs in order to live in the tropics. They also taught us how to develop literacy training materials and teach from them, how to translate Scripture, and how to evangelize and disciple new believers. Emphasis was placed on the importance of developing national church leadership as quickly as possible, in the belief that this would not only be better for the newly planted churches, but would facilitate our departure. Those who trained us were confident that we could accomplish any of these areas if called upon to do so. The goal was to plant churches based on the "three-selfs" model: that is, self-supporting, self-governing and self-propagating. Although by now we fully realized that planting tribal churches would not be easy, we nevertheless felt well-equipped for the task. And it was now time to translate our training into action.

Shortly after arriving in the Philippines I was invited into the office of Bob Gustafson, our field leader. He issued me a challenge: on the one hand he invited me to speak up when questions arose in my mind about comments I heard or practices I observed, noting that older missionaries sometimes tend to become entrenched in the way things have always been done. On the other hand, he reminded me that new missionaries have much to learn about living and working in a different culture, and that there may be valid reasons for the way things are being done. In effect, he challenged me to become both a *learner* and a *contributor.*

Observations

As a young missionary to the Philippines I questioned as many veteran church planters as I could about their ministry experiences on the different islands. It soon became apparent to me that a wide gap existed between what I had been taught about turning churches over to nationals and what actually happened on the field. In fact, I was unable to find even *one* national church that had been regarded capable enough to be given the responsibility of handling its own affairs. Reluctantly, I had to admit that my mission agency lacked a successful "three-self" model in the Philippines. No church planting team had successfully phased out of their ministries so that nationals could control their own churches—*and this after almost a quarter of a century of sacrificial missionary effort.*

Analysis

Trying to be a learner, I began to analyze my agency's activities over the years to see if I could identify reasons for such a dismal track record of turning churches over to nationals in the Philippines. My research revealed a number of factors that no doubt contributed: 1) field strategies evolved piecemeal, apparently to meet needs of new field members. For example, since language and culture were obviously the first tools required by missionaries to function effectively in ministry, these usually were given top priority. 2) Scripture translation and community development followed in the form of medical work and literacy. 3) Only as these two phases were cared for did the attention begin to shift to the matter of church planting.

Needs-based Strategy

This piecemeal approach tended to make each ministry component an end in itself rather than an intregal part to complete the overall task of planting churches capable of reproducing themselves. Thus the approach was needs-based or needs-oriented; a comprehensive field-wide strategy was lacking.

Individual team members, possibly because of the lack of an overall field strategy, tended to focus more on "phase-in" activities (e.g., evangelism and discipleship) than on "phase-out" activities (e.g., activities that would empower nationals to develop leadership among themselves with an eye toward ministry that reproduces). Team members, following the lead of field leaders, followed suit. They implemented the piecemeal activities individually instead of taking the stated objective of planting churches that reproduce and then integrate all the various activities, directing them toward that one goal. Team members tended to view ministry with "phase-in eyes" rather than "phase-out eyes."

A later survey of missionary writings confirmed the emphasis on various individual steps towards church planting rather than on integrated activities that bring closure to missionary involvement. Some literature focused on contextualization by way of emphasis on worldview and/or cultural themes; some emphasized strategies and communication techniques for evangelism and some emphasized biblical and theological perspectives. But in all the literature surveyed there was no model that integrated all the various perspectives (of theology, anthropology, linguistics, strategy, worldview, management principles, and communication) into a single comprehensive "phase-out" oriented model for pioneer church planting (see Appendix A).

Withdrawal

With the lack of an overall integrated strategy, it is not surprising that most team members never really knew when it was an appropriate time to leave. They had no basic checklist against which to measure progress. Missionaries rightly worried about departing prematurely, leaving congregations unable to carry on independently; and they worried about overextending their stay. They became frustrated as they knew that either decision could impede the development of the national believers.

Role Changes

In order for nationals to be released to carry on effective church leadership and church maintenance, it is important for them to pass through certain transition stages where ministry roles change. My colleagues lacked understanding of just what was involved in such role changes that help assure effective and successful withdrawal. But what are these anticipated role changes for expatriates? For nationals? Are there identifiable role changes that result in responsible phase-out (i.e., a national church capable of making it on its own)? What sort of church planting candidates should a mission agency select to assure effective role transitions? Is there a special kind of training that will produce church planters who think and act with an "empowering mentality?"

An Integrated Approach

My analysis of the Philippine field situation revealed a number of factors that no doubt contributed to the lack of even one church being placed completely in the hands of nationals. 1) On the team level, members lacked a comprehensive church planting strategy; one that incorporated role changes for withdrawal, dealt with key questions and faith objectives for each stage of the church plant, and provided a checklist to determine progress made toward the overall goal. 2) On the field level, a piecemeal strategy had developed over the years which meant that the strategy employed was determined by the changing needs of the various field members. 3) On the agency level, the candidate selection and training process tended to perpetuate and reinforce paternalistic church planting procedures.

Unfortunately, because a systemic approach to church planting was lacking, no criteria was in place for adequately selecting and building teams of church planters with a focus on empowering national believers to lead their own congregations. Inevitably, practices on the field will reflect an agency's philosophy of church planting, which in turn will affect, positively or negatively, the strategy chosen by the various teams on the field.

A Personal Case Study

After completing one year of studying the national language in Lipa City, Philippines, we moved into Dugyo, Ifugao to begin our ministry. There we joined Dick and Lou Hohulin, Bible translators affiliated with Wycliffe Bible Translators / Summer Institute of Linguistics, who had invited us earlier to shoulder the responsibilities of church planting and development among the Antipolo / Amduntug Ifugao. We looked forward to seeing how God would raise up nationals capable of multiplying the churches planted.

But in learning about the Ifugao we began to experience frustration. Throughout our time of language and culture study, we had become increasingly convinced that the tools for these two disciplines should be more effectively integrated. One could easily be tempted to focus on one or the other, depending upon personal preference. Although my preference would pull me toward culture study, I recognized both to be essential if personal acceptance, evangelism and church planting were to be effective.

To be personally accepted within the Ifugao community called for knowing a number of things: greetings, departures, etiquette; how to build relationships, demonstrate love, resolve conflict. Evangelism and church planting, on the other hand, called for familiarizing oneself with a number of key terms and topics the Ifugao use to express their view of the visible and invisible world. We knew we needed both language and culture.

We could assess our progress in language learning in two ways. The first involved the texts used to study the Filipino national language, Tagalog (all Filipino languages have similar grammatical patterns). The second involved Nida's (1950) five levels of language learning, subsequently revised by Brewster and Brewster (1976).

However, we found no equivalent tool to measure our progress in culture learning. Although we worked through the "Universals Outline" (an adaptation of Murdock's 1961 outline), provided by our agency, we found it difficult to gauge our level of cultural competency.

As more Ifugao responded to the gospel, we moved beyond evangelism to discipling new believers, but at the same time we felt we lacked clear direction. During this stage, neither my wife nor I really knew where we were relative to our overall goal. What should we accomplish before leaving the Ifugao? Perhaps some short-range objectives would provide a clue about our progress in reaching our long-term objective.

We were discovering that both Filipino and expatriate colleagues, who ministered among other people groups, were asking similar questions about when to leave a new congregation. Their frustration apparently was equal to ours. All of us felt handicapped by the lack of a comprehensive plan to attain an identifiable point at which to withdraw and the lack of tools adequate for analyzing the people we came to reach. At this point I began to formulate a simple, four-stage model to be used for pioneer church planting.

A Plan Evolves

Before we took up residence among the Ifugao in 1972, I discussed strategy with our field director for planting new congregations. Both of us were looking to God to break the emphasis on missionary-controlled church planting that dominated our field for over two decades. We were eager to see churches among the Ifugao that were *completely* and *responsibly* led by Ifugao believers. To avoid repeating this same control pattern among the Antipolo / Amduntug Ifugao, I proposed a specific plan designed to empower national believers to multiply their own churches.

After making two hiking surveys and an aerial survey, followed by conferring with the Hohulins, we decided to plant three churches in strategic areas, and then launch a force of believers to reach the rest of the area and even cross tribal borders. We set a target period of two terms (eight years) to achieve this goal. Our plan incorporated the idea that Ifugao Christians would continue to plant new churches after our departure. Because the geographical area in which the approximate 3,500 Antipolo / Amduntug Ifugao live was small, we believed our goal quite realistic.

Implementing our plan called for the following: the Hohulins agreed to provide the New Testament, a hymnal, and literacy materials. Our challenge was to learn the language and culture, work to meet felt needs, teach the gospel, develop respected local leaders, facilitate the planting of reproducing churches in key locations, tie the churches together and oversee the development of written and taped Bible study materials. If our plan succeeded, we were certain the Ifugao could continue on their own without outside assistance by (or before) the end of eight years. This result, of nationals directing their own churches, would be a "first" for the Philippine field.

As we reflected on our Philippine field's, and mission agency's closure strategy, we realized we desperately needed a church planting model that would not bog us down with unnecessary details, but instead keep us focused on a phase-out departure. To facilitate this I proposed a model that I believed would meet both these criteria. This proposal consisted of a comprehensive, phase-out oriented church planting model with five distinct stages: (a) Preentry, (b) Preevangelism, (c) Evangelism, (d) Post-evangelism, and (e) Phase-out. See Appendixes A and B.

Preentry Stage

The Preentry Stage addresses the matter of preparation for those individuals interested in cross-cultural church planting. This includes preparation scholastically and experientially, in Bible, the social sciences, in ministry (including cross-cultural), and in other related areas. During this preentry stage, the church planters establish their prayer and financial bases, and begin to form a multi-gifted team. Ideally, the team members spend time getting to know each other in social activities, as well as work-related activities. They also design strategies to foster team loyalty, unity and productivity. They then begin to learn the national language of their host country. They review literature on the target communities, they consult with national churches and mission agencies, they conduct various types of surveys, and design a preliminary overall phase-out strategy for reaching the target people.

Preevangelism Stage

The Preevangelism Stage begins when team members move into their target location. During this stage emphasis is placed on learning. More specifically, the team members strive to achieve level four in language and culture acquisition simultaneously. During this time, they also address felt needs, develop quality relationships with key individuals in the community, and ask penetrating questions which cause nationals to reflect on their worldview. All of these together lay the groundwork for the next stage: Evangelism.

Evangelism Stage

The Evangelism Stage finds team evangelists continuing to assist in meeting felt needs, setting a firm foundation for the gospel and presenting an accurate gospel message. All of these activities are to be done in a culturally relevant way. By identifying and focusing on key decision-makers of the community, the team's multiple efforts result in the birth of new communities of faith.

Postevangelism Stage

During the Postevangelism Stage, the team members work for quantitative and qualitative growth. Their aim is to provide a conducive atmosphere, and personal example, for the ongoing development of: (a) philosophy of ministry, (b) meaningful worship, (c) indigenous leadership, (d) biblical functional substitutes, (e) avenues for meeting social needs, (f) outreach strategies to reproduce themselves, (g) teaching, (h) pertinent literature, (i) effective means for literature distribution, and (j) church and mission associations. Strategically, team members begin to work themselves out of their respective ministries in the move toward phase-out.

Phase-out Stage

In the Phase-out Stage, the team members program longer absences from their respective ministries. This will help enable the eventual and total withdrawal of the team physically, but not relationally. Team members continue to work toward completion of the objectives established during preentry and preevangelism, and revised during the evangelism and postevangelism stages. Thus, the withdrawal comes a little at a time, until the various ministries are left totally in the hands of the nationals. Such a comprehensive model moves from *preparing,* to *perceiving,* to *presenting,* to *perfecting,* to *parting.* More importantly, it prepares the way for nationals to introduce the Christian world to new insights about God and Christianity.

The Purpose of This Study

The intent of this book, therefore, is to present a comprehensive, Kingdom-based, phase-out oriented church planting model designed for cross-cultural contexts. In this model, clear role changes for church planters and nationals are developed; basic tools for accomplishing each stage are provided. Included are illustrations from the author's field ministry among the Ifugao, along with other field data and literature to supply concrete examples for each stage. The book includes a partial checklist field workers can develop to evaluate their specific ministry from preentry to phase-out. Although this model originated with an application to tribal and peasant people, the majority of the principles, such as role changes and phase-out, phase-out oriented ministry teams, a comprehensive evangelism-teaching model based on story, leadership and followership models, the Checklist in Appendix F, principles to establish functional substitutes, along with cultural and planning tools are certain to be germane to all urban church plants. Nor must urban church planters overlook the increasing numbers of recent arrivals from rural settings, or the approximate 70 percent of the world's population who prefer the concrete medium of communication.

Three Key Definitions

This book focuses on crosscultural pioneer church planting. While some no longer see a role for western pioneer church planters, opting for a facilitator role, I believe the pioneer role will continue to exist until the last unreached people group is reached (in every generation). I define pioneer church planting as the planting of multiplying churches in unreached areas of the world by individuals engifted and committed to this goal (Rom. 15:20).

I believe in Kingdom-based church planting (KCP). This means church planters take seriously the Great Commandment and the Great Commission, incorporating both into the overall strategy. I attempt to accomplish this through a team effort (which can be international) that identifies *ecclesia* with *missio Dei.* I define KCP as a team effort of multi-gifted and committed people who address the social and spiritual needs of an unreached people, resulting in members of the target population placing their allegiance in Christ as Savior from sin, congregating together, and empowered by the Holy Spirit and church planters to mature in their gifts and skills so that they can repeat the cycle in other unchurched areas, monoculturally and cross-culturally.

This book calls for church planters to phase-out of their respective roles so that nationals can phase in to them, hopefully fulfilling them far better than the itinerant team members. Some argue phase-out should never occur because chruch planters should never place themselves in roles that would require this exchange to happen. This argument misses on several points. It fails to consider the power residing in anyone conveying new ideas. The exchange of ideas, for example, Bible stories, is in reality an exchange of power, requiring role changes of both the teacher and the recipient. Secondly, it misses the function played by status and role, something present in every relationship. Lastly, new tasks, such as evangelism or teaching the Bible, require new skills. Church planters model these tasks until the nationals feel comfortable doing the same. I define phase-out as programed absences by the church planters that encourage nationals to take up their rightful responsibilities as leaders and multipliers of the church planting movement. This is much more than what David Bosch calls granting them a "certificate of maturity." It is responsible mentorship, the type of care Paul demonstrated to those to whom he ministered.

The Limitations of This Study

This book has several limitations. Due to the broad scope of the model presented, the focus of necessity is primarily on areas related specifically to cross-cultural pioneer church planting. Topics such as linguistics, language acquisition, Bible translation, literacy, medical, and agriculture are discussed only as they pertain to church planting. This is due to the breadth of the area of church planting, not because I consider these factors unimportant or unrelated. The multiple ministry roles fulfilled by the Hohulins and ourselves testify to our concern for holistic ministry.

This study concentrates on completing a church plant primarily from an expatriate church planter's perspective. Further study, which views withdrawal of the church planters from the perspective of nationals, is needed.

While this book assumes partnerships in team formation it does not deal specifically with this area. Nor does it address partnerships post-phase-out, even though I consider this a valid possibility if empowerment remains the functional goal.

Mapping Out The Journey Before Us

The book is divided into six parts. Part One discusses the Phase-out stage. This section defines responsible phase-out by isolating its components, clarifying role changes that are necessary for phase-out to become a reality, and developing a specific phase-out oriented church planter's profile designed to select church planters who desire to empower others.

The second part considers the Preentry Stage. This section points to certain inadequacies in my training: building a phase-out oriented team, processing the team's vision into action, and equipping team members with tools necessary to accomplish their vision.

The Preevangelism Stage is discussed in Part Three. Two socio-cultural aspects that call for attention in this stage include: integrative study guidelines, and interfacing the oral and print mediums.

Part Four addresses the Evangelism Stage. This section discusses two essential ingredients: an accurate presentation of the gospel and a comprehensive teaching model that will provide a firm foundation for that gospel.

The fifth part examines the Postevangelism Stage. Studies in this section focus on ways to develop national church leaders / planters, men and women capable of discerning biblical principles and applying these principles in culturally relevant ways.

The proposed five-stage church planting model moves beyond church growth. With roots embedded in an anthropological theory that stresses commonalties, church growth calls for dynamic equivalence. With such an emphasis, conflict and contradiction often receive inadequate attention. For this reason, this model includes contradictions as well as commonalties. The comprehensive model moves beyond an emphasis of planting a single church to an emphasis on multiplication of churches; it moves beyond the study of worldview to include economics and social organization; it moves beyond evangelism to Kingdom-based church planting; it moves beyond pastoring to developing indigenous leadership; it moves beyond phase-in to responsible phase-out. This model refuses to allow church planters to substitute pastoral robes for apostolic robes while at the same time providing the necessary pastoral care.

PART 1

Phase-out

"But now, since my work in these places no longer needs my presence....Let us go somewhere else....so I can preach there also....now that I am far away be keener than ever to work out the salvation that God has given you with a proper sense of awe and responsibility...
you long to see us, just as we also long to see you."

(Rom. 15:23, Phillips; Mark 1:38, New International Version; Phil. 2:12, Phillips; 1Thes. 3:6, New International Version)

2

Defining Phase-out

My former mission agency began church planting in the Philippines in 1951 and presently works among 19 tribal groups. After almost 40 years of dedicated missionary effort, *only one tribal work has been completely phased out because its objectives were met.* Why? Because neither the mission agency nor the church planters started with a clear definition of and plan for phase-out.

Without such a definition of phase-out, the church planters had no way to identify their necessary role changes, much less work through them. Furthermore, the agency did not include a phase-out philosophy in its recruiting, selection and training of church planters. Consequently, most of its church planters stayed on as evangelists and teachers, rather than becoming partners; they emphasized phase-in rather than phase-out. The Philippine field would wait almost two decades before communities of faith were completed according to proposed objectives. We desperately needed a definition of responsible phase-out.

Of course, church planters who leave prematurely may harm the church. But they can also harm it by staying too long. In the following pages I will discuss ways to maintain the delicate balance between these two extremes by: (1) surveying various perspectives of phase-out; (2) isolating its components; and (3) defining responsible phase-out.

Surveying Various Perspectives of Phase-out

This section looks at phase-out from three perspectives. The first briefly reviews the missiological roots pertaining to exit strategies. The second perspective considers some current thinking in relation to phase-out, while the last examines a New Testament perspective of departure.

Reviewing Exit Strategy Roots

The debate over when church planters should leave a group of believers is not new. Rufus Anderson and Henry Venn, both late nineteenth century mission strategists, were the first to expound the three-fold formula: self-government, self-support and self-propagation. (See: Williams 1990 for a helpful discussion.) They argued: missionaries who followed this formula would develop national led churches. While not everyone agreed with them, their formula stimulated phase-out thinking.

John Nevius (1829-1893) built on the "three-self formula" from a pragmatic perspective. Nevius used the three-selfs in China because they worked. Roland Allen (1868-1947) concluded that the formula was not only practical, but biblical. Allen argued the church expands spontaneously as the Holy Spirit is allowed freedom to work in the missionary (as he did in the life of Paul) and the converts. Much later, Alan Tippett added to the formula self-image, self-functioning and self-giving.

Others, William Read, Victor Monterroso, and Harmon Johnson (1969), promoted the idea of churches reaching autonomy from agencies by changing roles over time from apostolate to administrator to partner to servant to consultant. C. Peter Wagner (1971) argued no mission should be content to go out of business after a church is established. Rather, missionary work should move through four phases: (1) going to non-Christians, (2) church development, (3) becoming a consultant and (4) launching another mission. Harold Fuller (1980) saw mission-church relationships advancing through four stages: (a) pioneer, (b) parent, (c) partner and (d) participant. While these writers may not totally agree with Anderson, Venn or Allen, they nevertheless are not content to control new churches, or remain in a maintenance role.

Current Perspectives

A mission executive recently told me his leaders continue to struggle with responsible phase-out. While they often talk about turning things over to local Christians, much of their work continues as it has for 20 to 50 years. This executive, however, wants to empower local believers to take control within a much shorter time.

Another mission leader laments his organization's failure to focus on a church planting exit strategy as opposed to an entry strategy. He recognizes there is no way the church will keep pace with burgeoning world population if church planters are reluctant to release power swiftly to those they have come to reach. Like the first executive, he seeks to change the worldwide dependency patterns being instituted by his organization's people.

Doubtless the time is ripe for a new look at our inherited departure strategies. We must correct and modify them if local believers are to receive and reproduce a church planting model that responsively empowers others. It is time we move beyond the cliche, "Our goal is to work ourselves out of a job," and start to make it happen on the local church level.

The New Testament Perspective

The book of Acts records a number of different reasons Paul and his team left cities in which they ministered. Obviously, sometimes they left for their own safety (e.g., Pisidian Antioch, 13:50; Iconium, 14:6; Lystra, 14:19; Thessalonica, 17:10; and perhaps Ephesus, 20:1). But, more importantly for our purposes, they also departed because of their desire and plan to reach as many people as possible with the gospel. After residing briefly in certain cities, they returned to previously visited areas to strengthen the believers and appoint elders (Acts 9:32; 14:21-22; 15:36, 41). See Table 1 for time periods. In some cases, Paul sent his team members to do this (e.g., he left Priscilla and Aquila in Ephesus [Acts18:19]; later he sent Timothy to Ephesus before sending him on to Corinth and Thessalonia [I & II Tim.; I Cor. 4:17; I Thess. 3:2], and sent Titus to Crete [Titus 1:5]). When revisits were delayed or inconvenient, he wrote letters of instruction and encouragement to the new communities of faith.

Table 1. New Testament Stays Were Usually Brief

Antioch - three visits over approximately four years

Corinth - several visits over approximately four years

Ephesus - three years

Caesarea - two to three years

Rome - two to three years

Paul and his team also left places of ministry when they had completed their work for a particular visit, i.e., evangelism, discipleship, or both (13:13; 18:1,18,21,23; 19:21) because their objectives had been met.

So, departure occurred for a number of reasons: Satanic hindrances, completed objectives and the designation of local leaders. As we plan our own phase-out strategies, we should take into account not only planned, but also unplanned withdrawals due to political and economic necessities. We should also take into account Paul's genuine care and concern for all the churches he left (2 Cor. 11:28). *Paul believed in responsible disengagement.*

Key Components Surrounding Responsible Phase-out

For an accurate definition of responsible phase-out, a church planter should isolate all related components of the ministry, including: (1) a definition of a local church; (2) the number of local churches to be planted in a given area; (3) the generational cycle of a local church; (4) the roles of team members, local believers and God; (5) theological training for leaders; (6) when to begin phase-out; and (7) ways of maintaining relationships after phase-out. We begin with a definition of a local church.

How one defines a local church determines the product one looks for. What takes place in worship, instruction, sociality, evangelism, and the written and taped curricula to support these activities, all help determine when phase-out begins. For me, a local church consists of a group of people who trust Christ as their Savior and organize their corporate life (defines leadership and followership) according to indigenous and biblical principles. Their purpose is to glorify the Triune God through worship, instruction, sociality and evangelism, which leads to new churches. They try through the power of the Holy Spirit to reproduce themselves in unreached areas, locally and at a distance.

Another component is the total number of churches required for the entire people group to hear the gospel. Several factors determine this number, one being demographic studies. These studies should indicate: (1) the route Christianity most likely will spread; (2) the number of church plantings required to place churches strategically in the entire people group; (3) the number of church leaders required on the local and itinerant levels; (4) whether an association of churches and/or a missionary training center is necessary; and (5) the ties the target community has to other subcultures and communities.

Discovering what constitutes a significant group within the target people will tell us how many churches we ought to project for the future. This requires cultural analysis. Add to this the demographic studies and your definition of a local church, and you establish the broad parameters for a church planting strategy that leads to responsible phase-out.

Cycles of vitality, lukewarmness, and sterility in the local church are important for church planters to identify. Like all institutions, churches go through various stages. First-generation believers often pay an unusually high price when they switch allegiance to Christ, but their strong commitment makes taking such a risk possible. But when second-generation believers join the church, passivism tends to set in. They do not face the same burning issues their parents did, nor are the lines drawn that differentiate believers from unbelievers so clearly defined. While their parents often experienced a sudden, dramatic conversion, second generation conversions tend to be more gradual and less emotional. Structure often replaces spontaneity. Third-generation Christians often face theological and ethical breakdowns. Nominalism tends to set in while this generation of believers seeks its cultural roots.

Church planters must be alert to generational issues when they define phase-out, i.e., by placing second generation expectations on first generation believers, or vice versa. Therefore, church planters must be adept at recognizing church cycles, and define their phase-outs accordingly.

The fourth component of phase-out calls for church planters to isolate the different roles played by team members, the national believers and God. As church planters move through social concerns, evangelism, discipleship, leadership development, organizing the church, and church reproduction, their roles change as national believers participate in the same things, imitating the models set by the expatriates (see Figure 1). The church planters' roles include: learner, evangelist, teacher, resident advisor, itinerant advisor and absent advisor.

When the newly established church reproduces another church close to home ("Jerusalem"), or cross-culturally ("Judea, Samaria, ends of the earth"), phase-out should be underway. National believers demonstrate their abilities to address social concerns, evangelism, teaching, meeting felt needs, giving, administering church ordinances, implementing church discipline, and developing leaders for both local and itinerant ministries. Their role changes include accompanying, participating, leading, and training. In all these activities both expatriates and national believers must recognize God's sovereign hand on themselves and those whom they are reaching.

The Trinity is committed to spreading the Kingdom of God around the world. The Holy Spirit's role is to convict unbelievers

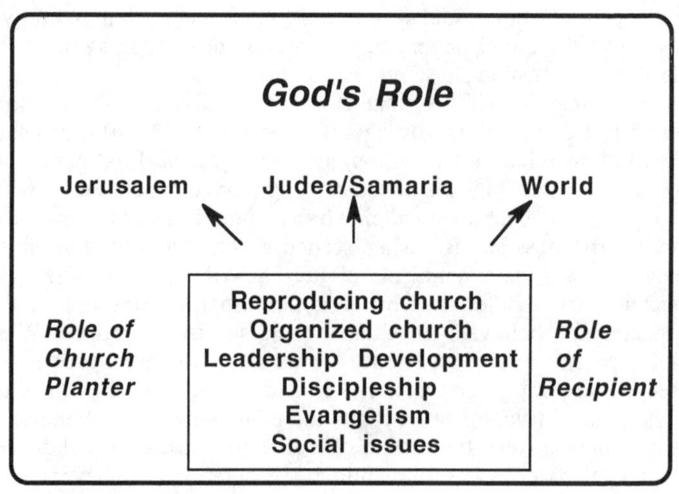

Figure 1. A model for determining phase-out

of sin, righteousness, and judgment (John 16:8). As for believers, the Holy Spirit provides power and comfort while residing within them. Jesus Christ paid the ultimate price to secure salvation for all who believe in him and for the physical universe. He promises to build his Church from "every nation, tribe, people and language" (Matt. 16:18; Rev. 7:9). The Father represents a true father figure who loves and disciplines his sons and daughters. The Father, Son, and Holy Spirit, promise to fulfill their roles. The Trinity expects teams and national believers to do likewise.

The fifth phase-out component is theological training. To be successful, it should provide a solid foundation for the gospel, be comprehensive (Acts 20:27), focus on the material as well as the spiritual world, and address cultural themes, cults, and political ideologies relevant to the community.

Theological training must move from the simple to the complex, from the known to the unknown and be presented through viable cultural means. From the perspective of phase-out, it should include everyone from the start, emphasize church planting evangelism rather than simply individual evangelism, be owned by the national churches, and be reproducible. The aim is to train theologically oriented church leaders who will model to their flocks the importance of starting new churches.

Sixth, church planters must decide when to begin their phase-out. They start by setting realistic timetables for the new community of faith to reach its goals. This is critical because it gives the team a specific goal.

Of course, one must be flexible. We set an eight-year goal knowing that health, subversive elements, or stony hearts could change the projection. The timetable, like the strategy statement, must regularly be updated to allow for new developments and understandings. *Phase-out begins when the stated objectives are met, not when the prescribed time arrives.*

The seventh and final component is determining how church planters can maintain good relationships after the phase-out. *Church planters work themselves out of a job, but not out of relationships.* Continued fellowship includes prayer, visits, letters of challenge and encouragement, videos, sending other people to visit, and cautious financial assistance.

Defining Responsible Phase-out

First, let me say what I do not mean by phase-out. I do not mean abruptly abandoning maturing believers, even when they reach a certain level of maturity and Bible knowledge. Or when they appoint their own leaders. Or when things seem to be going well, with problems at a minimum.

Phase-out oriented church planters build in their absences over time so they can have interaction with the church throughout the disengagement process. They plan their disengagement. They start with short absences and move toward longer and longer ones until they completely withdraw physically, but not relationally.

Church planters normally begin phase-out by stepping back from active leadership. By this time the believers are doing evangelism, discipleship, and leadership development and organizing the church, as well as starting new churches. The seven components surrounding phase-out begin to converge. It is now time for the church planters to distance themselves geographically from the believers.

Of course, any phase-out strategy has to start long before the church planters enter the ministry context. Closure must be designed before their ministry starts, because a planned phase-out affects all the steps in church planting: preentry, preevangelism, evangelism and postevangelism. Such planning provides team members a global picture, direction and a checklist toward closure. Just as a blueprint illustrates to construction workers the finished building and the steps to get there, so a planned phase-out strategy helps a church planting team. Without such a prefield plan, phase-out will be continually delayed, or, in all too many cases, never achieved.

Phase-out must be integral to the entire mission agency strategy. It is a comprehensive organizational approach that starts with the end product and works back to those who are responsible for producing it. It affects everything: how candidates are recruited, selected and trained, how they plan, form teams, handle social programs, evangelize, develop leaders and curricula. When a mission agency works with such a definition of phase-out, it is not likely to wait 40 years to achieve its first phase-out from a new group of believers.

Conclusion

Responsible phase-out does not mean abrupt pull-out. Rather, it is the planned absences of church planters, protracted over time, so that national believers can immediately strengthen their spiritual roots and wings, as responsibility for the church shifts as quickly as possible to them from the church planters. In time, the exploring believers will provide the universal body of Christ new insights for understanding the Christian faith. Responsible exit strategies do not typically call for abandonment.

Responsible phase-out begins with a *strategy of closure* for the overall people group, and for each subculture within that community. Well-honed phase-out strategies call for planting clusters of churches that have a contagious enthusiasm for reproducing themselves. Moreover, it encourages the national believers immediate freedom to execute this. While the expatriate team members transition through various roles which lead to their physical departure, individual members maintain personal relationships through prayer, visits, limited financial assistance, letters, and pictures.Responsible phase-out strategies create believers whose allegiance remains on the Holy Spirit, not team members.

Such a strategy of closure, crafted over time and seasoned with prayer, determines to a great extent whether the team will accomplish its goal in a realistic time. It stands in good stead to produce believers whose reliance remains on the Holy Spirit, not on team members. If we are to move beyond phase-in to phase-out, our agencies must be permeated from top to bottom with this kind of thinking and action.

A strategy of closure calls for ministry role transitions, of which I will now consider.

3

Preparing For Role Changes

If church planting is to become a way of life within and without a particular people, national believers must own this vision and be trained to accomplish it. To facilitate this objective, church planters must be prepared for a series of changing roles that will swiftly propel national leaders into ministry roles, hence allowing them to become proficient. I will now consider the various roles expatriate church planters pass through as they advance toward phase-out, and the stress and conflict surrounding such role changes. Key issues pertaining to preparation for role changes are raised through an analysis of my role changes among the Antipolo / Amduntug Ifugao church plants.

Role Changes Leading to Phase-out

Phase-out oriented church planting requires church planters to engage in planned role changes. The first role, that of "Learner," begins in the Preentry Stage and continues through Phase-out. During the Preentry Stage, church planters spend significant time learning and practicing biblical truths, missions, the social sciences and studying the host country. Through language and culture analysis (Preevangelism Stage), they learn to view life from the host people's perspective. Participating in cultural events enables them to gain first-hand insights, the results of which can be compared to previous studies done during the Preentry Stage. By being willing to learn during the Evangelism Stage, expatriates may avoid syncretism, and find ways to communicate the gospel so that the nationals can in turn relate it easily to others. An attitude of learning during the Postevangelism Stage provides ways to equip trainers, facilitate biblical functional substitutes and develop relevant curricula. Even during Phase-out the attitude of learning must continue. The fast changing conditions of a people and different generational needs all demand a learner role. Effective church planters never allow themselves to be lulled into believing they know their target audience; they remain hungry learners.

The church planter takes on the role of evangelist in the Preevangelism Stage through practicing Christianity in daily life and asking penetrating questions that cause the listeners to reflect upon their worldview. Once fluency in language and culture is gained, the expatriate launches the Evangelism Stage ministry. By verbalizing the gospel message in a culturally relevant way, yet without compromising the gospel, the objective of winning key members of the target people to Christ can be met, establishing a solid foundation upon which to build a church.

The church planter must adapt his role in evangelism from *doing* to *modeling* to *releasing* national Christians. The modeling phase takes place during the Postevangelism Stage as the evangelist no longer just wins nationals to Christ, but rather models evangelism in such a way that new believers feel comfortable in imitating this aspect of ministry. Therefore, the church planter always takes others along, encourages their participation, and provides time for debriefing.

Effective church planters never allow themselves to be lulled into believing they know their target audience; they remain hungry learners.

During the release phase of evangelism the church planter encourages the local Christians to evangelize on their own. Rather than accompanying them, he or she anxiously awaits their return to see how it went and to offer advice and inspiration.

The active work of the church planter shifts in emphasis. As he or she becomes more successful in modeling evangelism to others, the expatriate begins a teaching role, initiating the Postevangelism Stage ministry. As with the evangelism role, the teacher role involves a process of doing, modeling, and releasing national teachers.

The emphasis on doing finds the church planter actively teaching a holistic curricula developed with the target audience. Following the church planter's example, and being encouraged to do so immediately, local teachers begin to expand their comfort zone in the area of teaching. Written curricula and visual aids assist them. As the teachers gain experience it is again time for the church planter to release the ministry of teaching to nationals; he or she now becomes a "resident advisor."

The resident advisor role is one of the most difficult a church planter must pass through. During this time the church planter becomes a coach on the sideline rather than a player on the field. The goal for this role is to allow local Christians to win or lose the game on the basis of their own efforts, not enter the game to save it for them. When the team is winning, coaching is fun. But remaining on the sideline when the team is losing is much more difficult. Nevertheless, the church planter must never do for the national believers what they can do for themselves. Rather, he must provide advice and encouragement. The lessons learned through mistakes encourage the spiritual and ministerial skill development of local leaders much more effectively than the intervention by a church planter, even with the right answers.

During the resident advisor role the local leaders take the lead. They decide what subjects to teach, who evangelizes where, how to institute various biblical functional substitutes, who assists in the development and dissemination of curricula, who should be baptized, who handles the ordinances, how the collections are dispersed, who should become deacons or elders, and other church-related activities. The church planter simply remains available to offer encouragement and advice, not to control the game through manipulating the players.

The effective resident advisor will now begin programmed absences, becoming an "itinerant advisor." Allowing for intermittent contact between the two parties over ever-expanding periods of time, these programmed absences empower national believers to march ahead in their respective ministries, depending on the Holy Spirit. Periodic visits provide church planters opportunities to discuss pertinent issues and offer encouragement.

The itinerant advisor role frees the church planter to enter a new ministry on a part-time basis. To affect this, the mission agency must be prepared to provide ministry opportunities for itinerant advisors, ministries that allow for periodic absences so they can periodically revisit the fledging churches.

The mission agency should base new ministry assignments on an individual's gifts and skills, not availability. For example, evangelists and teachers could be placed in other church plants (where language and culture permits). This cross-fertilization of ideas should be beneficial for both parties. Some may qualify as consultants for field activities, or trainers of other nationals to reach other people groups within their own country. Curriculum writers and literacy specialists could also serve as field consultants, training new personnel and nationals and assisting veterans. Some could continue working on curricula with the people they left. Team members heading for furlough should be challenged to take studies related to the type of ministry to which they will return.

Effective mission agencies prepare relevant part-time ministries for itinerant church planters because this fulfills their goals in several ways: (1) National churches are encouraged to grow on their own; (2) ministry vacancies are filled, expanding the agency's influence; and (3) the new ministries often take less time because previous mistakes are corrected. They also protect family relationships by taking into consideration the concerns of spouses and children.

In the final role change, the church planter becomes an "absent advisor." This role usually takes place when geography makes consistent return visits virtually impossible. But physical separation does not necessarily mean spiritual separation. The absent advisor's periodic contact through letters, tapes, videos, pictures, or visits does much to encourage the nationals' continued growth.

As in the itinerant advisor role, the mission agency must be prepared to offer absent advisors ministries that will challenge these experienced veterans. Should an agency fail in this area, it will lose one of its most valuable commodities, seasoned combatants. The absent advisor pool of personnel provides mission agencies area leaders, field leaders, team leaders, and veteran team players.

In sum, phase-out oriented church planters pass through six role changes. Using an American football analogy, one assumes the learner role before his rookie year, yet continues throughout his entire football career. The church planter begins ministry as "evangelist" and "teacher," playing all the positions on a team. But as new believers mature (which can be a fast or slow process), the church planter becomes the leader or quarterback, calling the offensive and defensive plays. After the team has gained experience and developed leadership, the church planter retires as a player and takes up a coaching role or becomes the resident advisor. While the coach provides direction, criticism, and encouragement, the win / loss column is decided for the most part by the players on the field. Even as coach, he is not content to remain forever, but distances himself as he trains coaching assistants, until he can turn that role over to a new coach and become the "general manager." In this role he helps with tough personnel decisions and team planning, but is absent periodically (itinerant advisor), and aloof from day-to-day operations. Finally, he moves on to a new team. As absent advisor, the church planter's role remains to be a friend and prayer partner in ministry, but his interests are refocused to another ministry.

Contrasting Proposed Role Changes

As noted in the first chapter, Read et al. (1969) and Fuller

(1980) have discussed the problem of departure and suggested various solutions for church-mission relationships. The phase-out oriented model presented below differs from their suggestions in several significant ways. (See Figure 2.) First, it begins with emphasis upon the role of "learner" which continues until the church planter completes the work and departs. This role enables the church planter to earn the right to be heard through demonstrating his acceptance of others; it begins by living among the target audience rather than making periodic visits.

In contrast to the learner approach, Read et al. (1969) begin with "apostolate," painting the picture of a person in authority with the answers to life's questions, the exact opposite role of a learner; the apostolate role focuses on "answer-theology" rather than "life-theology."

Secondly, the phase-out oriented model avoids the errors of colonialism by starting partnership very early in the church planting process, and gradually withdrawing. Read et al. call for an "administrator" ("outside control") role while Fuller prefers "parent," both of which can carry colonial overtones. While these

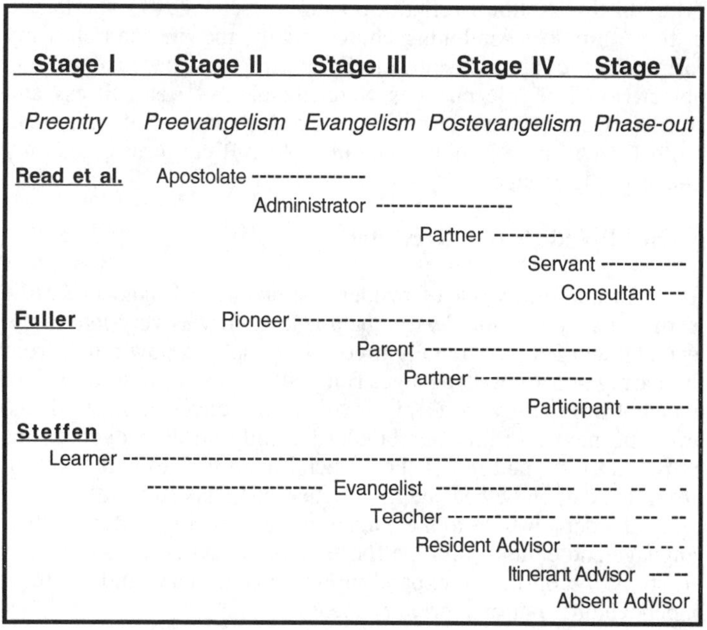

Stage I	Stage II	Stage III	Stage IV	Stage V
Preentry	*Preevangelism*	*Evangelism*	*Postevangelism*	*Phase-out*

Read et al.
Apostolate ---------------
Administrator -----------------
Partner ---------
Servant -----------
Consultant ---

Fuller
Pioneer -----------------
Parent ----------------------
Partner ---------------
Participant --------

Steffen
Learner ---
--------------------- Evangelist ----------------- --- -- - -
Teacher ------------- ------ --- --
Resident Advisor ----- --- -- -- -
Itinerant Advisor --- --
Absent Advisor

Figure 2. Phase-out oriented role changes

writers seek a common outcome (i.e., independent, indigenous churches), my proposed model prepares national believers for departure much earlier, a process facilitated by intentional, planned phase-out rather than a politically precipitated pull-out, created by mission/church tensions.

Finally, the learner, partner, advisor roles emphasized in the phase-out model avoid the struggle of major role redefinition required by the other two models. Individuals serving first as apostolates and administrators often experience personal identity crisis when they transition to partner, servant, or consultant, and many, if not most, fail to make the transitions. The same dilemma faces church planters who see themselves as parents and are later forced to become mere participants. The phase-out oriented model keeps church planters in a servant model throughout, learning, modeling, partnering, in the *early* evangelism and discipling stages of ministry. The Advisor Role begins very early, as will be evident in the following case study.

Stress and Conflict in Role Changes

In this section I reflect over the role changes I experienced in the Antipolo / Amduntug church plants, the *first* churches my former agency phased-out in the Philippines because of met objectives. The role changes were not always easy. Stress and conflict were a natural result. Using the analogy of American football I will now recount some of those difficult times when my ministry role changed.

From "Rookie" To "Recruiter"

In our first week of residence among the Ifugao in 1972 I learned a very valuable lesson, be a learner. It was very late in the evening, and I was extremely tired. My mind was now numb from the barrage of a new language. But I was not sure how to excuse myself from the group deeply involved in conversation, so I just left. The next morning our landlord calmly strolled over to our house and informed me of the proper Ifugao way to exit a group. From that day on he became my teacher, and I his student.

To demonstrate to the Ifugao my learner role, I studied their language and culture full time for ten months. After the ten months of study I continued expanding my vocabulary and cultural understanding, but on a briefer schedule.

Taking the learner role enabled me to receive invitations to attend a number of functions, some never witnessed by other expatriates. At these events I heard new phrases, observed nonverbal behavior cues, handled paraphernalia, and watched different leaders perform in a number of social settings. For example, as I observed one sacrifice I asked various participants to explain the events transpiring. They eagerly explained the intricate nuances of the sacrifice and volunteered why certain individuals were selected to oversee the sacrifice. Their explanations often challenged my hypotheses, which caused continual juggling of my church planting strategy. My participation also enabled me to develop close relationships with influential individuals.

Discussion. My willingness to become a learner of Ifugao language and culture, and continually adjust my church planting strategy accordingly, opened the door for the Ifugao to learn from me. Becoming a student resulted in having students. But taking the learner role also raised a number of problems. For example, the tools I received for language and culture study were not well integrated, nor ministry directed. Our study efforts resulted in a description of the culture, unconnected to ministry, and not integrated to language study.

In that neither the language nor culture study approaches related directly to ministry in a tangible way, I often became spiritually dry. My time was consumed with study but without a familiar ministry role. With the added stress resulting from the newness of the situation, not always being understood by the Ifugao, or understanding them, I struggled to find balance in my learning role and my spiritual walk. The trialogue of ministry, spirituality, and acceptance presented a number of problems to me.

Another area that provided me problems was relating animism, decision-making, and leadership structure to ministry. I lacked models to analyze these events, and relate them to evangelism and church development. As I reflected on the ethnographic data I had gathered I wondered what insights this information held for effective evangelism, discipleship, and leadership development. Whom should I target? How are decisions made? What aspects of animism could serve as stepping stones for the gospel? for the Christian life? Which would have to go?

Lastly, I realized church planters must possess a certain type of attitude. They must be willing to learn and continually recraft their church planting strategy. Mission agencies must therefore select personnel who possess a learner attitude and are willing to take judicial risks, deviating from traditional approaches to ministry while not neglecting the lessons of history.

From Playing "All Positions" To "Quarterback"

My foundational teaching for the gospel began in early January 1973. I asked key individuals in the village where, when, and how we should begin evangelism. I did this because I wanted the Ifugao to know from the beginning I highly valued their input.

Leadership development had begun. They were my teachers. Their input, however, caused me to rewrite my strategy statement numerous times. Even though I often felt my ideas were better than theirs, I backed off, often reluctantly.

Our evangelistic meetings included singing, teaching, and lengthy dialogue, all of which I led. Once the Ifugao learned the songs, I invited different individuals to lead them. Following the traditional Ifugao meeting patterns I encouraged dialogue during all our evangelistic meetings.

After several weeks of teaching lessons about God from a topical study approach, I made a startling discovery. I noticed the Ifugao's interest level jump dramatically when I inadvertently added an Old Testament story. While I preferred a more analytical approach to Bible study, I had to make adjustments if the Ifugao were to comprehend my message and tell it to others. Changing teaching styles resulted in increased comprehension, instant evangelists and a new appreciation of the effectiveness of stories in evangelism.

It is customary for Ifugao to review the discussion in a meeting for latecomers so they feel included. To facilitate the Ifugao's learning and leadership skills, I asked key individuals who had heard the discussion to update the latecomer rather than do it myself. This encouraged participation, revealed future leaders while at the same time providing feedback. While this approach proved effective, it was not an easy step for me to take. Rather than waiting for someone to stumble through a summary of the lesson it seemed so much easier and faster to provide the latecomer a concise, accurate version of my view of the subject. I had to consciously repress this urge.

Written curricula also facilitated the Ifugao's comprehension of the gospel. The Ifugao requested written copies of the lessons prepared for evangelism so they could study in their own homes and show to their friends.

Recruiting several of the Ifugao to work with me in the production of these studies, together we incorporated in the curricula questions raised by the Ifugao during evangelism. These joint productions were the first step in reaching one of our long range goals, the Ifugao producing their own curricula. But this joint adventure proved to be time-consuming. It took a concerted effort on my part to put aside my bent towards time efficiency so that these individuals would have sufficient opportunity to develop their own skills in this area.

In November 1973, we began the meetings for new believers as we had for evangelism, by asking the Christians where, when, and how, we should meet. During the meetings the Ifugao led all the singing, read the Scripture, and gave the announcements. I continued to encourage dialogue during all teaching sessions. As for praying, I handled this for approximately two months until several Ifugao felt comfortable praying in public. After that I seldom prayed publicly. When the Ifugao asked me to pray I would always suggest that someone else pray unless special occasions dictated otherwise. I felt sadness as another one of my roles ended abruptly.

In February 1974, a number of the Ifugao believers requested baptism. So we (expatriates) invited an Ifugao Christian leader from a distant northern Ifugao tribe to oversee the baptisms. By having another Ifugao (from an acceptable area) conduct the baptisms we felt a precedent could be set, Ifugao can, and should, handle their own baptisms.

When the second group of Christians requested baptism in September 1974, some of the male leaders who were baptized by the visiting Ifugao oversaw the ordinance. Since that time, the local Ifugao have performed all baptisms, including two of our daughters. While this approach accomplished our objective, it was not easy to stand by and watch someone else baptize the converts you had prayed for, and labored over for months.

Before our first communion service in July 1974, we corporately discussed for several weeks what we would do and which elements to use. I led the first communion service with a number of Ifugao assisting. During our debriefing sessions we addressed any questions the service surfaced. By our first furlough the Ifugao handled everything by themselves. I once again found myself on the sideline, observing rather than leading. The transition from major player to quarterback resulted in a bittersweet feeling.

One of the older believers died during our absence on a brief trip to Manila in March 1974. I had covered little teaching on the subject of death so the Ifugao were virtually on their own to figure out how to conduct a Christian funeral. The resulting funeral was a mixture of traditional Ifugao beliefs and Christianity; they prayed God would take the dead person's spirit to heaven so that it would not roam aimlessly around the village looking for a life to claim as their worldview taught them. Prayers to God replaced appeasement sacrifices.

Upon our return from Manila, villagers informed us about the funeral. We gathered to discuss death and the Christian's response to it. We also talked about other areas of life in need of biblical functional substitutes. During each of these discussions there was always a strong urge to say, "The best way to handle this is..." I had to make great effort not to control the discussion.

Harvest time in July 1974 became another critical time for Ifugao believers. They desired to demonstrate a Christian perspective of harvest but were not quite sure how to go about it. Long meetings were held to work out the details. The believers decided that all harvesters would meet early at the home of the family who planned to harvest. They celebrated harvest by singing Christian harvest songs, reading Scriptures relating to harvest, and offering corporate prayer to God.

During another one of our absences in 1977, an Ifugao Christian couple moved into a newly constructed home. The young family held an open house to thank God for his provision. A number of the Christian guests prayed, asking God to bless the resident family, and all who might stop by or spend the night. They then sang a number of hymns. Another biblical functional substitute had replaced traditional Ifugao custom, this time without any assistance from us. I struggled with the fact my presence was no longer required.

My evangelist role continued but now emphasized modeling so the Ifugao Christians could eventually become evangelists. In June 1974, we received an invitation (necessary for a formal visit) to present the gospel in a village to the south, so around a dozen of us went weekly to begin laying a firm foundation for the gospel. We spent significant time developing basic themes related to the gospel so that the message would be understood as restoration of a relationship broken because of practiced and inherited sin.

In the beginning my companions would only answer questions posed by the host village. I handled everything else. I wondered if the Ifugao would ever become effective evangelists; I often lacked needed patience. But by the time of our first furlough in May 1975, approximately three years of residence among the Ifugao, the believers advanced beyond accompanying me, to participating confidently with me; they sang, gave testimonies, and handled some of the evangelism. During our furlough they continued this outreach which eventually resulted in the birth of the second church in the tribe.

A major concern I had nine months before our first furlough was who would take over my teaching role during our absence? I offered to work with any of the men during the week so they could handle the Sunday services. Six months before furlough around a dozen men took up the challenge. Five of these were young (15-20 years of age) who just came to listen. Today, most of them are active leaders in the churches.

I met with the prospective teachers every Saturday night for study. Afterwards, they decided who would handle the bulk of the work on Sunday, and who would assist. Two were always involved. After the service we would meet again for debriefing. This enabled us to provide constructive critique without public shame. Nevertheless, I found it especially hard to wait for the debriefing times when I heard totally erroneous statements being made by one of the teachers during a service.

The young Christian leaders experienced tremendous criticism in their inability to find certain passages quickly, and their lack of formal Bible training, but they persevered. We left for furlough wondering what we would find upon our return. Could they make it on their own? Would the believers accept home grown leaders? How long would it take the young leaders to become comfortable with their new role? With no replacements for us during furlough they would have to. We hoped the Bible study materials produced would encourage and direct them during our absence.

When we returned from furlough in 1976 we found a number of the Ifugao men doing an excellent job in leading church activities and outreach.They were ready for ordination. Traditional Ifugao villages are led by a number of part-time practitioners, so we followed that model for the churches. During our Saturday meetings with the teachers we discussed the appointment of church leaders. The Ifugao suggested we do it the traditional way, i.e., after much discussion we just point the finger *("lindeng mi")* at the chosen individual. During the next four weeks I lead studies on church leadership, their duties and qualifications. We set July 3, 1977 as the date to appoint the first Ifugao church leaders.

As the day for appointment drew near my co-worker argued that six leaders should be appointed by ballot. After several hours of discussion, I left for home, unable to persuade him differently. The next morning when I returned for the service my co-worker informed me there would be no ballot. During the night one of the Ifugao leaders, who had heard about the voting proposal, convinced him this would conflict with Ifugao culture.

On ordination Sunday, and after lengthy discussion, the believers chose six men to lead them. While I had deep reservations about one of those selected I was able to keep quiet. After I prayed for the newly appointed leaders, we all went to the river where they baptized a number of new Christians. Their duties as recognized leaders began *immediately,* and *publicly.* After the baptisms a celebration feast followed.

My public leadership role changed drastically with this ordination. From that time on the majority of my time was spent with the elected and potential leaders attending the Saturday meetings. I began to feel the isolation from public ministry as I took on the coaching role.

Discussion. My learning role intensified as I progressed in the Evangelism and Postevangelism Stages. In that Christianity is a way of life I had to learn about all aspects of Ifugao life. For example, how the Ifugao selects leaders; how their religion relates to death, harvest, and house construction; how to conduct various types of meetings; how they learn. In some of these areas my training provided excellent direction. For example, my U.S. teachers encouraged us to train nationals immediately to take over every aspect of the ministry: evangelism, prayer, baptism, communion, and leadership. My teachers also taught me to provide a firm foundation for the gospel so that the good news becomes interpreted as Jesus' efforts to restore our broken relationship with God because of sin (supracultural need) not some other pressing need being meet, such as health or protection from spirits (felt needs).

My training also had some shortcomings, among which were the lack of tools to communicate an accurate gospel so that the hearers could communicate it effectively to others. Without exposure to principles of cross-cultural education, I never questioned a topical teaching approach for the Ifugao. What is the best teaching approach for concrete relational thinkers (approximately 70 percent of the world)? Can they reproduce what they hear? If they can not, evangelism, and more importantly, Ifugao evangelists, will be stifled.

My training also failed me in the area of curriculum development, even though this became one of my first tasks upon gaining fluency in the dialect. Should the oral and print mediums be integrated? How shall I train national writers? What curricula should be produced? Who decides this? How should this material be disseminated? Do I need an overall teaching curricula that builds upon a solid foundation for the gospel? I was left on my own to find the answers to these questions.

The idea of biblical functional substitutes was also foreign to me. Forced to discover for myself, I struggled to discern biblical issues from cultural issues. I remember no models being presented during my training in this vital area of church development.

Directed training in a team approach to ministry proved to be another weak area of my training. While in the case of ordaining Ifugao leaders, my co-worker and myself worked out the situation without conflict, not all situations went as smoothly. The impact of differing expectations and ministry philosophies was never discussed as possible sources of conflict prior to forming our partnership. If I did not understand the process of team development within my own culture, how could I be expected to effectively train national teams to replace us?

From "Quarterback" To "Coach"

Periodically during our first term I took the role of a coach or resident advisor so that the Ifugao could stretch their gifts and skills. They did quite well.

By 1978, six years after entering the Ifugao community, I became a full-time coach, pacing the sideline as I observed the Ifugao believers create their own church history. When the Ifugao played well, I liked to coach. But when the Ifugao did not play well I wanted to suit up and bench the quarterback so I could replace him. But whether the team played poorly or well, it was hard and lonely remaining on the sideline. It always seemed so much easier and faster to just do it myself and in my way.

The Ifugao leaders had advanced from accompanying me, to participating with me, to leading effectively, to training others, without much outside assistance. While we continued the leadership meetings on Saturday night I noticed on Sundays the teachers adding substantial material not covered Saturday night. They became confident in their teaching role. And members of the community of faith were accepting them.

When we left on trips the Ifugao continued teaching in our absence. They met on their own before Sunday, decided who would lead the service, and discussed the chapter or topic under study. Some became effective trainers of younger teachers, encouraging them to take small parts of the Sunday service.

In the area of outreach the Ifugao decided where to go and who would participate. They always tried to include young believers. The believers made all decisions concerning the collections, handled the ordinances of baptism and communion, oversaw all functional substitutes, mediated disputes, and continued to assist me in the development of curricula.

While I continued to receive requests to administer the ordinances, handle the Sunday services, or accompany them on evangelistic trips, I seldom participated in such activities. I did accompany them numerous times on evangelism trips to the north because my presence opened a door that was socially difficult for them to open. I became a lonely Resident Advisor.

During the construction of the church building in October 1977, I mistakenly returned to the quarterback role. The increase in the number of Ifugao believers called for a central meeting place, especially since rainy season was just around the corner. Since we could no longer fit under a house, I challenged the men to cut lumber before the arrival of rainy season. But dry season did not inspire the Ifugao to hurry to cut wood.

Rainy season arrived with only a few pieces of lumber sawed, consequently, we spent an uncomfortable wet season worshipping together. I let the leadership know what I thought about their delay, even though I knew the construction of an Ifugao home or granary may take a decade to complete. Speaking for several of the leaders, one individual politely informed me to ease up, the church building would be built when the church was built. My goal orientation came through too strongly.

From 1978-1979, I focused almost 100 percent of my time on equipping the Ifugao leaders so they could move beyond leading to become trainers. I encouraged evangelists to not only evangelize, but also develop evangelists.

When the leaders returned from the church plant in the

south I would always ask how the trip went, how potential leaders for the church were developing, and what they personally learned from the trip. I encouraged them to include potential leaders in the activities whenever possible.

Because of the Ifugao's continual visits to the church in the south, the local leaders matured quickly. It was time for their ordination. This event took place in December 1980, following the pattern of the first ordination service. While I attended all the preparatory meetings for this event, they did not ask for my advice. Even though this is what we had prayed for for years, it hurt nevertheless. The Ifugao no longer found necessary the advice of the "father of our faith," as they affectionately called me.

The two churches joined together to begin a church plant in the southwest in early 1978, and one in the north by June of the same year (completing our overall church-planting strategy). The church plant to the north became the toughest but they never gave up, and today there are over 40 believers, having their own ordained leadership. They also began a church in a neighboring tribe in the southwest. In July 1989, the Ifugao informed me they planned to ordain a number of church leaders there. The number of Christian leaders continued to grow, developing as effective church leaders / planters, dependent upon the Holy Spirit rather than upon me.

We made a concerted effort to be out of the tribe for two to three week periods of time during our resident advisor role. This enabled the Christian leaders time to function without us. When we returned we spent considerable time answering questions that arose during our absence.

While I attended all the preparatory meetings for this event, they did not ask for my advice. Even though this is what we had prayed for for years, it hurt nevertheless.

Discussion. During this very difficult role change I came to realize several important things. The first had to do with the extreme difficulty I felt in releasing a national team to handle their own affairs. I had to work through my own reasons for being reluctant to release the Ifugao. I had to be willing to leave the quarterback uniform behind no matter what the score. I had to realize my stepping in to complete a ministry more quickly and efficiently did not really save time in the long run, nor did it contribute to the maturity of leaders. I had to realize they could lose games, but remain strong contenders in the league through the power of the Holy Spirit. Nevertheless, I was totally unprepared for this lonely role.

Secondly, I realized the importance of knowing my own leadership style preference and that of my Ifugao friends. What type of leadership style did I prefer? The Ifugao? When did they match? When did they conflict? What adaptations were necessary? Once I reached a coaching role in a certain area, should I ever return to quarterbacking in the same? I needed some tools to answer these questions so that Ifugao leadership could be developed, capable of addressing all aspects of church life and multiplication.

From "Coach" To "General Manager"

By mid-1978, due to the increased maturity of the Ifugao church leaders, and the planting of new churches, I discussed phasing out of the Ifugao ministry with our mission leaders. We felt our continued residence among the Ifugao fostered dependence on us rather than on the Holy Spirit. Our presence allowed the Ifugao to look to us for solutions, even though they could adequately solve the problem themselves. We were told to continue living among Ifugao for another year.

When the year passed I again discussed an itinerant role with our mission leadership. They sent the following prerequisites for departure: (1) the believers should stop serving rice wine or other intoxicating drinks; (2) the believers must be able to deal clearly with the cults in the area; (3) establish a schedule for outreach; and (3) complete the curricula.

> I had to realize my stepping in to complete a ministry more quickly and efficiently did not really save time in the long run, nor did it contribute to the maturity of leaders.

While not wishing to address the merits of the four prerequisites here, it became very apparent they defined leaving a people quite differently than we did. We began a continuing dialogue as to the appropriate time for church planters to phase-out of a church plant.

In May 1979, we moved out of the area to become itinerant advisors. During this time I divided my time equally between the Ifugao and service to other church-planting teams. My work among the Ifugao called for periodical visits to see how things were going and conduct various seminars. During each of our visits, I repeatedly challenged them to think about developing new leaders.

From these visits requests came for new curriculum. I worked on their requests when I returned home. Ifugao would visit us periodically to work on the same. This role continued until we returned to the States in May 1986.

Regarding service to the mission, I spent most of my time consulting with other church planting teams working in Luzon, Palawan, and Mindanao. My travels eventually took me to Papua New Guinea, Thailand, and Indonesia. I later chaired a committee that provided direction and training of all the agency's church planting teams in the Philippines.

Discussion. Because the mission agency lacked a sharply honed definition of responsible phase-out, a lot of avoidable stress occurred between us. What are the necessary components of a definition of phase-out? Should only one church be planted in each people group? Should the expatriates plant churches in all key areas of a people group so that a church is geographically available to all? What are the roles of expatriate? Nationals? The mission agency? God's? Can expatriates begin phase-out in five years? Seven years? How does an agency create a phase-out mentality? How does it protect the family while providing legitimate part-time ministries for absent advisors?

From "Current General Manager" To "New General Manager"

The church plants among the Antipolo / Amduntug Ifugao, from the Preevangelism Stage to Phase-out, spanned approximately seven years (1972-1979). During these seven years we resided outside the community around twenty-eight months. See Table 2 for specific dates.

Phase-out began in May 1979, with periodic visits continuing until our departure from the Philippines in 1986. In our Absent Advisor role we have maintained our relationship through written correspondence, pictures, and personal visits in 1989 and 1993. It took a total of 14 years to plant the three churches within the tribe, providing a church within walking distance for the total population. Presently there are 10-12 churches.

My visits to Ifugao in 1989 and 1993 highlighted three areas in relation to phase-out. The first was the necessity of repeating the basic truths of Christianity. After years in the Absent Advisor role, the Ifugao continued to ask the same questions they asked during my Itinerant Advisor period. One reason for this was the aggressive work of the Ifugao believers as evangelists. When a number of new believers met with us, the veterans asked questions for the benefit of someone in the audience (Ifugao custom). I concluded phase-out calls for continuous repetition of the basics of Christianity by a respected teacher.

- *Learner Role:* Fieldside - 1971
- *Evangelism Role:* Jan 1973
- *Teacher Role:* Nov 1973
  Baptism - Feb 1974
  Communion - July 1974
  Harvest functional substitute - July 1974
  Church building - Oct 1977
  Leaders ordained, Church #1 - July 1977
  Leaders ordained, Church #2 - Dec 1980
- *Resident Advisor Role:* Jan 1978
- *Itinerant Advisor Role:* May 1978
- *Absent Advisor Role:* May 1986

(Permanent residence from 1972-1979 [28 months absent])

Table 2. Ifugao time frame for role changes

Another area that caught my attention was the Ifugao Christians' desire for consistent contact with itinerant church leaders from outside their dialect. While this is no longer possible for me, this need can be met in several ways. One is through the Association of Evangelical Churches of Ifugao. Leaders from the association visit the different areas several times a year. Another way is to have mission agencies working in the area include them as guests and/or speakers in seminars and conferences. The Ifugao believers desire continual association with believers from outside their territorial boundaries.

A final area that impressed me was the renewed spiritual motivation stimulated by a set of pictures for the Gospel / Acts curriculum which I presented to the three churches. The periodical introduction of new materials during phase-out may be instrumental in rejuvenating spiritual motivation (as it did during the Postevangelism Stage). New materials introduced over time may play a major role in rekindling local believers. It also makes it possible to address second generation needs.

Discussion. Perhaps most crucial to the Absent Advisor role is the agency's need to provide new ministry opportunities that will challenge seasoned team members. Without such a challenge the veterans are likely to become attrition statistics. How should agencies utilize the gifts and skills of veteran church planters? What specialized training should individuals receive to enhance their abilities? What arrangements can be made that would allow veterans to visit the churches they helped flourish? Phase-out oriented mission agencies should do all they can to retain their tested veterans by offering them ministries that challenge their gifts and skills.

Conclusion

Responsible phase-out oriented church planters pass through a number of role changes. These transitions call for relinquishing one's own power so that others are empowered to mature in character and ministry skills. Such role changes facilitates the church planting cycle in that local leaders are encouraged to mature under the power of the Holy Spirit.

Church planters must be willing to die to self-serving ambitions so that national believers can live up to their full potential.

But these role changes come with a high price, as evidenced by my own experiences. Role changes call for cutting the umbilical cord. They call for separation of the parents from the maturing adolescents so that one day the two can meet as peers. It is only natural for the team members who helped birth the various ministries to want to continue controlling them. But this approach cripples the development of young believers. Church planters must be willing to die to self-serving ambitions so that national believers can live up to their full potential. They must be willing to move beyond phase-in to phase-out. This requires a certain type of individual, someone who is phase-out oriented.

4

Selecting Phase-out Oriented Church Planters

Bill and Nancy (names are changed) eagerly joined a church planting team but soon found their gifts and abilities did not match their assignment. Although frustrated they refused to quit, feeling compelled by personal guilt to continue. Were they not qualified according to their mission agency's selection process? In time, the frustration they felt began to infect other team members. Conflict among team members resulted, and this did not go unnoticed by the host community.

It was at this point that the team members discovered just how much of their energies were being focused on each other rather than on the people they came to reach. Instead of working toward phase-out, team members of necessity spent significant time trying to resolve inter-team conflict. This pattern continued for several years until finally Bill and Nancy felt they should drop out of the team. Today, Bill and Nancy still experience pangs of guilt; they believe they failed themselves, the team, their supporters, and those they went to reach with the gospel.

What was the cause of Bill and Nancy's failure? Was it due to lack of dedication? Was it due to inability to get along with others? Or was it due, at least in part, to an inappropriate selection process? What type of individuals best qualify for phase-out oriented church planting? This chapter addresses selection of church planters with phase-out in mind. In selecting phase-out oriented church planters one should consider role confusion that can cause attrition, the cost of attrition, ways to organize to cut attrition, how to conduct a job analysis, and criteria for selecting a phase-out oriented church planter.

Confusion of Role: A Cause of Attrition

Responsible phase-out requires a well articulated strategy of closure (Chapter 1). It also demands the church planter transition through a number of role changes so that national believers can become adept at leading their own churches and planting new ones (Chapter 2). For such an outcome to occur on a regular basis, a selection process based on a specific profile is needed.

One weakness we noted in our agency's selection process was the absence of a comprehensive profile to identify a phase-out oriented tribal or peasant church planter. The qualifications set before our candidates had focused on two areas: (1) spiritual qualifications (I Tim. 3; Titus 1); and (2) present ministry involvement. As a result, these two criteria served as the qualifying benchmarks for the selection of *all personnel,* including church planters, and support workers (e.g., pilots, dorm parents, teachers, office personnel).

Our mission's selection process in effect produced a confusion of roles because it failed to distinguish between the differing roles various ministries require. The matter of role changes was also overlooke, role changes that church planters must pass through before phase-out can become a reality. As a result, a number of church planters perceived their roles to be long-term pastors. Moreover, local believers were trained to assist the expatriates in fulfilling their objectives rather than in training nationals to take over from them. Too frequently, expatriates assumed that many years of training and ministry experience were necessary in order for nationals to lead their churches effectively, let alone plant new churches.

Because the qualifications of church planters were indistinguishable from those of support workers, it was easy for support workers to see themselves also qualified for church planting. This idea was reinforced overseas in that their field leaders had assigned them to a team as church planters (teams were formed on the respective fields.) Thus many team members had been assigned inappropriately. Like Bill and Nancy, they became discouraged when they (as well as their teammates) realized their personal gifts and abilities did not match the tasks required of them.

Sadly, although mission agencies send dedicated Christian personnel into cross-cultural church planting situations, many are not really adequately qualified, and the end result is catastrophe for all involved: e.g., the individual, the family, the team, the target community, the supporting churches, the mission agency, and the host country. Bewildered expatriates pack their bags while they ask themselves what went wrong. Families experience tremendous stress. Staggering teams may try to regroup. Meanwhile, the community forms its own opinion of expatriates and the religion represented. Supporting churches too wonder why things turned out as they did. Hopefully, the mission agency begins to reevaluate its selection process and the host country reconsiders the mission agency's status within the country. All this can delay the phase-out progress. But why was there such failure? Is it possible to avoid such failure today? If so, how?

> How a mission agency selects its church planters will reflect its values and priorities in relation to specific job assignments and phase-out orientation.

From the above case study we can conclude that spiritual qualifications and ministry involvement are key components for any church planter. Yet more should be said about specific qualities required for a phase-out oriented church planter. It is therefore necessary to develop a profile that takes into account the specific tasks of a phase-out oriented church planter. Apart from such a profile, team conflict can easily result. When personal or corporate expectations are not met, and when evangelist and pastor roles become long-term personal ministries rather than ministries designed to empower nationals, phase-out is inevitably delayed and the body of Christ suppressed. How a mission agency selects its church planters will reflect its values and priorities in relation to specific job assignments and phase-out orientation.

The Cost of Attrition

Studies show that when unqualified personnel are sent to evangelize and plant churches in a cross-cultural environment, the result is detrimental to the spreading of the Kingdom of God. Graham (1987) calls attention to the fact that attrition results in at least six deficits in any type of church planting:

1. Lost souls are not reached.
2. Churches go unplanted.
3. "Windows of opportunity" are lost.
4. Missionaries experience a sense of failure.
5. Marriages / families experience stress.
6. Stewardship of resources is poor.

These costs are extremely high. Good stewardship demands they be minimized. One logical way to reduce the attrition rate is to send out personnel who are not only highly qualified for the tasks required, but those willing to progress through the various roles that will enable nationals to replace them. Like the Marines, we should look for, and send out, a "few good men and women." The key elements for reducing attrition are quality and philosophy, not just quantity and volunteerism. A church planter's profile, therefore, must be based on the tasks required to accomplish a church plant, along with a willingness to change roles.

Organizing to Cut Attrition

We need to recognize at the outset that it is difficult to formulate a list of criteria because of the different types of cross-cultural church planting situations, the demographics involved, and individual agency's distinctives. So it is advisable for each sending agency to formulate its own criteria based on the target people. The resulting profile should then become the agency's guide in recruiting, selecting, and training candidates in terms of phase-out objectives.

Even though an agency's criteria for selecting cross-cultural church planters may not be articulated, this does not mean that such criteria does not exist. Candidates, pastors, and mission executives usually have such lists, if only in their individual and/or collective minds. But in order that pertinent criteria not be missed, false criteria must be deleted, and poorly defined criteria must be focused. It is therefore important for an agency to produce a well-honed profile, particularly if phase-out is to result.

What preliminary steps can be taken to assure a composite list of desired qualities for successful church planters? First, each agency should have a carefully worded mission (or vision) statement. This statement will help identify the types of jobs required to accomplish the stated purpose. For example, New Tribes Mission's purpose statement reads: "Reach new tribes until we have reached the last tribe." To accomplish this, a number of job slots have to be filled (e.g., linguists, translators, church planters, community developers).

Second, an agency must determine the characteristics and qualities that are needed for the particular job descriptions. By completing these first two steps, an agency can slow the attrition rate among its church planters while still working to accomplish its phase-out goal. Figure 3 demonstrates the flow from the initial Vision Statement to setting the criteria for selecting personnel.

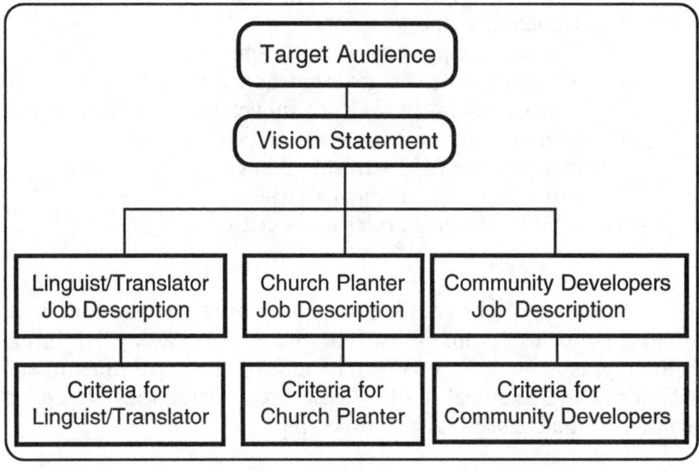

Figure 3. Organizing to cut attrition

Establishing Criteria by Isolating the Tasks

What are the minimal entry-level requirements for those anticipating an urban church plant? A tribal or peasant church plant? For our purposes here I will conduct a cursory job analysis with tribals and peasants in mind. (How will this differ for your target audience?) This will isolate the types and/or groups of tasks that such church planters must perform regularly. As I thought about the necessary activities in my ministry, and compared them with my colleagues around the world, I isolated the following tasks:

1. Study of culture
2. Study of language
3. Work with a team
4. Building mono-cultural and cross-cultural relationships
5. Leading mono-culturally and cross-culturally
6. Training mono-culturally and cross-culturally
7. Teaching the Bible and other subjects mono-culturally and cross-culturally
8. Mediating conflict mono-culturally and cross-culturally
9. Living / working / traveling in a different climate
10. Developing contextualized curricula
11. Assessing demographics, making surveys

12. Strategizing, implementing, evaluating
13. Updating supporters
14. Maintaining personal / family spirituality
15. Mediating between government and society
16. Ministering in the midst of subversive activities
17. Building and/or overseeing the construction / maintenance of airstrips, buildings
18. Providing basic medical assistance
19. Ability to change roles continually

The above tasks can be grouped according to the following broad categories: communication, planning, leading, training, following, spirituality, survival in a foreign environment, and vocational and practical skills. These broad categories suggest a profile that includes at least the following:

1. Commitment to God's call
2. Spiritual maturity
3. Managed household / singleness
4. Psychological maturity
5. Evangelistic experience
6. Discipleship experience
7. International political awareness
8. Empathetic contextual skills
9. Servant leader / follower
10. Effective action planner
11. Flexibility and adaptability
12. Physical vitality
13. Basic medical skills
14. Financial support maintenance / expansion

Such a lengthy list (of fourteen criteria!) often intimidates candidates for none see themselves possessing all of these admirable characteristics, or at least at an acceptable level. Therefore, agencies must incorporate in the selection processes three strategies to counteract such an intimidating job description: (a) utilize a scale that ranks each individual's ability in the fourteen criteria, (b) construct a composite ranking of each candidate relative to other candidates, and (c) place emphasis upon training for teamwork.

With the above structure in place, selection can now begin. The best way to evaluate a match of the criteria to the candidate would be to observe him or her in a church plant over a period of several years. Time, of course, makes such analysis virtually impossible. An optional effective selection model would be to conduct assessment in a more controlled environment, i.e., add to the traditional selection process of references, interviews, and psychological tests, an extended time for simulation exercises that highlight the fourteen criteria in specifically designed exercises. During each exercise, candidates would be ranked by a team of experienced assessors according to a simple five point system (see Appendix D for a flexible document). [See Graham (1987) for a succinct overview of an Assessment Center for Church Planters.]

The second strategy calls for an overall ranking by the assessors of each candidate relative to other candidates. At the end of the assessment, each assessor is provided a copy of the averages determined by the other assessors. The assessors then agree together on a final rating of each candidate's anticipated abilities as a church planter, using a prescribed form that covers 10-12 specific areas.

The third strategy, the matter of working as a team, is developed in Chapter Four.

Defining the Criteria

The above fourteen criteria become bench marks of commitment and competency in evaluating potential tribal and peasant church planters, and determining how effective these candidates may be in attaining the objective of phase-out. I will now examine each of the above criteria in greater detail. How should these differ for urban church plants among the upper-class? The middle-class? The lower-class? Different ethnic groups?

Spiritual Maturity By this is meant that a candidate evidences an unwavering confidence in a sovereign God who is active in his own life and in the world. At the same time the candidate recognizes his/her own humanness and need of Supernatural power. This charateristic provides the motivation for consistent Bible study and times of prayer, and for reliance on the power of the Holy Spirit, for power to demonstrate the fruit of the Spirit. Those individuals evidence the character qualities found in I Timothy 3 and Titus 1. The joy of the Lord becomes their daily strength; they stand in awe of God. They do whatever they can, including forfeiting public roles, if by doing so others can develop spiritually.

- Does the candidate evidence anxiety?
- What biblical principles are evident in the person's actions?
- Which fruit of the Spirit have you observed in the person? Which have others observed?

- Does the candidate expect God's intervention in his life?
- How does the individual react to his/her own sin?
- Is the candidate thankful?
- Is there evidence the candidate is willing to encourage others into ministry roles so that there is growth in their ministry gifts and skills?

Commitment to God's Call With such a commitment, individuals know beyond a shadow of a doubt God has called them to reach the lost for Christ. They set their courses accordingly, allowing nothing to deter them from this goal. Their personal aspirations become secondary to what they believe God wants of them. These individuals gather information on the target people, associate with them, take appropriate studies, pray for the people and missionaries working among them. They also look for other committed Christians and try to learn from them. If candidates are married, their spouses share their conviction.

- Does the candidate evidence anxiety about his/her call? Does the spouse?
- What ministries or preparation has the individual participated in that indicates movement towards the goal? Does the candidate think long range?
- What would stop this candidate from fulfilling his/her call?
- Do others confirm the candidate's call?
- Who are the candidate's spiritual heroes? Why?

Managed Household / Singleness Here the candidate's family models God working in the midst of close relationships. The husband consistently demonstrates love for his wife, as does the wife for her husband. Couples seek to maintain a satisfactory sexual relationship. They encourage each other to utilize their gifts, even if this requires one of them to take a back seat. Parents discipline their children through love and correction but do not inhibit their development by overly protecting them. The children respect their parents. People enjoy visiting their home because it reflects Scripture.

Singles view singleness as God's sovereign plan for their lives thereby providing maximum time for ministry. The desire for a mate does not control daily activities. They control sexual desires through the help of the Holy Spirit and perhaps a trusted mentor. They give themselves for the growth and development of others. They demonstrate the fruit of the Spirit.

- How does the husband evidence respect for his wife? Does he

encourage her spiritual, emotional and intellectual growth?
- How does the wife evidence respect for her husband?
- Is there evidence the children fear either parent?
- Do the parents inhibit their children's development through over protection?
- Which fruit(s) of the Spirit are evident in the candidate's life?
- Does each partner feel sexually fulfilled?
- Why do people like to visit the candidate's family? Why don't they?
- How is the single person handling his or her singleness?
- Does the single see God's sovereignty in his or her present status?
- How does the single find fulfillment in the growth and development of others?
- Does the single maintain an accountability relationship with someone?

Psychological Maturity Psychological mature persons recognize their own uniqueness; God made each one for a special purpose. Consequently, these candidates utilize to the fullest their God-given gifts and talents to further the Kingdom of God; they thank himfor the privilege of being co-laborers with him. They acknowledge their weaknesses and try to improve them through the power of the Holy Spirit. At the same time they consistently refuse to be controlled by weaknesses or dwell on the past. The individual candidate's anxiety level is consistently stable; they know who they are before God. They not only tolerate the behavior of others, but they do everything they can to help others develop psychologically; that is, another's growth encourages them.

- Does the candidate focus on the past?
- How does the individual handle group activities?
- How tolerant is the person of others? Is he a team player?
- Does the candidate encourage others to grow psychologically? Does the growth of others bring jealousy? Joy?
- Is the candidate teachable? Defensive? Racist?
- Is competitiveness necessary for the candidate's self-worth?
- Does the person experience mood swings?
- Does the individual evidence a balanced self-confidence?
- Does the candidate take judicious risks?

Evangelistic Experience Candidates aggressively look for opportunities to witness for Christ through their walk and talk. They pray consistently for opportunities to witness, and also pray for those to whom they witness. They understand one's lost condition before God, the remedy of the gospel, and take time to study the world's great religions and cults. They can determine an individual's understanding of the gospel and can move them towards Christ, using appropriate biblical principles and captivating illustrations. These candidates are personable and influential; they succeed in leading people to Christ and aggressively train others to do the same.

- How does the person define the gospel?
- Is there evidence the candidate prays for opportunities to witness?
- Is the person adaptable in his witnessing methodology?
- If the individual has witnessed to someone of a different culture, what problems were encountered?
- Do people like to talk with the candidate?
- How familiar are they with the world's great religions? Cults?
- Does the candidate have a track record of witnessing? Winning people to Christ?
- Has there been involvement in a team evangelistic effort? How did it work out?
- Has the candidate successfully trained others to evangelize?

Discipleship Experience Here there is a desire to see others grow in their Christian faith. They understand the steps involved in moving new Christians from babyhood, through adolescence, to adulthood. These candidates ask God for individuals and/or groups to disciple. They demonstrate care and compassion with gentle rebuke. They demonstrate tough-love. They adapt their approach to the needs of their disciples. Their discipleship abilities give evidence of assisting others to mature in their Christian faith, and of training others with positive results. They are team players, willing to release their roles so that others can grow.

- Who disciples the candidate?
- Who looks to the candidate for spiritual advice? Encouragement?
- How adept is the person in pinpointing someone's spiritual need?
- What does the candidate do to enhance his discipling abilities? Has there been discipling through a team effort? How did it work out?
- Does the person rebuke his disciples as needed?
- Is there a track record of individuals whose faith grew because of the candidate's efforts? Of disciples who have then discipled

others?

International Political Awareness Here individuals are aware of the effects of the major political ideologies on the world. They have investigated the value of Capitalism, Marxism, Liberation Theology, from a biblical perspective. They are able to identify the strengths and weaknesses of each ideology. Moreover, they have examined their own socialization to capitalistic values and are aware of the latent values within the models they propose to implement in a cross-cultural setting, and are capable of making the necessary adjustments. They recognize that nationals really want to control their own destiny, and are willing to work to make this become a reality. Their aim is to become internationally astute.

- When was the last time the candidate voted?
- How does the candidate react to critiques of Capitalism? Marxism? Liberation Theology?
- Can the person articulate the strengths and weaknesses of Capitalism? Marxism? Liberation Theology? Deconstructionism? Postmoderism?
- Is the candidate aware of class structure in relation to the various ideologies?
- How willing is the candidate to train nationals so they can lead the churches? Is s/he a team player?
- Is there evidence of uncritiqued (from a biblical perspective) capitalistic values in the candidate?
- How does the individual keep current on political affairs?

Empathetic Contextual Skills The desirable candidates not only communicate or lead effectively within their own context, but they will also seek out opportunities to hone their skills within new contexts, with equal effectiveness. They show similar interest in knowing other languages and cultures. They recognize the value of learning, teaching, and leadership / followership styles within and outside their own culture, and make appropriate adjustments. Rather than being judgmental of differences they seek to learn from them; they also seek to become incarnational models of Christ. Their lives motivate others to action regardless of the ethnic context because they moved beyond outward adaptation to inner empathy and identification. Lifestyle does not inhibit their ministries.

- Has the candidate effectively taught children?
- Has the candidate effectively taught adults?
- Does the candidate evidence a desire to learn other languages

and cultures? Is their evidence of cultural discernment?
- If the individual has worked with people of a different culture, what problems arose? How were these handled?
- Is the person aware of preferring his/her own learning, teaching, and leadership / followership styles? Is he willing to adapt them?
- When in a group, does the candidate listen respectfully to others? Observe nonverbal cues of others?
- Does the individual evidence the incarnational model of Jesus Christ in his methodology?
- Does the candidate exhibit an excessive lifestyle?

Servant Leader / Follower Leadership and followership abilities are viewed as gifts from the Holy Spirit and are used to serve the body of Christ, not to further personal aspirations; these individuals see themselves as bond-servants of Jesus Christ. They have acquired an in-depth working knowledge of the Bible; they can sense the needs of individuals, find solutions, and resolve conflict. These individuals challenge others to stretch their own abilities by willingly delegating to them various responsibilities; they inspire vision. As team players they willingly change roles (become followers) so others can lead. They model a disciplined lifestyle and active faith; and meet the qualifications of I Timothy 3 and Titus 1. People follow them willingly.

- Does the candidate have a mentor? Is he/she willing to be a follower?
- Do his/her questions cut to the heart of the issue?
- Do people seek out the candidate for spiritual and/or practical advice? Would you?
- Does the individual take initiative in situations calling for leadership?
- How does the candidate handle competition? Is he/she a team player?
- Does the individual delegate responsibilities to others willingly?
- How does the person handle conflict? Does the candidate listen to others?
- Is the candidate an effective steward of personal resources?
- Does the candidate evidence an insatiable hunger to learn from anyone?
- Is there ample evidence the candidate is willing to change roles so others can grow?

Effective Action Planner The desired candidates possess abilities to formulate goal-oriented plans and are able to execute them successfully. They can integrate a number of programs and see the big picture, yet are able to analyze and articulate various components, set goals, and evaluate both the process and the overall effectiveness of the proposed plan. Moreover, they are adept at organizing ideas and are consulted about step-by-step implementations. In addition, they are able to train others to formulate and execute plans.

- Does the candidate tend to become enmeshed in details?
- Can the individual plan long-range goals as well as short range?
- What evidence is there of the successful action plans?
- Do others seek the person's assistance in forming action plans? Would you?
- Does the candidate actively seek out and train others to become effective action planners?

Flexibility and Adaptability Successful candidates evidence tolerance for ambiguity. Instances of unmet appointments, breakdowns on the freeway, lack of precise instructions, unexpected visitors, someone breaking into a line in front of him at the grocery store, geographical moves to a different state, disorganization, different personalities, all these are accepted as challenges for growth rather than sources of irritation. Patience, flexibility, and adaptability characterize these individuals. They more easily laugh at their own mistakes and are tolerant of the mistakes of others. They view the necessary role changes as opportunities to strengthen the gifts and skills of others; To this end they give of themselves willingly in working together with others.

- Does the candidate evidence resiliency?
- Is there evidence the person is sociologically mobile? Is the same true of the spouse?
- Does the person demand perfectionism of himself/herself? Of others?
- How has the candidate handled separation from his/her extended families? The spouse?
- What is the candidate's opinion of ethnic groups? Working as a team? Does his/her spouse agree?
- Is the candidate (and spouse) controlled by cleanliness? Time? Food preferences? Privacy? Orderliness?
- Is the candidate willing to give up his/her rights so others can be reached?
- Does the individual seek personal role changes so others can grow? Can he/she release? Is he/she a team player?

Physical Vitality Desirable candidates enjoy good health, keeping themselves physically fit through consistent exercise, adequate sleep, and an appropriate diet. Knowing their body's endurance limit they take appropriate breaks and vacations. They care about their appearance and physical condition. Being able to delegate keeps them from punishing their bodies to the point of unnecessary burnout.

- Does the candidate's physical appearance evidence discipline?
- Does the candidate have physical deficiencies that would disqualify him/her?
- How often is the person sick?
- Does the individual participate in a personal exercise program?
- When was the last time the candidate took a vacation? For how long?
- Does the candidate make it a habit to eat a balanced diet?
- Is the individual prone to delegate when the workload is heavy?
- Has the candidate experienced burnout? Under what circumstances?

> The resulting profile should then become the agency's guide in recruiting, selecting, and training candidates in terms of phase-out objectives.

Basic Medical Skills The candidate has a working knowledge of basic first-aid and tropical medicine (if needed) and then is able to assist tribal and peasant people with preventative medicine. As Christ met the physical needs of people, so the expatriate is motivated to meet the physical needs of community members by means of his or her own abilities, or through the assistance of others. The candidate will also want to teach basic medical skills so that community members can work toward transforming their own world.

- How has the candidate prepared in the area of medicine?
- Can the individual administer basic first-aid?
- How is the candidate preparing in the area of tropical medicine?

- Is the candidate capable of transferring his knowledge of medicine to others?

Support Maintenance and Expansion Individuals look to the Lord to provide prayer and financial supporters. As the teams form, they assemble a packet of materials to introduce themselves, and their church-planting goals to potential supporters. They then contact family, friends, and interested contributors to communicate the vision of their future ministry, and to solicit partnership in prayer and finances. The candidates should maintain consistent contact with these backers, using a variety of means, while at the same time trying to enlarge their network to off-set inflation. These individuals are confident that God will supply all their needs, and challenges others to believe the same.

- Does the candidate have a plan to locate supporters? Is he/she working the plan?
- Does the individual evidence trust in God to meet his/her daily needs?
- Does the candidate view "living by faith" as subhuman? The spouse?
- How does a person overcome the fear of asking others for financial support?
- Are others growing in their Christian faith because of the candidate's model?
- How has team efforts to raise prayer and financial supporters worked out?

Applying the Criteria

Since 1983, associates of the Center for Organizational & Ministry Development have conducted over 125 Church Planting Assessment Seminars. More than 2,500 candidates have been evaluated. Of these, approximately 66 percent were recommended primarily for church planting in urban settings. Research conducted on these church planters demonstrate a positive correlation between this approach to selection and the successful plants of national led churchs.

Conclusion

If mission agencies set goals for their personnel of attaining phase-out, they must first recruit and select candidates that are capable of such a task. To do this, they will need to conduct a job analysis and identify the criteria that specifically relates to the job at hand. Among other things, this will include a willingness to be part of a team that expects to develop national teams to take over from them.

Taking such an approach to recruitment and selection will help assure an agency that the candidates they approve are the kind that possess the qualities needed to complete the task, and institute phase-out. It will eliminate the temptation to place unqualified personnel (e.g., Bill and Nancy) in a church plant situation. Guilt and frustration can be avoided by selecting individuals who are not intimidated by required role changes. Clearly, how a mission agency handles the recruiting and selection process will play an important role in phase-out possibilities.

The fourteen characteristics of an ideal church planter's profile may appear formidable and even somewhat unrealistic. Admittedly, it is idealistic. But don't give up on being a church planter just yet. Recognize that few, if any individuals, will be gifted with all the qualities listed above. It should also be noted there are levels of attainment for each criteria, and that a team is required to meet all the criteria at a minimum level.

Yet these fears should not deter sending agencies from formulating such a ideal profile at home, nor church planters from developing the same with nationals. If the baton is to be passed to national church planters, it should be passed to qualified people. What would the national church planter profile look like? How would assessment differ in a cross-cultual setting? For apart from setting high goals and standards, not much of significance is ever accomplished.

The church planter profile also points out the need to form a team that comprises all these qualities at a minimal level.

PART 2

Preentry

"It is not good to have zeal without knowledge....Commit to the LORD whatever you do, and your plans will succeed....Go and make a survey of the land and write a description of it....Writedown the revelation and make it plain on tablets so that a herald may run with it."

(Prov. 19:2; 16:3; Josh. 18:8; Hab. 2:2, NIV)

5

Assembling A Phase-out Oriented Team

Church planting that empowers nationals responsibly usually requires more than an individual effort, it requires a team of qualified men and women. Unfortunately, my preparatory studies incorporated little opportunity for teamwork. That is, we were not required to be involved in planting a church, nor write church planting strategies corporately. We could only conclude that it was assumed that the socialization aspects of our training, together with specific theoretical teaching on the subject of church planting, would produce unified teams automatically. This combination seemed to be all that was needed to empower qualified nationals to take leadership and eventually plant new churches. Sadly however, experience has shown otherwise.

To be fair, we must concede that the considerable emphasis placed on conflict resolution (following procedures outlined in Matthew 18) did help preserve a team's longevity once it was formed. However, too little attention was given to all that goes into building or dissolving a team. For example, we were not alerted to: 1) the sequence of phases whereby team members become effective contributors; 2) the changes in style of leadership for the different phases; 3) the impact of different personalities on the team; 4) the wisdom of writing strategies and job descriptions (for both team leaders and key players); and 5) how to dissolve a team.

In addition, when I arrived in the host country I soon became aware of the tremendous internal pressure that the teams of expatriate and national church planters, translators and community developers were working under. For some, this inordinate amount of stress turned to disillusionment and resulted in a giving up and a return to the homeland.

How were we to account for this? Might some of this be due to the fact that so few had previous experience with team activities of any kind, let alone any related to church planting? Were personal agendas (due more to ignorance than to intent?) taking the place of team agendas? What perceptions do these leave with nationals?

Building a phase-out oriented team of qualified individuals involves consideration of at least the following: foundations and precedents for team-building, strengths and weaknesses of a team concept, the definition of a team, and the process by which effective teams produce national churches capable of reproducing new communities of faith.

Foundations and Precedents for Team Building

At the outset, we note the concept of teamwork that appears in the Trinity, where the Father, the Son, and the Holy Spirit not only make significant individual contributions, but also work together as a team to accomplish a common objective.

In the Old Testament, Nehemiah provides a prime example of a team builder. After he himself inspected the destruction of the walls of Jerusalem, he took a small band of men with him to assess the situation. Nehemiah then assumed strong leadership when he challenged this select group—a motivated team—to remove Israel's disgrace by rebuilding the walls. Apparently the group accepted his challenge because they replied, "Let us start rebuilding" (Neh. 2:18, NIV). As a result the walls were restored in just fifty-two days!

Later, Jesus committed his plan for reaching a lost world into the hands of a twelve-member, personally selected, team with widely differing personalities and backgrounds. We know about one team member who failed, and we read of conflict among some of the others. Yet all were called by Jesus to work together to fulfill a common objective. The account in Mark states, He "sent them out two by two" (6:7, NIV).

Interestingly, Jesus' team approach carries over into the book of Acts. Murphy (1976:113) has identified eleven of the most notable teams:

Barnabas-Saul-Mark (13:4-13)
Paul-Barnabus and their "companions" (13:13-15:12)
Paul-Barnabas-Judas-Silas (15:22-34)
Paul-Silas (15:40ff)
Barnabas-Mark (15:37-39)

Paul-Silas-Timothy (16:1-9)
Paul-Silas-Timothy-Luke (16:10ff)
Paul-Silas-Timothy-Luke-Aquilla-Priscilla (18:2-23)
Paul-Silas-Timothy-Luke-Aquilla-Priscilla-Apollos (18:24 -29)
Paul-Silas-Timothy-Luke-Erastus-Gaius-Aristarchus (19)
Paul-Silas-Timothy-Luke-Sopater-Aristarchus-Secundus-Gaius-Tychicus-Trophimus (20:4)

A study of these teams can provide much information that is significant. In the first place, we learn that not all team compositions were successful. For example, Paul and Barnabus' team broke apart due to differences of opinion, yet neither of them abandoned full-time ministry. Second, although the previous experience of the team members varied considerably, every team had at least one experienced leader. Finally, successful teams may be comprised of multi-national members (Acts 20:4).

Recognizing The Strengths and Weaknesses of Teamwork

In recent years the idea of teamwork has grown in popularity. Mission agencies too are taking greater interest in a team approach, believing it may be the best way to reach a lost world for Christ. Proponents of the team concept point to potential mathematical possibilities where two plus two may equal seven (Lev. 26:8; Eccles. 4:9-12). Others argue, however, that two plus two may equal one.

Thus, the team approach should not be viewed as a panacea, for it has weaknesses as well as strengths. In fact, its potential weaknesses may derive from its very strengths. For example, while loneliness may be decreased by team relationships, the possibilities of friction among members will increase. For some, teamwork may enable a balanced ministry, but at the same time bring disagreements about priorities. (See Table 3 for a list of tensions found in the team approach.)

Defining A Phase-out Oriented Team

Building on Francis and Young's (1979) definition, I propose to define a phase-out oriented team as: An energetic group of people committed to God, who strive for team unity while completing a common objective, and who enjoy their working relationships and intend to settle only for quality results.

Table 3

Strengths and Weaknesses of the Team Approach

Strengths	Weaknesses
1. diminishes loneliness	1. increases friction
2. provides balance in ministry	2. produces disagreement as to priorities
3. provides continuity in ministry	3. creates dependency
4. includes various generations	4. includes potential for conflict and statuses
5. provides protection and solace	5. becomes ingrown
6. provides collective strength	6. stifles individual initiative
7. produces quality decisions	7. produces power cliques
8. has stated objectives	8. leads to inflexibility

There may be other important components in the definition of team, but in this definition four stand out:

1. An energetic group committed to God,
2. Strive for team unity while achieving a common objective,
3. Enjoy working relationships,
4. Goal of high quality results.

All four of these components readily apply to expatriate church planting teams worldwide. The first calls for an action-oriented, physically healthy group of individuals who like to accomplish things *for,* and *through,* the Lord. By means of their collective synergistic efforts they seek to facilitate a responsible phase-out. *To accomplish this, the team members must recognize at the start that there is an end to their work.*

Perhaps the key to implementing the team's phase-out objective is the combination of these components: commitment to God, to each other, and to the task. Their commitment to God is the anchor that will hold them fast in the midst of inevitable storms. Their commitment to a team means a willingness to recognize, respect and enjoy the diversity of personalities, and the variety of spiritual gifts and skills each member brings to the team (Rom. 14:19). Their commitment to the task denotes a willingness to stick with the job until its completion.

The last component reflects professionalism. As responsible team members, they shoot for high quality professional results. They will hold each other accountable, by refusing to tolerate slothful behavior or sloppy results. In other words, their is a mutual concern for faithfulness and accountability (I Cor. 4:2; I Pet. 4:10).

In summary: a responsible, phase-out oriented, church planting team recognizes it exists to accomplish certain objectives and then move on. To do this the team members commit themselves to God, to the team and to the task. More specifically, they agree at the outset to a stated set of objectives; together they modify them as necessary; they unite to make a professional effort to expedite them; they expend the necessary energy to maintain positive interpersonal relationships within the team; they celebrate collectively the team's quality accomplishments; and ultimately form successor teams (of nationals) to replicate the effective church planting.

Assembling A Phase-out Oriented Team

What kind of individuals do phase-out oriented teams require? Actually, these teams call for a special kind of mindset with a willingness to relinquish one's own area of ministry to national counterparts. Such giving up of personal ministry however can be very threatening. On the one hand, it can result in a win-lose situation if team members tenaciously hold on to their power because this stifles the nationals' growth which then impedes phase-out. On the other hand, it can be turned in to a win-win situation if team members share power readily, for sharing power often multiplies power. In the latter instance, capable leadership among national believers can emerge as church planters which then frees up the original church planting team to focus their efforts elsewhere.

Team leaders should therefore search for individuals who can view ministry from a long-term perspective, not just the short-term. They will seek those who demonstrate flexibility, a willingness to follow as well as lead, and possess a strong self-image that allows them to empower others without being threatened themselves. Finally, they will search for individuals who enjoy assisting others grow.

Timing too is important in building a responsible phase-out oriented, church planting team. It is beneficial for such a team to form *before* leaving the home country to plant churches abroad.[1]

Because of the many possibilities that exist today for ministering among ethnics in both the United States and Canada, assessing a candidate's ability to work on such a team is possible in a cross-cultural setting here without having to wait until an individual arrives in a foreign country.

Ideally, some pre-field, cross-cultural church planting experience in a team context should be required of every candidate. Such a requirement would allow an agency to assess a number of pertinent qualities prior to sending the individuals to a field, particularly the following: (1) the ability to work as part of a team; (2) the ability to identify with others of different cultural backgrounds; and (3) the ability to empower others responsibly. Mission agencies who can send teams abroad comprised of personnel who have already worked together on a team project will undoubtedly be better equipped to work with nationals on a team and undertake a cross-cultural church plant assignment.

Pre-field experience also benefits the team as will as the agency. As team members, they become acquainted with each other through work, play, and ministry—all in an environment that is common (or at least familiar) in which they can share their personal and team expectations (e.g., doctrine, methodology, child rearing). Test instruments that help team members understand themselves and each other include: the Personal Profile System (work style preference), The 4MAT System (learning style preference), and Disciple Leadership Profile[2] (leadership style preference). These tools are helpful in identifying individual strengths and weaknesses, and they can assist in assembling a balanced team where members complement one another.

Organizing A Phase-out Oriented Team

A number of pertinent questions should be asked before the formation of a team is finalized. Five come to mind at this crucial time in the team's development:

1. Who will lead the team?
2. Why do we exist (purpose)?
3. How should we organize ourselves to fulfill our vision?
4. How will we resolve conflict?
5. Who will back us?

Selecting the Team Leader

While there are a number of key factors that influence a team's effectiveness, probably the most important is the selection of a capable leader. Sometimes it is the mission agencies who select the team leaders, and they in turn recruit their own team members. In other cases, a few individuals may begin to form relationships, out of which a team will form, and a leader will emerge. Regardless of which way team leaders assume power, they should possess skills in two basic areas: (1) in building relationships; and (2) in accomplishing tasks.

To be effective, a team leader must first of all know how to work with people, and be able to motivate them to work productively with others. For this reason, leaders of teams must know and understand themselves as well as the other team members. In their key roles, they will be called upon to: model servanthood, build trust, be encouragers, mediate conflict, be supportive, keep communication of feelings and issues flowing, and exhibit a willingness to learn.

The second area of importance for a team leader relates to the task to be undertaken. A team leader must understand the various components that comprise the tasks, and know how to prevent blockages. Key attributes for team leaders in this category include the following: they should be persons who seek as well as provide information, stimulate ideas, delegate, manage human resources, craft strategy, and be able to evaluate.

In addition, the more effective team leaders demonstrate a flexible leadership style. They change their style to take into account the current stage of team's development: that is, whether the team is being assembled, sustained, or dissolved. Effective leaders possess the wisdom to know when to delegate, and how to guide their teams towards closure.

Verbalizing the Team's Vision

Beyond adequate leadership, teams need a Vision Statement that zeroes in on their overall objectives. Among other things a Vision Statement articulates the team's direction, and it alleviates false guilt when some worthy concerns do not receive equal attention; it is useful for specifying direction for resources (both personnel and financial); it helps refocus goals if the team strays off course; and because the established goals are stated, it is easier to determine the present position, which then makes the timing of passing the baton (phase-out) much clearer.

Team member(s) compose their Vision Statement based on current knowledge of their target people. Although specifics of this statement will need adjustments over time as the data base increases, the initial writing provides direction for the team. To illustrate, the Vision Statement we prepared for the Ifugao church plants reads:

> The long-range objective of the Antipolo / Amduntug Ifugao team is to see three New Testament indigenous churches, capable of maintaining their physical existence and reproducing themselves spiritually,established in the areas of Dugyo, Pula, and Amduntug, within eight years, at a cost of $750,000.

A Vision Statement will serve to keep all of its members headed in the same direction, particularly if a team is multi-gifted. Without such a statement—along with a commitment to it—team members will tend to drift into doing what is right as each sees it, which often results in chaos (Judg. 17:6). Team unity is threatened, love for one another dims, and the nationals (with their uncanny ability to read people), fail to perceive Jesus (John 13:35). Can team members continually state conscientiously: "Look at us!" (Acts 3:4)? If they have agreed together on a team Vision Statement, the goal of unity and phase-out can be facilitated.

Organizing the Team

The third question asks how should teams be organized so that individual gifts and skills are maximized? Conducting a job analysis will answer this question.

Conducting a job analysis. The Vision Statement can be translated into its specific jobs and tasks (which at the same time considers all environmental factors) through conducting a job analysis. While agencies should take the lead in conducting such a study to be sure they recruit the right type of personnel, the team members too will benefit from conducting their own study. Such studies clarify how jobs relate to each other, then help identify the various components of each job and the order of priorities, and they help identify the qualifications needed for accomplishing them. (See Bemis [1983] and Gael [1983]) for detailed specifics on conducting a job analysis.)

Designing the team's organizational chart. Because cross-cultural church planting calls for a team of multi-gifted people, individual teams may include:

1. Linguist / Translators
2. Anthropologists
3. Evangelists
4. Disciplers
5. Ethnomusicologists
6. Community developers (medical / agricultural / educational)

It may be that some team members will be gifted in more than one skill, which could reduce the number of members needed.

Also, some types of specialization may not be required for certain people, e.g., literacy personnel in a literate area. Alternately, personnel may be seconded from other agencies to complete a team. For example, WBT/SIL may supply a linguist / translator. Just how many members are necessary for a team, and in fact how many teams are needed for specific people groups, are determined by reference to previous demographic studies. Figure 4 depicts a possible organizational chart.

Writing job descriptions. Job descriptions clarify the role expectations of both leaders with followers, and of followers with other followers. Such a document helps diffuse potential conflict by removing the fog that so often shrouds job assignment boundaries. See Appendix E for a Job Description form.

Projecting time lines. The team's Vision Statement can also help determine the length of time needed to complete the project. Timetables can be produced for each of the four stages of church planting: preevangelism, evangelism, postevangelism and phase-out (See Figure 5.)

All time projections should be revised annually, since elements like health, or calamities may impact them. But timetables must never be allowed to jeopardize professionalism. Rather than compromise the quality of results, timetables should be extended. Timetables should serve as allies when striving for responsible

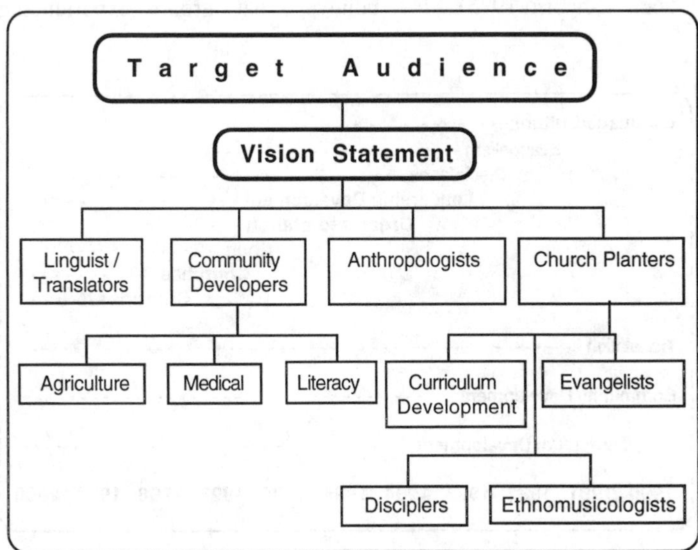

Figure 4. The team's organizational chart

phase-out.

Contingency plans. Church planting teams frequently find themselves living in dangerous areas of the world. Therefore, sending agencies and team(s) should develop ahead of time a manual that establishes evacuation criteria, including a list(s) of those to be contacted, procedures for a hostage situation, responses to ransom demands, communication codes to signify the degree of urgency, and suggested escape routes. Matthew (10:16) recommends that Christians be shrewd as snakes and as innocent as doves. Having contingency plans, in lieu of Matthew's advice, may someday prove crucial in protecting the lives of innocent team members.

Planning for Team Conflict

Although history teaches us conflict is inevitable, team members often fail to learn the skills to resolve conflicts. Even the Apostles could not agree which one was the greatest (Matt. 18:1). Social differences caused friction in the early church (Acts 6). While team members may be close friends at the outset, conflicts between individuals all too often alter relationships. Team members should anticipate conflicts and learn how to deal with them *before* they become a reality.

Skillful handling of conflicts can actually prove beneficial to a team (Shapiro 1975). He believes that groups experiencing

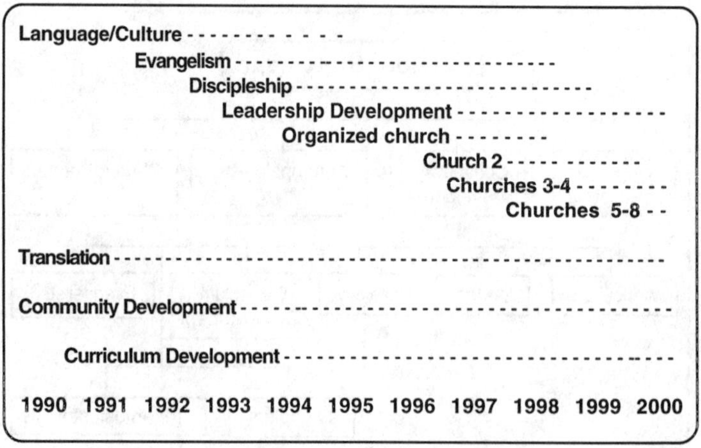

Language/Culture - - - - - - - - - - - -
Evangelism -
Discipleship -
Leadership Development - - - - - - - - - - - - - - - - - -
Organized church - - - - - - - -
Church 2 - - - - - - - - - - -
Churches 3-4 - - - - - - - -
Churches 5-8 - -

Translation -

Community Development -

Curriculum Development -

1990 1991 1992 1993 1994 1995 1996 1997 1998 1999 2000

Figure 5. Project level time projections

conflict are apt to be more creative in their problem solving than groups experiencing little or no conflict, and they tend also to be more effective decision-makers. Moreover, the greater the conflict, the stronger their commitment to the agreed-upon decision, once the conflict has been resolved.

But we need not assume all conflict results in a win-lose. Win-win situations are possible, particularly for teams who share a common Vision Statement and similar methodology. Effective teams plan ahead by thinking through creative approaches for meeting conflict resulting from both human and Satanic influences; these effective teams strive to use conflict creatively so as to facilitate rather than delay phase-out. This kind of creativity can provide national teams with excellent models to replicate.

Team Life Cycle. Potential conflict may be reduced if team members recognize there are various phases through which teams pass. The first phase is a time when team members feel each other out while trying to avoid friction. I call this the ***discovery*** phase. (See Figure 6.)

In the second phase, members begin to ***disagree*** with each other. Tensions arise as individuals articulate methodological preferences and vie for control. Personalities are attacked. At this point some team members may opt out, especially if they believe no resolution is possible, or if their ideas seem to be unappreciated.

The third phase is characterized by organizational ***development.*** Roles and accountabilities become clarified. Team members establish procedures for handling business, including resolving conflict. They commit to a shared vision, goals, and priorities. When disagreement arises, they try to focus on issues rather than personalities. Team members begin to really listen to each other. Servanthood becomes the team's model.

In the fourth phase, maturing teams demonstrate an interdependence as the individual members work together toward a joint objective. Team commitment and synergy now make it possible to ***deliver*** on established priorities. They understand their roles as leaders and followers. They commit to established methodology yet remain flexible. When conflict arises, team members provide descriptive feedback and demonstrate active listening. Team members write slogans, create ritual, and relate success stories to keep the vision alive. They actively seek to serve each other.

Dissonance can set in at any time in the team life cycle (center circle). Vision and commitment can be lost. As new members come on board or former members leave for one reason or another, role and accountability lines tend to become ambiguous. Personal agendas begin to replace the former team objective. Communication deteriorates causing mistrust to build. Some feel unwanted. The team must recognize the deterioration taking place and return to phase four as soon as possible or face premature disbanding. (The return to phase four will most likely require a leader with expertise in group renewal.) In that most teams will find themselves addressing these issues a number of times before reaching their ultimate objective, demonstrating a servant heart at all times must become and remain one of their greatest priorities.

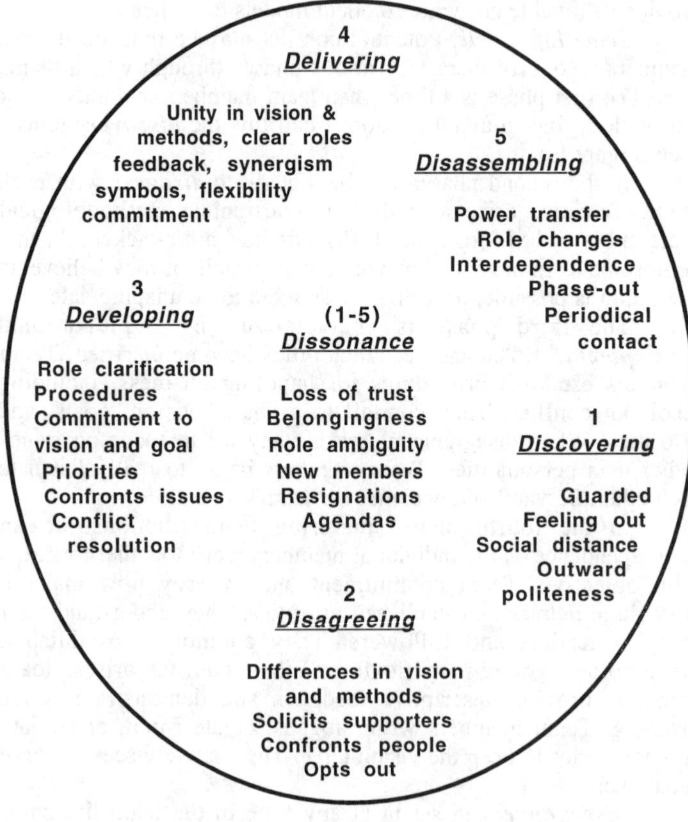

Team goal: Servanthood demonstrated in each phase.

Figure 6. The Life Cycle of a Team

To be sure, phase-out oriented teams will reach another phase, ***disassembling***, particularly when nationals begin to assume responsibilities of the various ministries and expatriates begin to withdraw. Role changes take place as power transfers into the hands of the nationals. Some team members may be invited to work under the nationals. For others, periodical contact will continue as deep friendships are hard to break. An understanding of these five phases will go a long way in helping teams complete their phase-out vision.

Fostering a climate for growth. The body of Christ should be a living, loving, challenging, and loyal community, with a goal of fostering a positive climate for character development and performance. This is a climate that honors God while at the same time challenges followers to righteousness and justice in a world controlled by Satan. Effective teams should reflect these same characteristics. They too need to help each other grow by fostering a climate favorable for growth, and by building each other up in Christ. Only in this way is a positive and visible model evident for nationals to follow (see Table 4).

Rapid bonding of new members. Sickness, disillusionment, singles marrying, and death—all have a way of changing a team's composition over time. This is another way of saying team members who begin a ministry seldom finish together. However, it

Table 4

Fostering Climate for Individual Growth

Creating climate	Building potential
1. active listening to their ideas and fears	1. admonishment (Rom. 15:14)
2. acceptance (Prov. 17:17; Rom. 15:5)	2. guidance
3. encouragement (I Thess. 5:11)	3. exhortation (Heb. 10:24)
4. hospitality (I Pet. 4:9)	4. commitment to goals
5. prayer (Jas. 5:16)	5. use of spiritual gifts (I Pet. 4:10)
6. forgiveness (Eph. 4:32)	6. teaching (Col. 3:16)
7. focus on behavior, not personality	
8. equal concern for each other (I Cor. 12:25)	
9. joy (Neh. 8:10)	

is possible to minimize the trauma of changes in a team's composition by "bonding" the new members as rapidly as possible. Graham (1988) argues that unless a team's "kinning" process is well underway within sixty to ninety days, the newcomer may easily remain an outsider. He identifies six objectives he believes must be in place if newcomers are to function fully as contributing members:

1. Complete understanding and support of the team's objectives.
2. Understand the team's basic strategy for meeting its objectives and their role in it.
3. Active participation in team meetings.
4. Active participation in ministry assignments.
5. Name seven new national friends made since they arrived.
6. Identify three unchurched nationals with whom they are taking specific steps to bring to Christ.

The need for immediate bonding is equally true for new members of national teams as for new members of expatriate teams. Although the fifth and sixth objectives above may be less applicable in the case of the former, the need for immediate bonding of new members remains indisputable for both.

> *...team members must recognize at the start that there is an end to their work.*

Celebrating the Team's Covenant. To be effective, phase-out oriented teams are more than just groups of individuals who work together; they are unified groups with shared objectives. But because unity and purpose in any relationship may be eroded by time and familiarity, it is especially helpful if teams schedule an annual event to remind them of their commitment to God, to each other and the growth of the team, and to the task before them. One way to accomplish this is to develop a Team Covenant that is then signed and celebrated annually.

A Team Covenant should designate the approximate number of years it will take to complete their objectives of ministry. Today, long-term commitments are not common, yet it seems only reasonable that each member contract before the Lord, and together with the others on the team, for the years expected to complete the task. This commitment then can be renewed each year. Annual celebrations of recommitment will do much to avoid or resolve conflict, and help promote the team's longevity.

Conclusion

Phase-out oriented church planting teams are not born, they are developed carefully over time. Ideally, they begin with ministry on the home front, in a cross-cultural setting. Each team should have a talented leader, a phase-out oriented vision statement, and—most importantly—be composed of a group of gifted individuals willing to defer to each other and to nationals. Their established group think becomes "entrepairneur," rather than "entrepreneur." As church-planting teams accomplish these goals, and replaced by newly developed national teams with like objectives, the Vision Statement will be fulfilled, nationals will reach their full potential, responsible phase-out will be a reality, and Jesus Christ will be honored.

But how do team members walk through the Vision Statement? Its time now to reflect on how to process vision into action.

1 Should a multi-ethnic team be formed, nationals and/or other nationalities would join most likely when the team reaches the host country. This will require that time and energies be spent to incorporate the new members' insights in overall objectives and day-to-day operations discussed prior to arriving. See: Harrison's *Developing Multinational Teams* for helpful insights.

2 Copies of these instruments may be obtained from the publishers as follows: Personal Profile System Performax Systems International, Inc. 12755 State Highway 55, Minneapolis, MN 55441; The 4MAT System Excel, Inc. 600 Enterprise Dr. Suite 101, Oak Brook, IL 60521; Disciple Leadership Profile Center for Organizational & Ministry Development. 120 E. La Habra Blvd., Suite 107, La Habra, CA 90631.

6

Processing Phase-out *Vision Into Action*

In rethinking the experiences of a number of my mission agency's church planters I came to realize that most of us were unacquainted with much that goes into the process of planting and developing churches. (Many of us, however, had experience in church splits.) It had not been suggested to us during our training that we design a strategy, nor were we introduced to models that could help propel our vision into phase-out.

Without this kind of training many of us launched naively into our church plants. The assumption seemed to be that by taking a step-by-step approach toward phase-out, our vision would be fulfilled eventually in God's time. There were some who questioned spending the time required to formulate such a detailed strategy, believing it to be poor stewardship. As they saw it, the urgency of fulfilling the Great Commission demanded immediate action due to the fact that so many people remained without the gospel. However sincere this concern, the absence of national led churches challenged this thinking.

In light of my past experience I will now propose a "user friendly," seven-step planning model designed to assist church planting teams reach the phase-out objective. This model builds upon the initial steps of assembling and organizing a team covered in Chapter Five (Step One). In this chapter, the model addresses: the benefits of strategic planning, internal and external environmental scans, defining a shared vision, model selection and faith objectives, action plans, results and evaluation (see Figure 7.)

Benefits of Strategic Planning

Strategic planning takes more than time; it takes perspiration. But it pays great dividends, especially when the objective of phase-out results. Some of the previously mentioned church plant attempts required a second generation of planters to try to counteract the results of poor strategy. Sad to say Meskinmen's Law often applied: "There's never time to do it right, but there's always time to do it again."

What are some of the benefits of strategic planning? First and foremost it can provide purpose and direction in that it states the team's reason for existence. Once the team understands its purpose and direction, priority tasks begin to emerge. Members can then set priorities and inquire if any member will need additional specialized training to accomplish them.

Strategic planning also provides a guide for evaluating a team's progress. It acts as a scorecard to measure wins and losses. It also can foster team unity in that team members come together to think about and plan the entire church plant process, including agreement on common terminology and symbols.

Relationships Scans

Steps two and three call for team members to conduct environmental scans of the internal and external relationships. These two steps answer pertinent questions, such as, What should team members expect from each other? Who is concerned about the team's successes and failures? The internal and external scans also provide important information that can help build quality relationships, enhance the communication process, and provide specificity to strategic planning.

Wise teams will want to identify who cares about the success or failure of their efforts, both internally and externally. By internal relationships, I mean the individual, the families, and the other team members. By external relations I mean the target community, the collaborators, and competitors. How members of a team relate to each other and those outside the team, and plan the strategy, is certain to affect their ability to implement and also complete the phase-out vision (see Figure 8).

Scanning Internal Relationships

Team leaders play a key role in scanning internal relationships. In that team participants—the individual, members, family members, and co-workers—all have personal expectations.

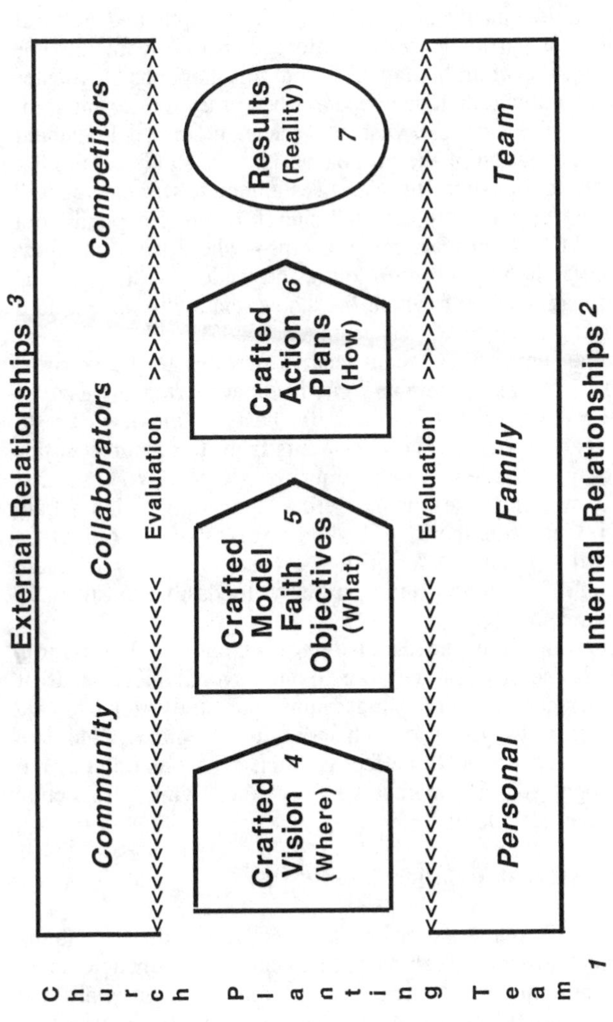

Figure 7. Processing vision into acton

Team leaders should identify the expectations early so as to utilize them constructively or diffuse them immediately. Team leaders also need to recognize each member's competency and commitment levels relative to specific job descriptions, and coordinate the team's collective efforts.

Depending on the population and geographical / cultural boundaries of a particular people, more than one team may be necessary for the church plants. When this happens, a master strategy and continual dialogue becomes necessary. For example, if a team with some evangelists wishes to focus on the Old Testament first in its presentation of the gospel, but the translator on another team decides to translate the New Testament first, conflict will result. Successful phase-out oriented church planting depends to a great extent on unified team relationships—where team members evidence servanthood, both as follower and leader. Without mutual submission, nationals with whom the teams relate will have a hard time discerning those on Christ's team (Jn. 13:35).

Another concern for team leaders pertains to the spiritual well being of the team members, members who find themselves entrenched in spiritual battle on a daily basis. If members are to hold to a clear conviction that God wants them to continue in this ministry, they will need daily feeding from God's Word so that unexpected circumstances do not erode long-range plans. Paul challenged team members to "take time to keep yourselves spiritually fit" (1 Tim. 4:7, Phillips). Team members who are vacillating in this area will find it virtually impossible to fulfill the Vision Statement.

Numerous other needs also require continual attention. These include the physical, emotional, and psychological needs of each team member. Attaining maximum team unity requires that holistic attention be given to each individual member. Complete team health is foundational to effective ministry, for as Bavinck has astutely recognized, team members become the "living introduction to the message" (1960:89).

Scanning External Relationships

Key to external relationships are members of the community the team plans to serve. Teams must become knowledgeable about the host community's historical background, its geographic and demographic particulars, and its language and culture, if they want to earn the right to be heard, particularly by the right people. (Chapter Eight develops this topic.)

By identifying the collaborators and competitors, team members can design the overall strategy with much more focus. Some of the collaborators and competitors would include the

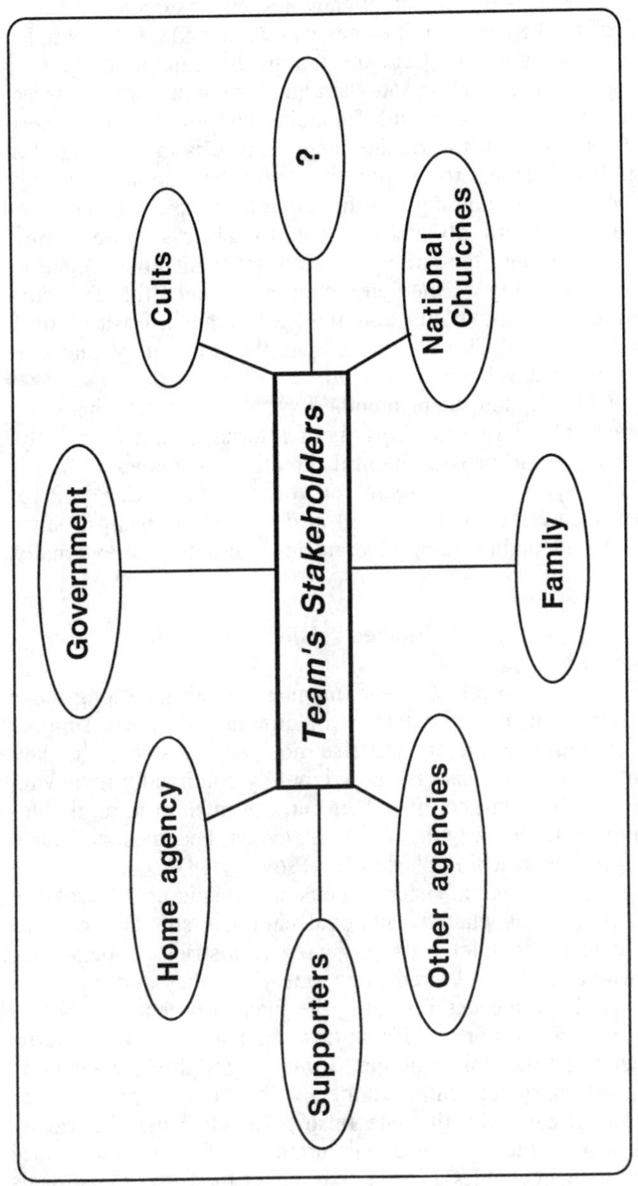

Figure 8. Identifying the team's stakeholders

mission agency, the national government, the national church, prayer and financial supporters, cults, Peace Corps, nonevangelicals, an association of churches, and insurgents.

Each of the above entities has its own agenda. For example, the team's sending agency has expectations that cannot be ignored; the host government and/or national church may or may not agree with the team's agenda; and financial supporters may exert pressures on the team to produce tangible results in exchange for funding. The people to whom the team has come also has expectations, to say nothing of other church groups or insurgents. Effective teams will do all they can to address these varied expectations through the strategies. How team members relate to outsiders, especially if they are unable to meet the expected expectations, will inevitably communicate either a positive or a negative meaning of Christianity to them, the community, and also to the national teams being developed.

For this reason, team members must constantly check the temperature of all relationships, both internally and externally. Paul's example can provide helpful direction in this area: "I will most gladly spend and be spent for your good" (2 Cor. 12:15, Phillips). Such efforts should result in deeper relationships, better communication, and meaningful strategies internally and externally.

A Shared Vision

The third step calls for team members to design a long-range Vision Statement, i.e., a statement of direction they can support whole heartedly. Such an exercise not only answers the key question of *where* the team is headed, but by continually reviewing it, team members will confirm their purpose in short term, day-to-day activities. In this way the Vision Statement becomes the team's driving force for reaching phase-out (Prov. 29:18).

The team's shared Vision Statement paints in broad strokes a finished portrait of what the national churches should look like when the team completes its projected ministries. It began by stating where the team desired to go, not where they currently find themselves. Its value lies in seeing the plan in its entirety *before* dividing it into parts or specifying how the team is to disperse its personnel and financial resources. It also highlights the kinds of training necessary for team members in order to implement the vision, and it can help alleviate false guilt when certain worthy projects cannot receive the team's attention. Finally, the team's Vision Statement enables an easier passing of the baton to nationals because the completed picture becomes recognizable by both parties. (See Figure 9.)

If the Vision Statement is to be adequately implemented, when possible, all team members should participate in its development. A joint venture will foster commitment and unlock team synergy; it will test the members' foundational assumptions about church planting; it will enable future leaders to emerge; and it can help guard against short-term operations as well as create a positive climate in which change can occur. But team members should not only participate in the initial draft of the Vision Statement, they must continue to adjust it as they gain more specific information about the host people.

As team members continually craft the Vision Statement they will undoubtedly encounter vision fatigue. It is easy to lose sight of the original vision when the tyranny of the urgent begins to drain the vitality of team members. This problem can be overcome by establishing an organizational structure and symbols that continually strengthen it. Reiteration of stories and slogans, both

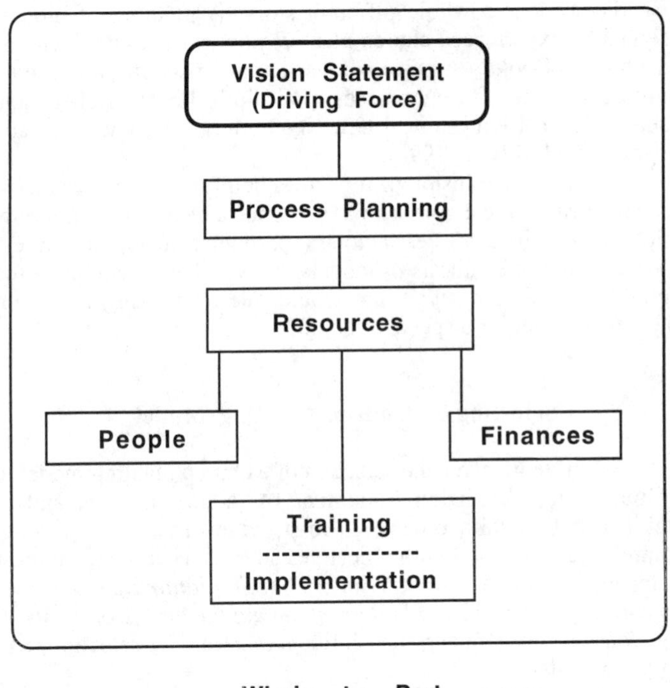

-- -- -- Whole to Part -- -- --

Figure 9. The Vision Statement as the driving force

formally and informally, can help. In any case, the team must persist in doing all it can to instill its structured vision in theminds and hearts of every team member, especially those just joining the team.

Once the team agrees on a Vision Statement, copies should be sent to supporters to solicit specific prayer. Prayer supporters can provide team members with some of the spiritual resources they need to claim a portion of Satan's territory for Christ.

Models and Faith Objectives

When we left for the Philippines in 1971 to plant churches among the Ifugao, no published church planting model existed of which I was aware. It would take almost another decade to pass before Hesselgrave (1980) would unveil his now well known 10-step model. We were on our own to develop a model that would fit our audience.

Today it is a whole different story. A plethora of models designed by experienced church planters now exist from which one can choose. Books espousing a particular cross-cultural model continue to roll off the presses (Faircloth 1991; Hiebert and Meneses 1995; Livingstone 1993; Neighbour 1990; Patterson and Scoggins 1993; Silvoso 1994).

While this explosion of models is helpful to church planters, it can also cause great confusion. How does a church planter know which model will work best among a particular people? Is there a specific model or synthesis of models that will best accomplish the team's Vision Statement? What would one be looking for when selecting a model for a specific people?

Selecting A Church Planting Model

Step five involves the selection of a church planting model to facilitate a team's Vision Statement for a host people, and to establish certain faith objectives to provide direction and bring closure. The model and faith objectives address *what* the team must do by asking the question, *Which church planting model best promotes the team's Vision Statement among the host people?* I will now consider three factors that influence the model selection, and suggest a model to evaluate models.

Church planters impact model selection. Church planting models tend to reflect the history, goals and aspirations of those who develop them. One could say the same of the models church planters select—they tend to reflect the history, goals, and aspirations of those who select them. Church planters who prefer to take a more controlling role throughout the church plant will select a model that reflects such a philosophy. Those who seek to phase-out, i.e., gradually turn the ministry over to nationals, or take a subordinate role under nationals will select models that support such aspirations. Models and church planters tend to find themselves intricately intertwined.

The type of church planters selected to launch new church plants determine to a great extent the type of churches produced. Nationality, ethnic backgrounds, personalities, leadership styles, followership styles, work styles, philosophies of ministry, skills, gifts, all impact the model selected and the type of churches produced. To illustrate, those overseeing cell groups tend to be strong leaders as do lone ranger church planters in the United States. Other models may require team players. Mission agencies and churches, therefore, should not underestimate the importance of spending significant effort selecting the personnel who will represent them. In that church planting is systemic, the type of church planters recruited will also play a significant role in the type of churches planted and developed.

The Vision Statement impacts model selection. As noted above, the Vision Statement becomes the driving force for the team. Team members will tend to select a model that will help propel their vision to closure.

Target People Impact Model Selection. There are three basic philosophies behind selecting a church planting model. Some prefer to single out a model that reflects personal gifts, skills and cultural backgrounds, and then find a people group that matches it. Logan's (1989) model exemplifies this. Others prefer to select a popular model advocated by a church planter guru and implement it among the target audience. Still others prefer to chose to conduct an environmental scan of a particular people group and craft a model to fit them. Cross-cultural church planters usually find themselves in the second or third categories.

While the second category should prove helpful for cross-cultural church planters (and what church plant is not cross-cultural to some degree?), category three, crafting a model to fit the target audience, is imperative. Until church planters have an in-depth understanding of a specific people group, selecting other than a generic church planting model can prove very ineffective. In that all models have strengths and weaknesses, wise church planters will conduct a thorough investigation of the host people so they can select or design a model that reflects the audience's worldview, as well as personal philosophy and theology. Even then, church planters recognize that future adjustments will be necessary as new cultural insights come to light. For Hesselgrave's (1980) 10-step model, Logan's (1989) ten principles, Neighbour's (1990) cell groups, Faircloth's (1991) 45-events or McIlwain's (1985) seven phases or my five-stage model to be effective among a specific people group, initial adaptation will be necessary, as well as, continual crafting.

With a host of church planting models existing today, how does one select a model for a specific people group? I propose a two-dimensional model for selecting a context-specific church planting model. The first dimension considers the model's comprehensivenss while the latter assesses its effectiveness.

Evaluating Comprehensiveness

What components should a comprehensive church planting model include? I have identified a minimum of five (See Table 5). As you read through these, and the "effectiveness" components below, ask yourself how well your model scores in each of the respective categories in relation to your target audience.

Foremost, a comprehensive church planting model will find itself rooted deeply in biblical principles. To evaluate this one could ask: Does the model promote the translation, study, and application of both Testaments of the Bible? Does it emphasize dependence upon the Holy Spirit and prayer? Does it take into account the past and present battles being fought between God and Satan? Does it present an accurate account of the gospel message?

Modeling the character of Christ should also be a prerequisite for the model. For example, Jesus "did not cling to His prerogatives as God's equal, but stripped himself of all privilege" (Phil. 2:6-7, Phillips) to reveal the Father's purpose to the world. Similarly, Christian workers should incarnate Christ's character in ways that will reveal the Father's plan to the host people. In part, this includes learning the language, understanding the culture and building solid relationships outside the team as well as within it.

A third component calls for Kingdom-based church planting; it includes strategies that address both the spiritual and physical needs of the audience. It incorporates the Great Commandment (Matthew 22:34-40) as well as the Great Commission (Matthew 28:19-20).

The empowering of nationals in all areas of ministry should also be included as a major component. Before responsible phase-out can become a reality, team members will have to release their own power to national counterparts. This power exchange should result in communities of faith led by responsible nationals. For this to happen, however, role changes become necessary for team members (learners, evangelists, teachers, resident advisors, itinerant advisors, absent advisors) and nationals (accompanies,

Table 5

Evaluating a Model's Comprehensiveness

Biblical
- Word (OT/NT)
- Holy Spirit
- prayer
- accurate gospel

Incarnational
- language acquisition
- culture acquisition
- team relationships with each other
- team relationships with host community

Holistic
- addresses felt needs
- addresses spiritual needs

Empowers
- church planter role changes
- national role changes
- long-term vision
- phase-out oriented

Reproduces
- community development
- evangelism
- discipleship
- leadership
- organized church
- reproducing church
- economically feasible

participates, leads, trains). This component helps ensure the overall goal is reached, maximizing the body of Christ by developing responsible national believers and phasing out of the respective ministries. While some team members may receive invitations to continue specific ministries, careful reflection should be given to ensure that dependency does not result.

The final component moves beyond empowering nationals to ensuring that a church planting vision that raises God's visibility in a community continues long after the Christian workers depart. To accomplish this, immediate reproduction of all stages of a church's life should take place: social concerns, evangelism, discipleship, leadership development, church organization, and the planting of new churches among similar people as well as cross-culturally (the mission arm of the church). All of this, of course, must be economically feasible for the target people or worked out judiciously through a partnership agreement.

Evaluating Effectiveness

Some church planting models are more effective in rural settings than in urban. Some work better among the upper-class than among the lower-class. Some induce better results among those living in more permanent settings than among nomadic or semi-nomadic people. Some are more effective than others among a particular ethnic group. Some produce better results among the youth than among an aging generation. Outside factors play a significant role in the effectiveness of any church planting model.

Inside factors play a significant role in effectiveness also. People create church planting models. The models therefore come packaged with certian values and assumptions. These must be identified and compared to those of the target culture.

Effective models will attempt to address a people's ethnicity, history, present worldview(s), socio-economic class, learning style, and gender preference. They will also try to accommodate the lowest skill level of the community of believers so that reproduction of all ministries becomes feasible for the majority. How then can one assess the effectiveness of a particular model for a particular people and class level?

Wise team members will investigate a number of church planting models before arbitrarily selecting the latest publicized model. Just because a particular model is promoted by an experienced church planting specialist in seminars or publications does not guarantee its success in a given team's milieu. Before choosing a particular model, or combining features of several models, it would be advantageous for Christian workers to ask themselves: What is the model's historical context? What key features does it offer? What basic assumptions drive the model? What are its strengths and weaknesses? In what types of communities is it most likely to succeed? (See Figure 10.) Consideration of these and similar questions are especially helpful for teams desiring to select or design a situational-specific model.

A point system could be developed for evaluating the comprehensiveness and effectiveness of any church planting model. Assigning 10 points to each of the ten categories (describing the model's history in the first column of the effectiveness model receives no points) would bring the total for a perfect model fit to 100 points.

100 - 95	Use the model!
94 - 90	Use with minimal adjustments.
89 - 80	Use with major adjustments.
79 - 0	Be very selective and keep looking!

The 10-point evaluation scale based on the church planter's satisfaction with the model could be broken down as follows:

10	9	8	7	6	5	4	3	2	1
Completely satisfied		Very satisfied			Moderately satisfied		Minimally satisfied		Totally dissatisfied

The five-stage model presented in this book offers a number of valuable features (see Appendix B). To illustrate, it recommends the need to look at church planting from a global perspective rather than isolated parts. It begins with the whole picture and then divides it into workable parts. It advocates selecting church planters that are willing to empower nationals responsibly. The model calls for a learner role through the entire church planting process. It views role changes as foundational to the empowerment of nationals. The goal of phase-out receives continual emphasis. Specific faith objectives are stated for each stage of the church plant. It includes a checklist and a tool for developing specific action plans for each of the faith objectives.

One must recognize, however, that this model originated from a particular historical context, i.e., no Philippine national churches had been formed that were run exclusively by nationals even though this remained my agency's stated objective for over twenty years. My own basic assumptions about life and ministry

History	Key Features	Assumptions	Strengths	Weakensses	Adaptability

Figure 10. Evaluating a model's effectiveness.

caused me to question this seeming failure. Some of these include: (a) God desires all believers to grow to their fullest potential, (b) the Holy Spirit is equally capable of leading national believers, (c) empowering others for ministry does not reduce one's own power but rather multiplies it for everyone, (d) mistakes will and should be made, (e) most cross-cultural church planting should result in phase-out, (f) church planting requires a learner mentality from beginning to end, (g) long-term process planning toward a stated goal can provide doable guidelines for short-term activities, (h) responsible phase-out depends on solid relationships being developed and maintained with national believers, (i) responsible phase-out requires constant realignment of roles for both expatriates and nationals, (j) church planting is systemic (i.e., recruitment, selection and training impact the type of churches produced), and (k) phase-out oriented church planting can be planned.

> A plethora of models designed by experienced church planters now exist from which one can choose....While this explosion of models is helpful to church planters, it can also cause great confusion.

An evaluation as to comprehensiveness and effectiveness of this model, or any model, will enable team members to determine its strengths and weaknesses in light of their own target audience. Such an exercise will also inform them of aspects of the model that should be retained, removed, or changed, and may lead them to consider the addition of others in order to effectively reach a particular target audience.

Establishing Faith Objectives

After a team designs its own church planting model and writes the Vision Statement, the faith objectives for each stage of the model can be identified. Faith objectives are intended to articulate what the team believes God will accomplish during each stage of the church plant as they implement the Vision Statement. To determine the faith objectives, team members should ask: What events must transpire so that phase-out will result? (See Appendix F for a partial list of faith objectives.)

Action plans

Action plans (step 6) set forth the steps that will turn the team's faith objectives into reality. Step six suggests *how* this can be accomplished, and provides answers to such questions as: How does the Holy Spirit enable us to turn our faith objectives into action? What obstacles must be overcome? Who is best qualified to accomplish this? What are the specific steps to be taken? What will it cost? How long will it take?

Other questions include: How will the team handle evangelism? worship? discipleship? leadership? missions? social efforts? Which plans should receive priority? Do the nationals concur with the team's plans? with the team's priorities? Do their ideas differ about how these activities should be conducted? Do their priorities match those of the team? When should nationals become involved in the planning? Will well-articulated, culturally sensitive action plans provide protection not only for the team—its unity, purpose, and closure—but also for the emerging national teams of believers?

Effective action plans call for *immediate* involvement by nationals in the planning and implementation. As teams plan strategy for evangelism with the nationals, they should encourage them to play constructive roles in answering questions that relate to who, what, where, when and how. As team members demonstrate a willingness to learn *before* they commit the action plans to writing, they provide positive models for national teams to follow at home and as they move into cross-cultural ministries.

Effective action plans inevitably involve compromise. Although team members usually have little difficulty agreeing on a common Vision Statement or establishing faith objectives, they often have trouble determining how to accomplish these (i.e., methodology). All team members therefore must be willing to compromise, or even sacrifice certain personal desires for the overall good of the team.

Because some members find it difficult to distinguish theology from methodology, there is considerable room for conflict, particularly when individual members stand firm for what they regard as "Truth." Teams must be able to work together not only theologically, but they must also be able to come to agreement on what constitutes prudent methodology. Someone cogently stated: "Our theology will determine the limits of the methodological possibilities, but it will *not* determine the precise methodology." If team members can recognize this fact, they will find it much easier to compromise on sticky issues and not become sidetracked in fulfilling the vision.

Effective action plans, according to Blanchard (1985),

require SMART goals. By SMART goals, he means those that are specific, measurable, attainable, relevant, and trackable. With SMART goals, teams can determine the obstacles to be overcome, and learn what they will need to know to accomplish them. They can also learn who the significant people are that should become involved, the necessary steps to take, the minimum results to be expected, and when to ask God to intervene.

Effective action plans place more emphasis on attaining objectives than on meeting deadlines. Although time projections are valuable and necessary, no one should become a slave to them. Calendars should be adjusted to match appropriate dynamic needs. Team members must remember to serve faithfully and wisely (1 Cor. 4:2; Matt. 10:16) while waiting patiently for God to give the increase (Acts 2:47; 1 Cor. 3:6).

> Church planting models tend to reflect the history, goals and aspirations of those who develop them. One could say the same of the models church planters select — they tend to reflect the history, goals, and aspirations of those who select them.

Unfortunately, shared action plans often tend to be substituted for the fulfilled vision. As with the team's Vision Statement and faith objectives, a modified copy of the team's action plans should also be sent to the prayer supporters. This will give the prayer warriors specific information to pray about while at the same time provide an update on the team's progress toward phase-out. (See Appendix G for a helpful instrument in developing action plans.)

Results

Team members should schedule reality checks periodically throughout the entire church planting process, along with a final check when they withdraw (step 7). Effective phase-out oriented teams create organizational structures that encourage opportunities for redefining or redesigning the team's plans.

Evaluation procedures should take place continually in both internal and external environments so that readjustments can be made immediately. These evaluations also make it possible to celebrate advances as they occur. Once the final evaluation takes place, the team can reflect on how well the phase-out vision was achieved. The evaluations should also prove helpful for preparing the next generation of church planters.

The more effective Vision Statements, church planting models, faith objectives, and action plans usually cannot be planned or formulated at one setting; they emerge over a period of time and through a stream of actions. Errors in strategy as well as unforeseen limitations have a way of surfacing along the way, but these can be cared for by immediate and creative alterations. Although initial, deliberate planning is a must at the outset, team members should accept the fact that the most effective plans are those that remain fluid. There must be a constant crafting of every aspect involved in processing the team's phase-out vision into action.

Conclusion

This chapter presents a seven-step planning model to assist church planting teams in reaching the phase-out vision. While acknowledging that adequate planning takes continual hard work, the benefits far outweigh the efforts.

No single strategy is an end-all-strategy. Constant evaluation, together with creative adjustments are essential ingredients for each phase whether it be the Vision Statement, the church planting model selected, the faith objectives, or the action plans. Each of these must remain relevant to the target audience. Learning to stay relevant will not only benefit a team's own ministry, but will also demonstrate to the national community of faith the importance of being learners in every aspect of ministry. Indeed, being learners is a practice nationals will hopefully emulate as they implement their own church plants at home and cross-culturally.

To help accomplish the vision, a number of exegetical tools become necessary. To these we now turn our attension.

7

Gathering Tools to Accomplish the Vision

A church planter recalled with great enthusiasm his team's evangelistic experience among a people group living in Papua New Guinea. The audience listened intently to the Old and New Testament Bible stories the evangelists taught them. Many attended the teaching sessions as no one wanted to miss any detail of a story. Soon the listeners became capable evangelists, recounting the stories to family members and friends. They took great pains to recite every line. The church planter was impressed deeply with the Papuans' spiritual hunger to learn every line of the stories and teach them to others.

As I listened to the church planter recount his evangelism experience my mind filled with questions. Why did the people have such a deep desire to memorize the stories verbatim? Were the listeners truly seeking God as the church planters believed, or, were they using the Bible stories as a new means of receiving an old dream—the elusive cargo? Did they believe someone would deliver the cargo if they learned the Christian stories adequately? Was the gospel message lost in their worldview? What tools exist that could help church planters better understand a specific people group?

Many of us knew we lacked helpful tools to analyze a people group, particularly tools that could help distinguish types of societies, identify basic values, isolate the social environments existing within a community, and discern the social integration taking place within the community. Most of us, therefore, came to believe naively that one basic strategy of church planting and translation would be sufficient for any people group in the world.

Most of our agency's translators, for example, translated the book of Mark first. They had been taught that this book was the easiest to translate first. While this may be true for the translator, it is questionable whether Mark is the easiest book for many people to comprehend. One reason for this difficulty is that Mark introduces thirteen individuals and eight locations in his first chapter. Beyond that, a number of other questions arise in the same chapter: What is a synagogue? a prophet? sin? repentance? baptism? the Kingdom of God? the Sabbath? the law? a desert? a fisherman?

The choices of translators impacted church planters as well. For those who intended to base the evangelism on the entire Bible, the only written Scriptures available usually came from the New Testament. Many found their evangelism limited due to the almost exclusive translation of New Testament texts.

Although some church planters attempted to incorporate material from the Old Testament, a lack of understanding of the different types of societies and their social environments resulted in a one-strategy-for-all approach. Our expectation of individual decisions, rather than by decisions made by groups, serves as one example. We later came to see that passages from Exodus, Joshua, or the Kings, represented a number of different types of societies and social environments, but at the time most of us had not seen this for ourselves, let alone make any application of it to our audience.

Not surprisingly, our lack of understanding in this vital area carried over to our teaching role as well. For example, we expected all churches to function better with a plurality of leadership rather than with a single leader. This philosophy led to little or no adapting of our evangelistic or discipleship methodologies. But this was due *not* to the lack of a learner's attitude, but to a lack of insight regarding alternative models that diagnostic tools could surface.

Because of church planting experiences like these, I want to present in the following pages a number of diagnostic tools that can assist church planters in identifying types of societies, values, social environments, and socio-cultural integration taking place among a particular people group. These tools will prove applicable to church planters ministering in urban or rural settings. They will help identify the bridges and barriers in evangelism and in discipleship training. Such understanding will facilitate a team's phase-out vision through relevant strategy design and responsible role changes.

Distinguishing Types of Societies

Four major types of societies exist: postindustrial,

industrial, peasant, and tribal. Knowing the most obvious differences between these major groupings can alert church planting teams to the not so obvious spiritual differences and sociological distances that exist between themselves and those they wish to reach with the gospel.

Appendix H distinguishes the four types of societies according to six cultural universals: material culture, social organization, political organization, economic organization, socialization, and science and the supernatural. This information should alert team members to the dangers of designing a single strategy of church planting or Bible translation for reaching every type of people. The fact of great diversity in societies calls for great diversity in strategies.

However, team members must move beyond a general understanding of the types of societies to an enlarged understanding of the *specific* target people. For this, competent diagnostic tools become essential.

Diagnostic Tools for Analyzing Social Environments

During our stay among the Ifugao we became involved in medical work, much of it with children who had a common skin infection *(gulid)*. By the time most Ifugao mothers brought their children to us, the skin infection was so advanced that extended medical attention became necessary. We tried in a number of ways to encourage the mothers to bring their children sooner, but no matter what we said or did, the children continued to arrive with the infection in advanced stages.

I discerned the Ifugao and I differed greatly when it came to crisis orientation. As I perceived it, a little advanced planning could prevent the children from having to endure a lot of needless suffering, but the Ifugao focused on the actual experience. Only when the child's infection became so bad that he or she could no longer sleep at night was it time for medical assistance. Since I personally detested nonplanning and unwarranted delay in such matters, it was hardly surprising that tension between us grew.

Discovering Basic Values

Later I discovered a useful model that helped me see not only what caused these tensions that existed between the Ifugao and myself in relation to crisis orientation; it also clarified for me a number of other important areas (see Figure 11). To illustrate, the model showed that I tended more toward crisis orientation, the Ifugao to non-crisis, with more than a two-point spread between us on the scale. I realized then that some changes were necessary, or tensions would only grow.

Lingenfelter and Mayers (1986:30-33) designed the two-dimensional model to expose certain value tensions and conflict existing between two culturally different parties. However, they intend the model to merely describe a people, not judge them. And

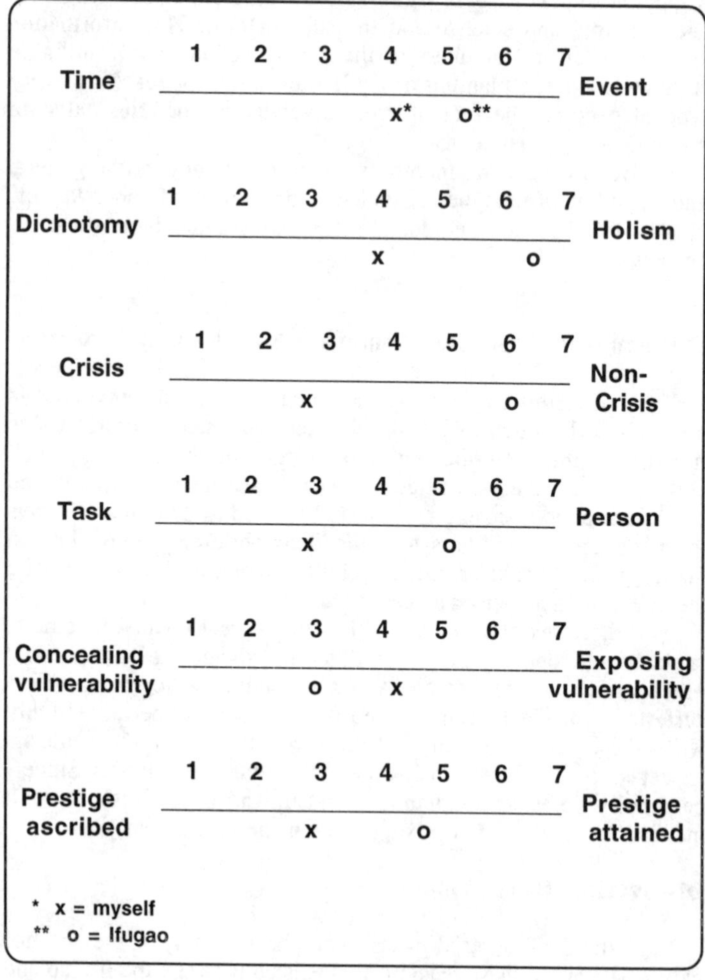

Figure 11. A Comparison of values

(Source: Adapted from Lingenfelter and Mayers 1986:35)

because any model can only approximate reality, the authors assume a smear range for each of the basic values.

Had I completed the questionnaire for this model of basic values shortly after entering the Ifugao tribe, there would no doubt have been a greater distance evident between myself and the Ifugao than is shown in the present comparison. Time and maturity no doubt helped draw us together. From this comparison, it would seem wise for team members to use this model soon after entering a people group, and again after several years.

Discovering Social Environments

Another helpful tool for developing a church planting strategy is Lingenfelter's (1992; 1996) grid / group model. He designed the four-quadrant model to distinguish social environments in relation to hierarchical relationships: Individualistic (A), Bureaucratic (B), Corporate (C) and Collectivist (D). (See Figure 12.) By social environments he means those narrower aspects of a cultural system in which one can observe regular occurring sets of relationship. For example, a researcher examining the hierarchical relationships in the Ifugao's cultural system would investigate such areas as property, labor, exchange, domestic authority, community authority, leadership, process, and decision-making.

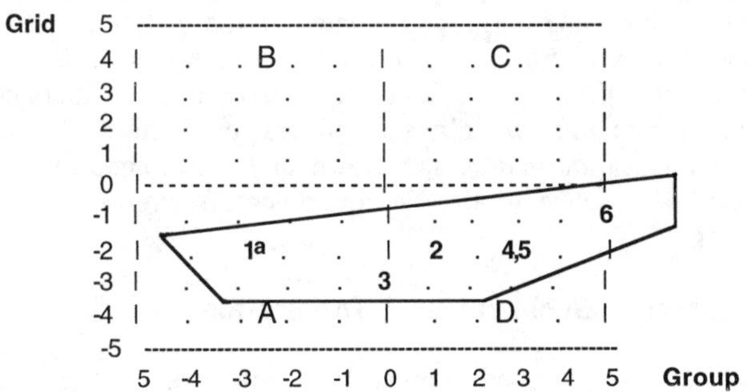

1a - Social environment of property; 2 - Social environment of labor; 3- Social environment of exchange; 4 - Social environment of domestic authority; 5 - Social environment of community authority; 6 - Social environment of leadership, process and decision-making.

Figure 12. Summary graph of the Antipolo / Amduntug Ifugao's social environments

Such an analysis will highlight the ways in which differingvalues act to restrain a people. In addition, it is possible to plot variations in the social environments. To illustrate, when I plotted the individual grid / group scores of the six social environments analyzed among the Antipolo / Amduntug Ifugao, I discovered a linear spread across the bottom of the matrix (see Figure 12). The Ifugao management of property, labor, and exchange, the economic factors of the model, show the Ifugao focusing on the private, domestic unit. The domestic unit operates in a low grid, weak group social environment. They emphasize individual property holdings, independent, profit motivated work activities, and organized labor and exchange for private profit.

An examination of domestic authority, community authority, leadership, process, decision-making, and the socio-political factors of the model illustrate that the Ifugao focus on public events. In the village arena, and on annual ritual occasions, the group becomes a more powerful force in Ifugao society. The group's ritual reinforcement is evident in the traditional activities of sacrifice, house building, planting cycle, and harvest. The Antipolo / Amduntug Ifugao, therefore, tend to oscillate between low group and high group orientation as they shift from domestic to village focused activities.

An average of the six variable scores place the Ifugao at low to moderate grid (-2) and moderate to high group (+1.5). The oscillation in social time shows up in the spread of the variable individual scores. This summary points out several important factors applicable for church planting among the Ifugao. The Ifugao place strong emphasis on domestic groups. But this produces factions that make large coordinated action difficult, e.g., a large association of churches. It also produces weakly defined leadership. At the same time, the Ifugao's emphasis on public ritual activities, such as baptisms, weddings, seminars, or conferences creates a group integration that cannot, however, be sustained by the social structure, because of the faction potential within the domestic groups.

Discovering Socio-cultural Integration

All people groups must deal with change because people change continually. This is particularly true in our modern world among tribal people. For example, among the Ifugao, some "traditional tribals" become "traveler tribals" in the search for wages or trade clients. But once the objectives are met, they return home (see Figure 13). Other Ifugao make a permanent move to Manila, or to other cities, to become full-time students, military personnel or wage earners.

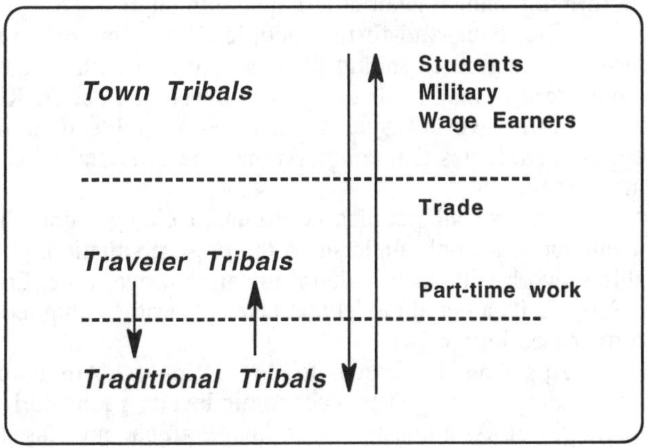

Figure 13. Transitional tribals: a global village

Even though a growing number of Ifugao move to the city, they tend to retain their home ties. For most, migration includes *a going and a coming*. Conn correctly challenges long-held assumptions that people migrate in only one direction, i.e., from the rural to the cities. He states: "Urban anthropologists more recently are looking at the links that bind cities to outlying communities. Cities are being seen more as essential cogs in a worldwide network that stretches to the rural area and far beyond" (Conn 1985:7). This is especially true of cities in developing countries.

The back and forth flow of tribal people raises several key questions for team members who are designing a church planting strategy in an urban setting: (a) What links exist between rural areas and the city which can be utilized in church planting? Educational institutions? Radio? Business? Military? (b) Who leaves to become wage-earners or students? Males? Females? Church leaders? Youth? (c) Where do they go? (d) Who returns to the villages or barrios? How often? For what purpose? (e) Who remains in the rural setting? (f) How will Christians in each type of society challenge the other's worldview? Ultimately, urban-rural networks demand urban-rural church planting strategies (Steffen 1993a).

What is true for tribal societies also applies to peasant societies, for many "urban peasants" also flee to cities in search of good jobs. The majority, however, end up living in slum areas, performing manual labor at less than minimum wage.

The back-and-forth "people flow" of urbanites from developed countries should likewise not be overlooked. What are the modern Roman roads today that connect the Pacific Rim? Other areas of the world? Such connections provide natural church-planting strategies that can maximize the gifts and talents of such mobile servants.

Because all peoples continue to change, church-planting teams must not only understand the present situation, but must be able to work with socio-cultural integration over time. Lingenfelter (1990) posits a tiered model that takes his grid / group model a step further (see Figure 14).

Applying this model to the Antipolo / Amduntug Ifugao finds them operating at two economic levels: a kinship level and a market level. As a kinship economy, the Ifugao are classified as an agricultural tribe since they produce basically everything consumed by the nuclear family. But, as the Ifugao raise more and more crops for exchange rather than consumption, they find themselves entering the more complex market level economy, particularly in the small surrounding towns (Feudal State). Some Ifugao have begun to ship their coffee to relatives living in Manila or Bagiuo, who know where to sell for the best prices—and through this activity, they find themselves participating at another level of complexity (Commerce State).

People groups undergoing rapid change require continuously crafted church planting strategies. In the case of the Ifugao, this calls for church planting strategies that address the rural-urban connections, but beyond that also address the various feltneeds experienced by different segments within their society, such as, animism, materialism, and loneliness. For church planters ministering in urban settings, this calls for formulating strategies for the urban-rural connections. With regard to the Ifugao, this strategy may also include international connections among Pacific Rim nations as a growing number of Ifugao move to Hong Kong and Singapore (headed for Canada) for work. Rapidly changing societies in today's global village calls for relevant church planting strategies—strategies that network all sectors of a people group of which each has its own distinct feltneeds.

Even if the world reaches a fifty-fifty rural-urban ratio shortly after the turn of the century as projected, numerous missionaries must choose to live in rural areas today (without feeling like second rate ambassadors) so that a generation of rural people will not be lost. But they should not, as I did, think of rural church planting in isolation from urban church planting. As transformation and technology increase, so will the networking between the rural and urban areas. Rural and urban church planters should strategize together so that all peoples have opportunity to worship the King of kings.

Several specific areas come to mind in which rural and urban church planters can benefit from the other's experiences and strategies. The first concerns those working with hunter-gatherers and the homeless. Because the lifestyles of these two groups have much in common, so should the church-planting strategies designed to reach them. Some of the parallels include: individuals travel set routes in small bands made up of those who can be trusted; their time focus is on the present rather than the future; their concentration centers on daily survival; they define private and public property differently than do landowners; and settling hunter-gatherers or the homeless brings a similar set of problems.

Another area where urban and rural church planters can learn from each other pertains to those working among urban gangs and those working within societies experiencing intra- or

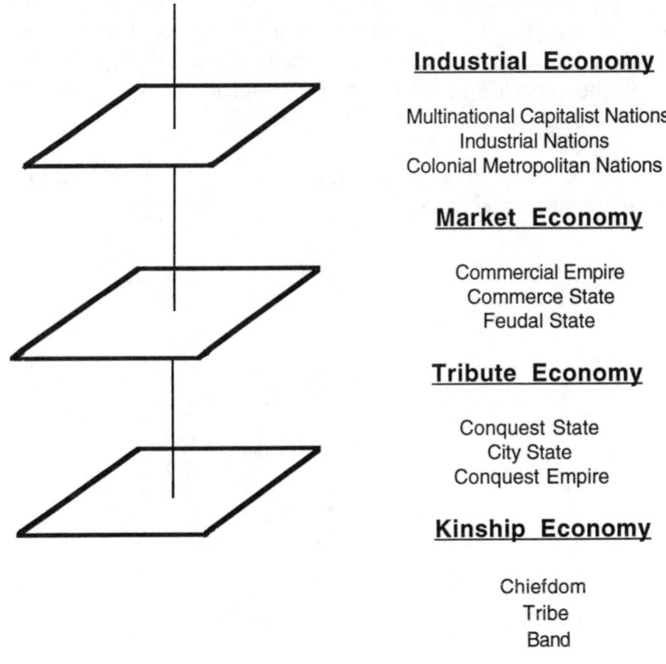

Figure 14. Levels of socio-cultural integration

(Source: Adapted from Lingenfelter 1990:45)

intertribal warfare. Some of the similarities between urban gangs and warring tribal factions or tribes include: a strong social organization; a common language; common symbols; initiation rites; the feeling of being trapped within territorial boundaries; hatred; killings which escalate revenge; the need to meet on neutral ground; respect for direct confrontation; and peace pacts. To avoid reinventing the wheel, urban and rural church planters should interact together where commonalties exist, and discuss church-planting strategies that best fit the intersocietal exchange taking place between rural and urban peoples.

Conclusion

Being able to utilize tools that distinguish various types of societies, identify value differences between team and community members, isolate social environments in biblical history, the target people, and one's own background, and measure socio-integration—all will assist the church planting team in designing a context-specific strategy. On the other hand, should team members fail to take these distinctions into account, team energies will most likely be spent on activities that will not relate well to the target audience.

We now turn to the matter of appropriate timing for utilizing these vital tools.

PART 3

Preevangelism

"He who answers before listening—that is his folly
and his shame....Though I am free and belong
to no man, I make myself a slave to everyone,
to win as many as possible....men of Issachar, who
understood the times and knew what Israel should do..."

(Prov. 18:13; I Cor. 9:19; I Chron. 12:32)

8

Utilizing Integrated Study Guidelines

As I talked with my church planting colleagues in the Philippines, and with others from around the world, about our mutual involvement in language and culture learning, I found that concerns continued to surface that matched my own. All had experienced a discontinuity between the study of language and culture. The study materials we received were not integrated well. Consequently, personal preference became the determining factor where one spent his or her time. Those preferring language study concentrated their efforts in this area while those preferring culture study focused on culture. Although all recognized the need for proficiency in both, the tendency was to place more effort in the area of one's preference.

Another area of concern centered around the exercises. Most considered the assigned culture studies too complicated and time consuming—even impossible to complete. While all began the culture study, few completed it. Even the condensed revision of Murdock's (1961) outline of cultural materials made the task too tedious. Moreover, the time required to file and cross-file all the newly acquired data seemed hardly worth the effort for the benefits gained.

The absence of cultural levels, similar to the five language levels designed by Brewster and Brewster (1976), brought a further criticism. Apart from establishing certain levels, investigators never knew what kind of proficiency they had attained. Team members begged for some kind of culture proficiency levels.

Many also found that the culture studies had no relationship to ministry. While the culture studies showed team members how analyze a community, they did not call for application to church planting. Consequently, the "So what?" question inevitably arose in the minds of those who were making a concerted effort to study a specific people.

During the Preevangelism Stage a number of team members admitted to feeling spiritually dead because of no longer being able to communicate the gospel verbally or participate in other former ministries. On the one hand, they wanted so much to become involved in ministry but, on the other hand, their minimal grasp of the language and culture prohibited it. They longed for study guidelines that would at least make them feel they were progressing towards an effective ministry.

By the time they reached the end of the language and culture studies, many felt unprepared to begin verbal communication of the gospel. While they had acquired the skills for communicating verbally, they realized their preparation for foundational teaching of the gospel had been neglected.

All agreed there was great need for more coordination between language study, culture study, and church planting. They believed that an integrated, progressive study would help them identify their proficiency level, and take the steps necessary to increase it.

In the next few pages I will attempt to define the general and specific goals of the Integrative Study Guidelines, provide an overview of the guidelines, and highlight some effective tools and models for investigating the external cultural environment. (I purposely limit myself here to an emphasis on the culture and church planting guidelines in that a number of scholars have adequately addressed the language area [Brewster & Brewster 1976; Davidson 1988; Larson 1984]).

Goals for the Study Guidelines

Effective Integrative Study Guidelines can assist church planting teams to perform ministries that result in changed lives. Thus, changed behavior becomes the overall goal of the Integrative Study Guidelines.

Specific goals for the Integrative Study Guidelines are at least fourfold: (a) to design a holistic, integrated system that addresses language, culture, and aspects of church planting; (b) to provide tools and models for effective analysis of cultures; (c) to build close relationships with the target audience; and (d) to provide a base for shared information. (Figure 15 depicts the general and specific goals of the Integrative Study Guidelines.) Nida astutely notes: "One cannot learn a language without

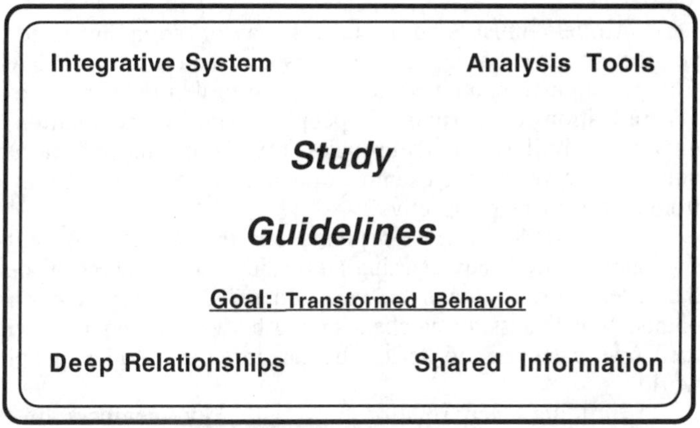

Integrative System **Analysis Tools**

Study

Guidelines

Goal: Transformed Behavior

Deep Relationships **Shared Information**

Figure 15. Goals for the integrative study guidelines

constantly hearing it; one cannot become acquainted with a culture without effective participation in it" (1950:270). It could be added, during the Preevangelism Stage, it becomes very difficult to maintain enthusiasm for ministry without some kind of participation in it. All three areas should be integrated if the team is to reach the final goal of changed behavior among the target people.

Since every tool or model will perceive behavior from its own distinctive perspective, each will raise its own set of questions. Therefore, team investigators will need a variety of tools and models to disprove all proposed hypotheses.

Moreover, team investigators should include historical models. Knowing the past enables one to better understand the present and make more accurate predictions about the future. Team members studying written historical and/or oral traditions are better able to note changes occurring within a people group in the areas such as, semantics, politics, economics, aesthetics, and religion.

Other external environmental scans should include models that relate to: (a) the individual, (b) homogeneous units, (c) the society, (d) surrounding societies, (e) the nation, (f) global influences, and (g) the spiritual realm. Neglect of models that address any of the above issues will undoubtedly result in incomplete data, ineffective ministries, and aborted Vision Statements.

Models must also surface behavior from an insider's perspective as well as an outsider's. Insiders tend to define behavior from within a community. Outsiders tend to define behavior from generalizations made about a people's behavior in relation to universal similarities. (Murdock's [1961] outline of cultural universals serves as one example of a study of a people's behavior from an outsider's perspective.)

Pike (1967) correctly points out that while one cannot accurately study behavior using an outsider's (etic) point of view, these "categories of convenience" do serve as helpful starting points. Nonetheless, researchers should be warned about allowing their own categories to define the categories of another people's world.

Building deep relationships with key members of the community requires that team members not only understand the new culture, but be realistic about personal and agency biases. Mayers' prior question of trust (PQT) is apropos here: "Is what I am doing, thinking, or saying building trust or is it undermining trust?" (1987:7). The guidelines should advance team members behaviorally from "Jesus loves you" to "We love you."

The team's attitudes and actions reveal an image of the incarnated image of God—that is, the target people's human picture of the invisible God. If church planters build close relationships with key individuals during the Preevangelism Stage, later, when they can verbalize the gospel message in the dialect (Evangelism Stage), it will be to *friends* rather than strangers.

Lingenfelter and Mayers (1986) challenge cross-cultural workers to become 150 percent people (i.e., 75 percent of their own culture and 75 percent of the target people's culture). Although team members will never become 100 percent like the target audience, they can become 75 percent. This means difficult changes become necessary as there can be no home field advantage.

Jesus Christ provides team members with the ultimate example in that he became the 200 percent person (i.e., 100 percent God, 100 percent man [Phil. 2:6-7]). On the human side, Jesus incarnated himself 100 percent as a Jew with his servant heart. Team members should imitate Jesus' example and attitude (Phil. 2:5). Being 150 percent messengers is possible through our Model's assistance.

Teams can share accumulated data on at least three levels: as teams, as field members, and as a Christian community. On the team level, each team should find ways to make its individual studies available to all current members, and eventual newcomers.

What is true for the team level should be reduplicated on a field level. That is, heads of mission agencies on the various fields should establish a base for sharing information. Team members working among a particular people can gain valuable insights through the studies made by other researchers working among geographically close people groups.

On the Christian community level, pertinent data should be published in missiological journals for the wider benefit of all. Such shared information can facilitate the phase-out process.

Components of the Integrative Study Guidelines

Areas that are highlighted in the Integrative Study Guidelines include: time periods; key words; time ratios between language, culture, and church planting; key activities involved within each of the levels surrounding language acquisition, culture acquisition, and church planting (with emphasis placed on the latter two); and activities outside the guidelines (see Figure 16).

Time Periods and Key Words

The Preevangelism Stage time period refers to the time elapsed between when the team enters a community to when it's members begin to communicate the gospel verbally (Evangelism Stage). Based on the experiences of one agency in the Philippines, this normally takes approximately one and a half years.

During the Preevangelism time period a number of words capture the ascending levels. The key word for level one is *familiarization.* Most team members reach this level within one to two months. Level Two will take another two to three months to reach, while Level Three will usually require an additional five to eight months. *Superficial* and *depth* serve respectively as key words for these latter two levels. Level Four will take perhaps six to fourteen months beyond Level Three. The key word for this level is *naturalness.* Few phase-out oriented church planters will remain in an area long enough to reach Level Five, which is identified by the key word *native.*

It is difficult, however, to set time periods for each of the levels because of the variety of situations in which church planters may find themselves. The particular country, an individual's personal health, the physical conditions, previous knowledge of the target language and culture, or of languages and cultures closely related, all influence the time factor. Nevertheless, all team members should set deadlines for each of the four levels and then strive to obtain them.

Proportional Time Ratios

The time ratios that exist between language study, culture study, and church planting will continue to change in each level. While these ratios are approximate, and may need to be adjusted for certain personalities, they can be very helpful in maintaining an integrated study that should facilitate life-changing ministries.

At Level One, the bulk of the Christian worker's time, 55 percent, is spent in language acquisition. Culture acquisition receives 40 percent of the time, while church planting receives 5 percent. At Level Two, the Christian worker's language study usually drops to 50 percent, and culture study increases to 45 percent. The church planting time remains constant at 5 percent.

Language study time drops to 45 percent in Level Three. Culture study time will remain at 45 percent while church planting increases to 10 percent. At Level Four, the Christian worker continues to drop the language study time to 35 percent. Culture study remains constant at 45 percent, while church planting time is increased to 20 percent.

The Christian worker's time ratios for Levels One and Two begin with a greater emphasis on language acquisition and very little on church planting. By Level Three, language and culture ratios level out, providing more time for culture study. There is a gradual increase in church planting time over all levels.

Guidelines for Language Activities

The guidelines for language learning challenge team members to learn language by way of concrete, social situations. By the time they reach Level Four, communicating the gospel effectively should not be a problem.

Completing the language guidelines should result from team effort. hose with expertise in language skills (including nationals) can assist other team members by serving as language consultants.

In Level One, the language learner solicits ten key texts surrounding daily activities. The texts will provide pertinent vocabulary, grammar, and cultural information. Culturally relevant dialogues should be developed from the texts so that language learning is grounded in specific situations. The language learner should internalize 300 words while on this level.

In Level Two, the language learner solicits another twenty key texts and writes dialogues, if none are available. A further objective for this level is a compilation of ten key terms, such as, faith, sin, God, reconciliation, forgiveness. The language learner also memorizes another 500-700 words, bringing the total

	Time	Level	Key word	Language	Culture	Church planting	
				55%	40%	5%	Ratio
PREEVANGELISM	1-2 months	*1*	Familiarization	300 words 10 key texts Dialogues	Demographics Basic values Property Annual cycle	Review Chronological Teaching model	
				50%	45%	5%	Ratio
	3-4 months (4-6)	*2*	Superficial	500-700 words (800-1,000) 20 key texts 10 key terms Dialogues	Social Labor and productivity Annual cycle	Bible study for Phases I, II	
				45%	45%	10%	Ratio
	6-10 months (10-14)	*3*	Depth	*700-1,000 words* (1,500-2,000) 30 key texts 30 key terms Dialogues	Exchange & generosity Domestic authority World picture Annual cycle	Revise church planting strategy Philosophy of ministry	
				35%	45%	20%	Ratio
EVANGELISM	6-14 months (16-28)	*4*	Naturalness	1,000-1,500 word (2,500-3,500) 60 key terms Concentrate where needed	Community authority, leadership, process, decision-making Cultural themes Ritual & mythology Socialization	Write Phase I Begin teaching Phase I	
		5	Native	-----	----	-----	

Figure 16. An overview of an integrative study guideline

vocabulary to 800-1,000 words.

During Level Three, the language learner tackles another 700-1,000 vocabulary words, bringing the total still higher, to 1,500-2,000. At this point, the language learner solicits another thirty texts, scripts new dialogues, and adds another thirty key terms. The total of sixty texts solicited by the language learners throughout the first three levels should result in approximately 300 pages of text material.

By this time, a number of the texts will deal with pertinent data found in Genesis 1-11. Such texts will provide foundational linguistic and cultural information for the Evangelism Stage. Some of the data would include terms and beliefs about: God, good and evil spirits, communication with the spirit world, the origin of the world, people, languages, animals, evil, death, the flood, and the rainbow.

The language learner focuses on weak areas in Level Four. He or she will memorize another 1,000-1,500 words, bringing the word total to 2,500-3,500, and add another sixty key terms, which brings that total to 100. At this point, the language learner should now be able to communicate quite effectively.

Guidelines for Cultural Activities

The five levels of proficiency for the culture learning guidelines move from the more concrete aspects of the culture to the abstract. As with the language lessons, this study should be a team effort that includes nationals. To illustrate, team members with expertise in anthropology can oversee the levels of study by assigning various individuals to collect data and draw conclusions. The cultural investigators can then write up the data and distribute it to team members, and promote the publication of pertinent data in missiological journals.

Just as levels of language learning are helpful to language learners, so are levels of culture learning to cultural investigators. Five comparable levels for measuring one's cultural progress and proficiency follow:

Level One - The researcher becomes familiar with the demographics of the area, mapping, kinship terminology, the social environment of property, the basic values, and begins to collect information on the annual work cycle. While he or she sometimes experiences severe culture stress, he or she nevertheless begins building friendships with key individuals of the community.

Level Two - The researcher's understanding of the physical environment continues to expand as does his or her understanding of the social organization of the community. His or he understanding of the social environment of labor and production grows. The rsearcher no longer feels completely alienated as he or she moves in and out of cultural situations. Friendships multiply and deepen.

Level Three - The researcher begins to understand the culture subconsciously; it is becoming a unified whole rather than a number of isolated parts. Culturally appropriate responses happen with more frequency. His or her understanding grows in the social environments of exchange and generosity and domain authority. Cultural stress continues to lessen as his or her friendships grow quantitatively and qualitatively.

Level Four - The researcher now finds himself or herself a transcultural person. He or she views life through the target people's worldview, resulting in cultural responses that are highly accurate. He or she gains understanding in socialization and the social environments of community authority and leadership, process, decision-making, and ritual and mythology. He or she experiences minimal cultural stress as friendships continue to multiply and develop.

Level Five - The researcher can respond to any cultural situation as well as native members of the community.

In Level One, the cultural investigator familiarizes himself or herself with demographics, kinship terminology, and with the physical environment of their surroundings (mapping). Mapping focuses primarily on the present, while kinship charts emphasize various relationships over past generations. Life histories are collected to gain further information about the past and enhance knowledge of personal histories.

The cultural investigator completes Lingenfelter and Mayer's (1986) questionnaire of basic values, as well as a major paper with ministry applications concerning the social environment of property study. This is followed by beginning a study of the annual life cycle, which charts weather conditions, division of labor, occupational, and ritual activities (see Appendix I). The chart can be updated on a monthly basis with additional circles added to incorporate events occurring beyond the one year, e.g., as Israel's seventh and fiftieth year did during biblical times.

In Level Two, the cultural investigator completes the study of the social environment of labor and production and writes up the data with suggestions for its application to ministry. He or she also updates the annual work cycle.

Selected team members prepare major papers with ministry applications on the social environments of exchange and generosity, and domestic authority. Another cultural investigator prepares a drawing of how the target community perceives the world (see Appendix J). The illustration should include how the world is tiered, connected, populated, and other important atmospheric phenomena and celestial bodies. After completing the annual work cycle, the cultural investigator analyzes the data to determine the best time to conduct evangelism, to take rest breaks, to learn when money is more readily available, to hold conferences, to ascertain the type of biblical functional substitutes required, and so forth.

Level Four finds the cultural investigator completing the formal study of culture. He or she completes major papers, along with ministry applications, on the social environments of community authority and leadership, process, decision-making, ritual and mythology. By now the cultural investigator should be able to list specific, major cultural themes that compete against each other (see Appendix K).

With evangelism just about to begin, the cultural investigator now completes a major paper on socialization with implications for evangelism and teaching. (See Appendix L for a matrix that contrasts the age development levels for insiders [e.g., birth to two years, three to six years, and so forth] with those of parents, others within the community, and those outside the community. Such a study can reveal the most effective type of teaching style for each age level.)

The above tools and models for cultural analysis pertain to individuals, homogeneous units, the society, societies that interrelate, and also to national, global, and spiritual influences. Moreover, the tools and models presented incorporate both the past and present life of a particular people.

Guidelines for Church Planting Activities

The Church Planting Guidelines focus on aspects of study that should be completed throughout the various levels so that Phase I of the Chronological Teaching approach (developed in

Chapter 11) may be taught effectively in Level Four. This dimension of the guidelines demands again a team approach. Church planting strategists, capable of overseeing the writing of a Church Planting Vision Statement and strategy, can provide leadership here. But the team also needs curriculum developers and persons who can design relevant teaching aids. Needless to say, it is important that nationals be included in these endeavors from the outset.

> Effective Integrative Study Guidelines can assist church planting teams to perform ministries that result in changed lives.

Level One begins with team members reviewing the Chronological Teaching theory (McIlwain 1987; 1988; 1989). In Level Two, team members study biblical passages related to Phases I-II of the Chronological Teaching model. During this period, the church planters internalize the phases, and discuss how the community is likely to comprehend the various stories.

Based on information from the language and cultural studies conducted during Level III, the church planters can now revise the Vision Statement and the philosophy of ministry. Should time permit, they, along with nationals, can begin to write curricula for the evangelism phase of the Chronological Teaching. Most team members will be able to complete the evangelism phase early in Level Four.

Activities Outside the Guidelines

It is helpful if mission agencies and/or denominations provide their teams with periodical checkups, workshops, and seminars during each of the levels of language, culture, and church planting. Checklists for language and culture, designed to indicate proficiency levels, can provide team members with confirmation of their progress and help them set goals for the next level. Periodic workshops or seminars that focus on language, culture, and church planting also provide team members opportunity for spiritual and intellectual reflection and stimulation. Academic courses, such as those offered by various institutions, is another alternative for in-depth study. Consultants from within and without the organization

Phase-out.

Conclusion

As has no doubt become apparent, the Preevangelism Stage provides team members a time to be learners. They are encouraged to model Christ during this period, while at the same time focus on ways to make their future ministries of evangelism and teaching relevant to the host community. Such understanding is sure to enhance the possibilities for changed behavior.

An integrated study of language, culture, and church planting can facilitate the learner role. Diligent study will help team members articulate a relevant Vision Statement, design an effective church planting model, and write comprehensive faith objectives and action plans.

The Integrative Study Guidelines set forth in this chapter advocate a team approach to the studies, so as to minimize the time factor, and maximize everyone's gifts and talents, including those of nationals. Undeniably, the learner role during the Preevangelism Stage may take time and tears, therefore, mission agencies would do well to provide incentives and direction for team members during this stage of development. How well team members succeed during this stage will have a tremendous impact on the journey leading to phase-out.

There remains another area that team members must not overlook, the relationship of the oral and print worlds. I will now investigate how these two interface, and the implications for cross-cultural church planters.

9

Interfacing the Oral and Print Mediums

After teaching a number of evangelistic lessons, I asked the Ifugao what they thought about the Bible's message. One of the older Ifugao responded, "What you are teaching us is good, but we cannot follow Christianity because we cannot read. It is all right for the younger generation to follow what you are teaching because they can read, but we are too old. We can no longer learn." Although I tried to explain it was not necessary to learn to read in order to become a Christian, my arguments apparently did little convincing. The Ifugao considered literacy an activity for youth who could still learn.

In time, a number of the Ifugao did become believers, including not a few illiterates and semi-literates. As the church grew, it desperately needed leadership. But legitimate religious leadership roles in traditional Ifugao society call for older, mature men. None of the older males, however, were interested in taking such a role, stating: "We cannot lead because we cannot read." By then I knew that merely offering literacy classes would not solve the problem because no one would join them. Somehow, I had to find a way to link the spoken and written mediums so that the pillars of the community could play a major role in the planting, development, and reproduction of national lead churches.

The dilemma I faced among the Ifugao is not so different from that which church planters face in more developed countries. As the Ifugao move toward a print culture, many of our urban cultures seem to be returning to an oral culture. Illiteracy is not only a problem in rural areas of the world, but also in urban areas, including the USA. Edward Wakin of Fordham University notes: "at least 22 million Americans can't read and write well enough to handle such basic daily tasks as writing checks, filling out an application, and following written directions." Maroney's study concludes that up to 72 million Americans are "functioning at a marginal level or below." Anderson, citing The *Popcorn Report,* alerts us to the following alarming statistics:

> We have assumed that the best way to educate is through reading. This is particularly true for those of us who read books, which includes you. But reading is in decline. Less than 10% of the population buys all of the books sold in America, although that's no guarantee that purchased books are read. The United States has become increasingly post-literate. Twenty-three percent of the US population is illiterate (1992:43).

Just as those having little literacy background in other parts of the world generally prefer the concrete mode of communication, so do those having similar backgrounds in the USA or other parts of the world. How does this reality challenge our existing teaching and training models?

In this chapter, I consider ways urban and rural church planters can enhance their evangelism and teaching through interfacing the oral and print mediums. To accomplish this, I will present literacy's present state along with some communication implications, differentiate the pertinent features between the oral and written mediums, highlight the various modes of communication used within the Bible, and propose ways to link the two mediums.

Literacy's Present State

The total number of illiterates and semi-literates in the world probably outnumber literates.[1] Barrett's (1997) figures, which do not include semi-literates, seem to confirm this (see Table 6).

Concrete Mode Dominates World

Unless training programs around the world can provide participants with a more positive experience, argues Klem (1982), educators will find that approximately 70 percent of the population will respond negatively to a literary approach to learning. Barrett's figures seem to support Klem's hypothesis. People with partial or no literary background tend to express themselves more through concrete forms than abstract concepts. If communicators rely too heavily on teaching strategies based upon literary foundations, approximately two-thirds of the world will be by-passed.

Table 6

World Literate / Nonliterate Population Projections

1900	mid-1997	2000	2025
1a 286,705,000	2685,031,000	3,003,971,000	5,093,494,000
2 739,233,000	1,374,770,000	1,238,926,000	1,135,556,000

1a refers to Literates; 2 refers to Nonliterates.
(Source: Barrett 1997:25)

Concrete Mode Growing in the USA

Our American culture is undergoing a major shift in communicative styles preference. One of the reasons behind this shift, and the illiteracy problem mentioned above, is the television. With the average TV sound byte now around 13 seconds, and the average image length less than 3 seconds, often without linear logic, it is no wonder that those under its daily influence have little time or desire for reading. Consequently, newspaper businesses continue to close down while video shops continue to expand.

Beginning in the 1960s a movement towards nature began among the youth of America that influenced communicative style preferences to move toward the concrete and transcendence. With the advent of MTV the shift became complete for a large majority—the verbal, concrete, short-term, multi-sensory experience, replaced the visual print media with its focus on logical, sequential format.

Reality-based TV has become popular in the USA. Shows such as 60 Minutes, 20/20, Inside Edition, Cops, Saturday Night Live, Rescue 911, The Oprah Winfrey Show, and the numerous soaps, testify to this fact. An introductory line from one reality-based show provides educators a possible clue as to the "why" of its popularity: "real stories of the Highway Patrol." Television (and videos), through dramatized life narrations, connects well with a growing number of Boomers, Busters and ethnics.

Contrasting Oral and Written Characteristics

A number of differences make it possible to distinguish the oral from the written. By identifying these differences, team members will be better able to understand not only their audiences, but themselves. For example, oral communicators tend to focus on hearing while members of literate communities tend to focus on seeing (see Table 7 for a comparison). The source of knowledge for oral communicators is nature, kinship, community, and the elders; they place great value on relationships and community. Literate peoples, on the other hand, tend to look to the printed page, and to those qualified to interpret it, for their source of knowledge. This latter emphasis rewards independence and individualism more than relationships and community. As individuals move from the oral to the written, levels of abstraction continue to increase. Goody (1987) identifies three levels of abstraction that move from the simple to the complex: (a)

Table 7

Contrasting the Oral from the Written

Oral Tradition	*Literary Tradition*
1. aural	1. visual
2. knowledge source: nature, kinship, community, elders	2. knowledge source: teacher, printed page
3. values group relationships	3. values individualism
4. actor oriented	4. observer oriented
5. multisensual	5. monosensual
6. learn through productive activities	6. learn in school
7. accumulation based on memory	7. accumulation based on multimedia
8. general analysis	8. high-detailed analysis
9. contradiction acceptable	9. contradiction unacceptable
10. creative reconstruction	10. verbatim memory
11. holistic	11. segmented
12. low chronology	12. high chronology
13. birth	13. achievement
14. receivers	14. transmitters

logograms ("word signs"), (b) syllables, and (c) an alphabet. The three levels, however, may not beas clear cut as theterms imply. But they are useful in that they indicate various degrees of abstraction. For example, if predominantly oral communicators were to jump immediately to using an alphabet, a major retooling of the mental processes would become necessary.

Oral communicators also tend to focus on the actor, that is, on those capable of communicating effectively by persuasion, intonation, dress, gestures, eye contact, space, or other nonverbal behavior. Feedback for these people tends to be immediate because of the dialogue that exists between the performer and recipients.

On the other hand, individuals of the literate world are usually observer-oriented. Reading a printed page raises questions, or it may bring to mind ideas and thoughts, all of which take place in the reader's mind. Feedback in this case is difficult because of the physical distance that exists between the reader and the writer. The former tends to be multisensual while the latter is monosensual.

Oral communicators actually prefer to learn by participating in activities that are productive. Under the apprenticeship model, individuals learn according to their level of competency, rather than according to a designated schedule. These individuals store their total library of life's experiences within the collective mind of the people group and retain it by continual repetition. However, repetition, over time, will result in changes in understanding.

The literate community usually looks to educational institutions as the source of information. Programs are set up by experts for the students to follow. Either the students keep pace with the program, fall asleep, or they drop out. As the knowledge bank increases, the wealthy construct libraries to contain it, making history tend to remain static.

Individuals in oral communities too often lack well developed procedures for systematic analysis. This may result in an inability to conduct a very detailed critical review (from the literate's perspective) of their own life, or that of others. Although contradictions may be common, this does not tend to upset them.

This lack of systematic procedures for analysis (in oral communicators) also affects their hermeneutics when they interpret Scripture. But they are not apt to make the same hermeneutical mistakes as do their literate counterparts (other than reading their own backgrounds into the text). For example, literates tend to take a word or verse out of context, thereby bringing to light a number of small issues or pictures. Illiterates, on the other hand, may capture the global picture of a text, but have difficulty isolating the parts that form the composite. Therefore, one's literate background (or lack of it) will influence one's hermeneutics.

In addition, oral communicators usually prefer creative reconstruction of an incident, rather than verbatim recall. More specifically, they seek recall *plus* invention. Because they tend to view life holistically, they may be easily led to syncretism. At the same time, however, they experience difficulty in maintaining long chronologies of peoples or events.

Once individuals in a literate community record a conversation or event, it is possible for all to engage in microscopic, critical analysis. Critics using a host of abstract, artificial divisions create new windows of perception. Alternative categories and classifications begin to emerge, challenging previously held assumptions and values. Criticisms can result.

For those who prefer verbatim reconstruction, accuracy may be maintained, but rigidity will very likely replace flexibility. They then tend to create a bifurcated world with division between the secular and spiritual. It also creates a world where extensive chronologies can now be built.

In oral communities, the status of one's parents often determines his or her position in society. *Whom* one knows supersedes *what* one knows. This tenet will be challenged in literacy oriented communities. In these communities, those who advance educationally become the caretakers and transmitters to those who lack such information. In oral communities, those who formerly transmitted knowledge now become the receivers. So, literacy not only challenges the status that exists within oral communities, but it provides social mobility for youth who will learn to read and write.

As oral communicators move towards literacy, a sequence of events takes place. Goody cogently points out that this transformation involves more than a simple binary shift from the oral to the literate. He points to three areas of change: (a) storage (intergenerational communication), (b) communication (intragenerational), and (c) internal change (cognition) (1987). Thus, literacy affects not only one's inner world, but also one's external world.

The literacy changes in the areas of storage, communication, and cognition also affect the social organization of the oral community by introducing new roles and statuses (see Figure 17). Whereas age and maturity had been the usual qualifications for leadership (as in traditional Ifugao society), now as newly literate young people gain abilities to read and write, the door is open for them to take leadership roles within that previously oral community. Their abilities to read, write, process data, store data—all introduced through literacy—become vehicles for social mobility that will eventually alter the social organization of the oral community.

A contemporary example of altered social organization may

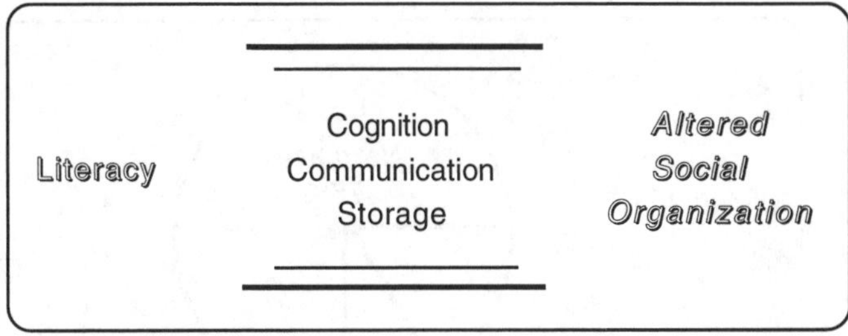

Figure 17. Literacy alters social organization

be seen among the many poor living in Sao Paulo. Their socio-economic position in society changed significantly, influenced by Paulo Freire's (1970; 1980) philosophy of education and literacy. Freire argued that a people's innate ability would enable them to change their own circumstances through critical reflection and action. He believed that education would not only cause people to become conscious of their problems, but would inevitably lead to revolution which in turn would result in a changed environment. Freire's sixteen years in exile demonstrate the power of his philosophy: *conscientisation* is meant to challenge the existing social organization of a society.

Three Basic Styles of Literature in Scriptures

Three basic styles of literature dominate the Scriptures: the narrative, poetry, and thought-organized format (see: Figure 18). The narrative sections are predominant, covering approximately 75 percent of the Bible. Writers over the centuries document the actions of a host of characters (and a few animals), from kings to slaves, from those who seek to follow God to those who live for personal or collective gain. Their life stories serve as mirrors to reflect our own, and more importantly, God's perspective of the situation. Koller astutely points out:

> ...the Bible was not given to reveal the lives of Abraham, Isaac, and Jacob, but to reveal the hand of God in the lives of Abraham, Isaac, and Jacob; not as a revelation of Mary and Martha and Lazarus, but revelation of the Savior of Mary and Martha and Lazarus (1962:32).

Poetry covers approximately 15 percent more of the sacred

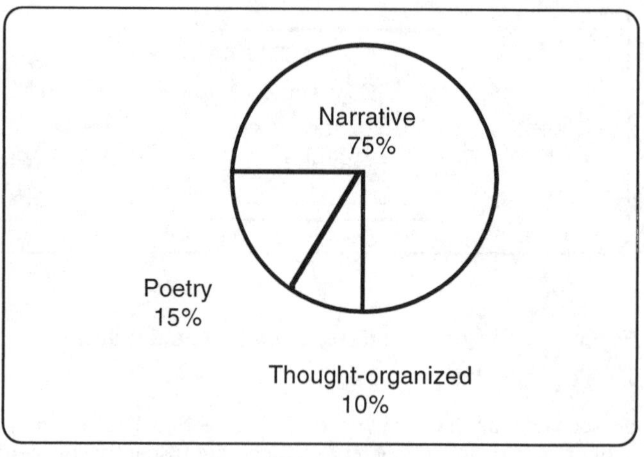

Figure 18. Three major literary genres of the Bible

text. Songs, laments and proverbs provide readers and listeners a variety of avenues to express and experience deep inner emotions. These portions of scripture demonstrate the feeling side of people and the God who created them (affective domain).

The thought-organized format comprises the remaining 10 percent. The apostle Paul's Greek-influenced writings fall under this category where logical, linear thinking tends to dominate. Interestingly, many, including the writer, preferred to spend the majority of time in the scripture's smallest literary style. It was time to expand personal preferences.

Concrete Mode Dominates Both Testaments

The concrete mode of communication dominates both Testaments, and is conspicuously evident in all three basic literary styles highlighted above. This mode of communication relies on objects and/or events to convey abstract concepts. Note how the following examples from the Old and New Testaments translate abstract concepts into concrete expressions (Table 8). The concrete mode of communication symbolizes God's message so that the literate and the illiterate can readily understand it.

Scriptures Integrate the Oral and Print Mediums

God communicated his word not only verbally through

Table 8

Concrete Expressions in Both Testaments

Old Testament	New Testament
rainbow (Gen. 9:13)	parables (Matt. 3:34)
circumcision (Gen. 17:10)	stories, children, lectures (Matt. 5-7)
angels (Gen. 18-19)	colt (Matt. 21:2)
burning bush (Exod. 3)	baptism (Matt. 28:19)
Passover (Exod. 12)	forgiveness feast (Luke 15:23)
singing, dancing, & timbrels (Exod. 15)	Passover meal (Luke 22:19)
ten commandments (Exod. 20)	rivers (John 7:38)
Urim and Thummim (Exod. 28:30)	foot washing (John 13)
sacrifices and feasts (Lev.)	fire (Acts 2:3)
stone memorials (Josh. 4:9)	word pictures, oral teaching (Acts 2:42)
drama proclamation (Josh. 8:33-35)	dreams and visions (Acts 16:9)
written accounts (Josh. 24:26)	creation (Rom. 2:15)
extra-biblical poetry & prose (Josh. 10:13)	poetry (I Cor. 15:33)
fables (Judg. 9:7-20)	allegory (Gal. 4)
riddles (Judg. 14:8-18)	architecture (Eph. 2:22)
musical instruments (II Sam. 6:5)	"psalms, hymns and spiritual songs" (Eph. 5:19)
torn robe, (I Kings 11:29)	creeds (I Tim. 3:16)
ewe lamb (II Sam. 12)	public reading (I Tim. 4:13)
forgiveness meal (Ps. 23:5)	extra-biblical book (Jude 14)
lots (Prov. 16:33)	numerous case studies
poetry, proverbs, linen shorts, a yoke (Jer. 13:1; 27:1)	
potter and the clay (Jer. 18)	
stories (Ezek. 17)	
handwriting on the wall (Dan. 5:5)	

prophets using a host of visual teaching aids, but also via the written media. He intended that his word communicate intra- and inter-generationally without losing any of its meaning over time.

God communicated his message by interfacing the oral and the written. As seen in Table 8, each emphasis in communication offer strengths and weaknesses. We who possess a literary background tend to neglect the oral dynamics of Scripture, and thereby risk losing the intended emotional impact. For example, we tend to rely on our eyes when we interpret Scripture. But Scripture should not be studied only with eyes; it should be heard with ears (Neh. 8:8-9; I Tim. 4:13; Rev. 1:3) and felt with hearts (Acts 7:54; 13:48).

Klem (1982) concludes that using oral communication that is indigenous can benefit either a print-oriented or oral-oriented people group in two ways: (a) it can internalize supracultural truth, and (b) enable effective propagation of the same. Western church planters should therefore learn to communicate orally as effectively as they do using the print media. Church planters will find that the combination will enable earlier and more effective phase-out. Many comfortable with oral communication will gain competence in using their gifts in literacy for church planting and development, and vice versa. In other words, the oral and the print mediums should be integrated.

Integrating the Oral and the Print Mediums

The use of the concrete mode of communication found in Scriptures and among ruralites can provide urban church planters valuable communication clues for ministry. Several suggestions for integrating oral and written modes of communication that will result in positive gain include:

Visuals

Wiseman (1982) argues that "visual literacy" (i.e., extracting information from a picture or illustration) usually is the first step in the acquisition of literacy skills. Use of visuals, together with directions, will gently move the oral communicator toward print media.

Pictorial stories have long been used to communicate religious messages in oral communities around the world. For example, in an outdoor courtyard of a Buddhist temple in Thailand, the life story of Buddha is depicted in a series of near life-size pictures. Another example is the dome of the Byzantine Basilica of San Marco where the biblical story of creation is depicted. The story unfolds in a series of twenty-four episodes, beginning with the top inner ring, and running counterclockwise. In Indonesia, Weber drew symbols while witnessing to tribal people. He called his approach "talk and chalk" or "drawn writing" (1957:84-86, 112-119). As his listeners began to draw the symbols and people inquired about their meaning, they became instant evangelists. Tippett (1987) noted that Old Testament stories had often been presented pictorially by way of Navaho sand paintings.

New Tribes Mission, Philippine Branch and the Philippine Baptist Mission, Southern Baptist Convention, produced 105 pictures designed for people living in developing countries who think in pictures rather than words. These pictures follow Phases I-III of the Chronological Teaching approach, i.e., Genesis through Acts (see Chap. 11).

The two agencies established certain criteria to ensure cultural accuracy. They wanted to avoid as much as possible any misunderstanding on the part of concrete relational thinkers. To illustrate, humans and animals are always depicted in their entirety within the picture's border. In addition, humans, animals, or trees, for the most part, are not superimposed over each other. Although it is possible that gestures, facial expressions, colors, and perspective may be misleading to different people groups, pictures with these precautions are far superior to those originating in the west.

The Antipolo / Amduntug Ifugao, for example, have used the pictures together with simplified printed study texts, to explain the events portrayed in the pictures when conducting evangelism and teaching believers. Tying the oral and print mediums together in this way not only preserves the Ifugao's preferred learning style but at the same time assures that key concepts are not lost.

A tribe in Papua New Guinea dramatizes parts of the evangelism phase of the Chronological Teaching approach (Walker 1988). They keep the props and costumes simple, and both youth and younger adults participate as actors. In this way, dramatization of the biblical text (previously read) becomes a powerful means of communicating truth, especially when accompanied by adequate interpretation.

The United Bible Society Asia Pacific Regional Center, in Hong Kong, currently produces a series of comics featuring Old Testament biblical characters. A number of these comics are being prepared for use with tribal, peasant and urban peoples within the Philippines through the auspices of the Philippine Bible Society.

Although some may consider comics a simplistic form of communication, they do contain certain complexities. Hatton alludes to several of these: (a) balloons, (b) kinesic communication, (c) sound effects; (d) surprise, questioning, or fear, (e) expletives, and (f) stressed speech (1985:430-437). Because the art work for the comics usually favors print oriented people, some problems may arise when these are used with oral communicators. That is to say, the medium of comics, which combines the visual and the written, is designed for a certain level of literacy sophistication.

Symbolism

For oral communicators who tend to be image-oriented, idolatry is never far away. For this reason, the church planting teams must utilize symbolism very carefully. Tippett (1967) relates the story of a missionary's surprise at observing a new Christian carving a half naked woman on the center pillar of the newly constructed church building. In answer to the missionary's query about why the artist was carving the woman, he cited I Peter 2:2: "Like newborn babies, crave pure spiritual milk, so that by it you may grow up in your salvation" (NIV). So that the symbolic is properly integrated with the written media, the text would need to be engraved somewhere on the carving.

Symbolism in the baptismal ceremony can be another effective way to communicate the meaning of this important rite of passage. For example, if those being baptized were to stand on the opposite shore from where the baptized believers stand, then after baptism they would move across to join their fellow believers on the other shore. The crossing of the river symbolically represents their passing from Satan's kingdom into God's kingdom through the death, burial, and resurrection of Jesus Christ. Reading Scripture portions related to baptism at some point during the ceremony adds the written to the symbolic.

For concrete relational thinkers, the use of symbolism also provides a powerful communication tool. In addition to the written ordinances, symbolism can be utilized with all aspects of the life cycle, such as birth, naming, initiation rites, marriage, death. Scripture reading, Bible study materials, or even brief captions used with symbolism, will help integrate the two powerful modes of communication.

Songs

The Antipolo / Amduntug Ifugao love to sing. During harvest activities and funerals they sing the *hudhud*. Although its content varies from area to area, this particular folk song records the exploits of ancestral heroes. Female specialists lead the nonpoetic narrative, and others join in on the chorus.

The *hudhud* serves a number of functions in Ifugao society: (a) It teaches Ifugao tradition informally to all within hearing distance; (b) it enables mundane work to be enjoyable; (c) it encourages group participation; (d) it allows for creativity as the leader presents tribal lore; and (e) it provides group solidarity during times of crisis.

The Antipolo / Amduntug Ifugao use the *Salidumay* tune to express some of their most inward feelings. The tune itself remains constant, but the words will vary according to the message the singer wishes to convey. The singer (either male or female) composes phrases to fit the meter of the tune. When the singer finishes each stanza, the audience joins in with the chorus, which also remains constant. This continues back and forth, until the singer completes the tale.

Young Ifugao believers soon began to use the *Salidumay* tune to communicate biblical truth and also personal testimonies. Before leaving for our first furlough, we spent our final evening listening to their testimonies in song. In due time, one of the Christians had composed a song with fifty-three verses (using the *Salidumay* tune). In it he told the salvation story from Lucifer through the ascension of Christ. He later taped it on cassette for distribution, and it was reproduced in the hymnal for all to enjoy.

The functions served by singing the *hudhud* are applicable for use among all Ifugao believers. For example, the creativity, leadership, participation ("partnership in communication"), and repetition used in their indigenous singing to provide encouragement and education in times of celebration and crisis should be adapted by the wider Christian community. This is true also for other people groups who prefer this type of creative, repetitious and participatory singing. Eventually, the placing of these songs in written form will allow multitudes to be reminded of biblical truths as they participate in singing the lyrics.

Stories

Ryken astutely asks:

> Why does the Bible contain so many stories? Is it possible that stories reveal some truths and experiences in a way that no other literary form does — and if so, what are they? What is the difference in our picture of God, when we read stories in which God acts, as compared with theological statements about the nature of God? What does the Bible communicate through our imagination that it does not communicate through our reason? If the Bible uses the imagination as one way of communicating truth, should we not show an identical confidence in the power of the imagination to convey religious truth? If so, would a good starting point be to respect the story quality of the Bible in our exposition of it? (1979:38)

Church planters ministering among oral communities around the world have long used Bible stories to win converts to Christ. More recently, McIlwain elaborated on this approach through what he calls the Chronological Teaching approach.

C. Kraft calls the Bible God's "inspired classic casebook." Rather than providing a theological textbook, God chose to promote "discovery learning" through historical situations common to all peoples. C. Kraft views the Bible as a series of redemptive stories designed to help listeners and readers understand God's interaction with humanity.

Myths and legends provide the basic philosophical foundations for many oral communicators. Bible stories should be contrasted with the group's indigenous stories so that the church planting team, as well as the target audience, can understand the similarities and differences.

Team members need to recognize the basic elements of these indigenous stories (including discourse features) so that misconceptions will be minimized between them and biblical stories. Brewer (in Olson 1985) provides a framework for examining stories when he charts the basic elements of a story. For Brewer, a story's basic elements include: (a) the opening, (b) setting, characters, events, resolution, epilogue, closing, and narrator. Discourse options cover: (a) the presence or absence of a particular element, (b) the explicitness or implicitness of the element, (c) the type of element, (d) when the element is introduced, (e) the repetition of the element, and (f) the order of the underlying event. Brewer's model can help the church planting team uncover the cultural specifics of a story.

> ...Scripture should not be studied only with eyes;
> it should be heard with ears....and felt with hearts.

Urban church planters should be as highly skilled in using stories as their colleagues who minister among oral communicators. They should ask: How does the target audience use stories? When do they tell stoires? What are the discourse features of a story? How much of their sacred book is narrative? For urban church planters, the more proficient they become as story tellers (about life in general and about God's interaction with good and evil characters in the Bible in particular), the more they can expect their audience to respond with excitement. An added benefit will be the gain of immediate evangelists and teachers as the listeners themselves repeat the stories to others (Steffen 1996).

Audio

It is a fact that the entire world now possesses cassette recorders and/or radios. Even TVs and VCRs may be found in the remotest parts of the world. These technological tools make it possible for church planting teams to reach people regardless of media orientation. Music, question and answer sessions, drama, films and talk shows provide new opportunities to plant churches among people groups all over the world. Scripts (of music, drama or Scripture) made available to listeners often legitimize the oral presentation.

The Antipolo / Amduntug Ifugao understood the *Jesus* film quite well, although among other groups the reception was not as positive. For instance, one group in the Philippines spent considerable time discussing Jesus' sex. Some felt his long hair indicated maleness, while others argued the dress (robe) made Jesus a female. They also found it difficult to accept the thin actors (due to width of screen).

The Genesis Project has produced a number of films that begin with the Old Testament. Many people who think concretely seem to experience difficulty comprehending the highly abstract creation story films. They would find the subsequent films more conducive to their learning style preference.

In sum, by researching traditional modes of communication of a people group, and then discovering those that augment them, team members will find communicational guidance for evangelism and teaching. The best approach for long lasting, inter-generational results seems to be a multi-media approach. It begins at a target people's level of abstraction(s) and expands to include those modes of communication that are absent. It integrates the oral and print medias through pictures, drama, comics, symbolism, singing, stories, cassette tapes, radio, videos, films, TV, and a host of other media forms.

Conclusion

God began with the spoken word, but soon added the written when he selected individuals to write all he wanted communicated. The written documents integrate a variety of communicational modes, which make learning about God, and living for him, possible for both print and oral communicators.

Church planters can demonstrate their respect for a people by using the indigenous modes of communication for evangelism and church development. But church planting teams must not stop there; they should go on to augment the traditional communication modes by using both mediums whenever possible. This gives the target people an opportunity to view God, and their own world, from different levels of abstraction, and enables them to relate to a different segment of the world's population.

Each of the modes of communication has its own strengths and weaknesses, but both are essential to a believer's growth and development. Although neither should be neglected, the starting point should always be the level(s) of abstraction apropos to the people targeted. Since such an integrated approach fosters instantaneous evangelists and teachers, church planting teams can move another step closer toward the phase-out objective.

Once the homework is done, an accurate gospel can be presented; it is time to tell the greatest Story ever told.

[1] Kurian documents the difficulty in defining literacy: "Literacy has conflicting definitions in different countries. UNESCO defines literacy as the ability to read and write a simple sentence. In some countries, such as Japan, Sudan, Uganda and Zambia, illiteracy is defined as never having attended school....Literacy is also qualified by the age groups to which they refer. Data for most countries relate to populations aged 15 and over; but in the case of others, such as Italy, the figures are based on the population over age six. Other kinds of error and bias include the exclusion of segments of the population, such as nomads in the Middle East and Africa and Indians in South America....Because of the great prestige attached to literacy, governments in developing countries have shown a tendency to inflate, or even fabricate literacy ratios" (1979:308).

PART 4

Evangelism

Then Agrippa said to Paul, "Do you think that
in such a short time you can persuade me
to be a Christian?" Paul replied, "Short or long—
I pray God that not only you but all who are
listening to me today may become what I am,
except of these chains."

(Acts 26:28-29)

10

Presenting an Accurate Gospel

Tradition taught the approximately 25,000 Palawanos living in southern Palawan, Philippines, to expect the arrival of a white person carrying a black book. When this person arrived he would be bringing God's message, which the Palawanos were to accept. So when the Sigfried Sandstrom family arrived in 1955, they found a waiting audience.

The Palawanos sensed Sandstroms' love for them in that they ate anything offered them, and in return, gave the Palawanos whatever they had. The Sandstroms spent themselves for the Palawanos; they incarnated the character of Christ. A year later, due to the ill health of Mrs. Sandstrom and their son, the family returned to the United States.

Before leaving Palawan, Sandstrom, using English, broken Tagalog, and a few Palawano words presented the gospel message. Hundreds of Palawanos responded, eager to do whatever the prophesied visitor asked. Sandstrom asked them to believe in Christ; to be baptized; to attend church; and to stop smoking, drinking, and chewing betel nut. The Palawanos responded willingly. Sandstrom baptized hundreds of Palawanos. Soon the Palawanos began baptizing their peers in more remote areas. A sweeping people movement had begun.

Tuggy and Toliver (1972) lament that evangelism was done so swiftly, causing the Palawanos to accept a form of Christianity without understanding fully the content, and that leaders baptized thousands of untaught people. Many Palawanos defined salvation as being "in God," evidently basing their salvation on what they did, or did not do, rather than on the meritorious efforts of Christ.

They then maintained their position "in God" by abstaining from alcohol and betel nut. Nevertheless, Tuggy and Toliver acknowledged some bright spots. Some church leaders met regularly for Bible study and then returned to teach in their respective areas. The authors attribute breakdowns in the people movement to a lack of shepherding and teaching.

From this case study, it becomes apparent that presenting the gospel message without providing adequate foundation in the receptor language can result in a false gospel. Because the seeds of destruction are inherent in any presentation of the gospel message, church planters must accurately present the foundational cornerstone of the household of God. I will now define the gospel, consider the relationship of felt needs to the gospel, suggest ways to accurately present the gospel message, and establish a means to measure comprehension.

Defining the Gospel

The Palawano case study, sad to say, is not an isolated incident. I have received letters referring to similar situations from church planters ministering in Brazil, Venezuela, and Colombia. Nor is the problem confined to rural areas. An inaccurate presentation of the gospel results in misunderstandings among people living in urban settings just as easily.

Was the problem among the Palawanos due to a lack of shepherding and teaching, as suggested by Tuggy and Toliver? Possibly, but that does not seem to be the case here. No doubt a prior problem existed—that of a distorted gospel message. An Asian proverb states that: if dirty water exists downstream, its source is also dirty. A clear presentation of the gospel initially will help maintain pure water downstream (correct understanding).

No one must be clearer about the definition of the gospel than the church planter. If he or she presents a distorted message, the entire message of the Bible becomes distorted. The fundamental key to understanding the whole Bible is a correct understanding of the good news of Jesus Christ.

A fellow traveler reminded Jesus' dejected disciples walking to Emmaus that the central message of Moses, the prophets, and the Psalms was Jesus Christ (Luke 24:27, 44). Paul claims unequivocally that, "The gospel is centered in God's Son" (Rom. 1:3, Phillips). Jesus Christ is the good news of the Bible.

The gospel involves power encounters because different powers vie for supremacy. A look at several of the verses that state Christ's purpose for visiting this planet will indicate the parties involved in the great spiritual conflict. Jesus came to:

- Destroy Satan's work (I John 3:8)
- Become the Savior of the world (John 3:17; I John 4:14)
- Seek and save that which is lost (Luke 19:10)
- Call sinners to repentance, not the righteous (Luke 5:32).

The above passages make it clear that power encounters take place between Christ and Satan, and between Christ and people. An invitation to receive the gospel message inevitably opens the door to spiritual power encounters.

The gospel is based on an historical event that can never be repeated. In the past, God revealed himself through prophets, but when Christ came to earth, he became God's final revelation to humanity (Heb. 1:1-2). Jesus Christ fulfilled the prophecies of the Old Testament by personally demonstrating the reality of the tabernacle, sacrifices, and ceremonies (Matt. 5:17; John 5:39). His willing sacrifice upon the cross superseded all other sacrifices ever offered, and made succeeding sacrifices blasphemous (Heb. 7:27; 9:25-16; 10:10). Jesus could therefore triumphantly shout: "It is finished" (John 19:30, NIV).

The gospel reveals humanity's true position before God: lost, dying, and facing severe judgment with eternal consequences. People not only inherit Adam and Eve's sin, they practice it, die, and face eternal separation from a holy God (Rom. 3:23; Heb. 9:27). Therefore, God classifies all Satan's children as his enemies (John 8:44; Rom. 5:10). Just as Satan faces eternal judgment in hell someday, so will his sons and daughters (Matt. 8:12; 13:42; Luke 16:24; Rev. 20:10). All people are without life, hope, inheritance, forgiveness, or excuse (Eph. 2:1,12; 5:5; Acts 26:17,18; Rom. 1:20).

The gospel message teaches the profound worth of people. Out of love, Jesus came to earth to restore our broken relationship with the Father. Through his death, burial, and resurrection, Jesus defeated Satan, conquered death, paid for our sins, and now offers eternal life, freely, to all who will believe (John 3:16; Eph. 1:7; II Tim. 1:10; Heb. 2:14). Because of Jesus' efforts on the behalf of humanity, God can now become their Father, and they no longer need fear death, or worry how to pay for their sins. God promises eternal life to all who believe. What people cannot do for themselves, Jesus did for them through the selfless giving of himself.

The gospel also reveals the profound worth of God's physical creation. Salvation is not limited only to those who place their allegiance in Christ, but it includes the decaying universe. Jesus' salvation extends to the physical universe (Rom. 8:19-22).

The apostle Paul received undoubtedly the fullest

understanding of the supernaturally revealed gospel (Gal. 1:12). In referring to the good news, he called it "my gospel" and "our gospel" (Rom. 2:16; II Cor. 4:3). Paul provides a succinct definition of the gospel in I Cor. 15:3-4 (NIV): "...that Christ died for our sins according to the Scriptures, that he was buried, that he was raised on the third day according to the Scriptures, and that he appeared to..."

The gospel did not embarrass Paul because it is "...the power of God for the salvation of everyone who believes" (Rom. 1:16). Although Paul believed creation points people to God, and their conscience bears witness to God, he considered the hearing of the gospel essential for obtaining salvation from sin (Rom. 1:20; 2:14-15). Paul boldly claims: "...faith comes from hearing the message, and the message is heard through the word of Christ" (Rom. 10:17, NIV).

> Because the seeds of destruction are inherent in any presentation of the gospel message, the church planters must accurately present the foundational cornerstone of the household of God.

In Galatians 1:8-9, Paul claims only one gospel exists, and warns that anyone tampering with this gospel can expect eternal condemnation. Paul uses sobering language to awake people to the preciousness and exclusiveness of the gospel.

In Galatians 3:1, Paul calls the Galatians "foolish" for adulterating the message of good news with legalism. Paul's strong conviction that only one gospel exists for the entire world did not sit well with many Galatians (1:10). Nevertheless, on this key issue, he refused to compromise. Whether Paul was addressing the legalists in Galatia, the proto-gnostics and antinomians in Colossae, or the idolaters in Athens, Paul preached that only Jesus Christ is able to solve humanity's dilemma before God.

The gospel requires repentance on the part of recipients. Jesus called for repentance, as did Peter before Jewish audiences, and Paul with his Gentile audiences (Luke 5:32; Acts 2:38; 3:19; Acts 20:21; 26:20). Orr warns that this is a "missing note in much modern evangelism" (1982). Team members would do well to heed Orr's warning in that the gospel demands repentance.

It is by faith that people appropriate the gospel, but faith itself is not the gospel. It merely provides the means of personalizing what Christ accomplished for us. Faith takes its value from an object, in this case, the One who declares believers righteous before God, i.e., Jesus Christ (Rom. 4:5; Eph. 2:8).

True reception of the gospel results in changed behavior in the lives of the recipients. Believers gain a new standing before God, receive the Holy Spirit, who, by dwelling within believers, empowers them to live a transformed lifestyle (I Cor. 6:19-20; II Cor. 5:17; Eph. 1:13). What Christ did *for us* provides the foundation for what the Holy Spirit produces *in us,* thereby making good works acceptable before God (Eph. 2:8-10). The gospel expects high standards of its recipients. Paul challenges believers to live "...in a manner worthy of the gospel of Christ" (Phil. 1:27, NIV).

Acceptance of the gospel also results in the birth of new churches. As the gospel spread from Jerusalem to Antioch, to Rome, and to the rest of the known world, communities of faith sprung up. Everywhere the gospel went, churches were born.

In sum, the good news of the gospel means that Jesus Christ became God's sacrificial substitute in order to meet his demands of love and holiness. His gracious efforts resulted in a way of salvation for all who believe and follow him, and the eventual restoration of a contaminated universe.

Felt Needs and the Gospel

There are at least three types of personal needs between which church planters should differentiate: basic, felt, and supracultural. Maslow (1968) posits five basic needs common to all people: physical, safety, affection, esteem, and self-actualization. Should one of the basic needs not be met satisfactorily, a felt need will arise. The supracultural need deals with restoring one's broken relationship with the Creator. Most people will experience all three types of needs at some point in their lives.

When Jesus Christ ministered on earth he addressed all three types of needs. He gave sight to the blind, healed the lame, raised the dead, caused demons and nature to obey him, and removed personal sin (Heb. 2:3-4). Later, Paul and other colleagues performed numerous miracles as they taught the gospel (Rom. 15:18-19).

The Bible commands believers not just to verbalize the love of God, but to demonstrate this love through good deeds (Gal. 6:10; I John 3:17-18). The Scriptures promote meeting people's physical needs as well as spiritual needs. The question arises as to whether the gospel is intended to meet people's basic needs...felt needs...spiritual needs...or all three?

In the United States (and other countries), many Christian

workers present the gospel as the answer to a person's felt need. One example of this is the "Four Spiritual Laws." The evangelistic tool, designed in the early 1960s for American university students, addressed the felt needs of love, acceptance, and security. These were needs that arose in a society that emphasized independence and mobility. Some Christian workers, confusing felt needs with supracultural need, interpret the good news to mean "God loves you and has a wonderful plan for your life."

A number of other examples of a felt need approach to evangelism often heard in the United States include the following: if a person is sick, the good news becomes: Jesus Christ will be your personal Healer. For those experiencing financial difficulties, the good news becomes: Jesus Christ will be your ultimate Provider. For those experiencing loneliness, the good news becomes: Jesus Christ will be your best Friend. For those experiencing sadness, the good news becomes: Jesus Christ makes sad people happy. For those experiencing low self-esteem, the good news becomes: Christ will return your lost self-esteem. This type of evangelistic approach defines the good news as Jesus Christ meeting people's specific felt need(s).

> The fundamental key to understanding the whole Bible is a correct understanding of the good news of Jesus Christ.

Not surprisingly, cross-cultural church planters often present a felt need gospel. For listeners who fear the spirits, the good news becomes: Jesus Christ will protect you because his power surpasses the power of all other spirits combined. For those needing economic assistance, health, or better crops, the good news becomes: Jesus is your Elder Brother. For those who lost a valuable object, the good news becomes: Jesus Christ, the All Knowing One, can find your lost object. For those facing social injustice, the good news becomes: Jesus Christ will liberate you. As in the United States, nationals often hear the good news defined as specific felt need(s) being met.

Dye (1980) speaks to the issue of felt needs through what he calls "Good News Encounters" (GNE). For him, GNE requires love, done "on the spot." It means taking action relevant to the need, and pointing an individual to God and/or to the Bible. For example, if a national expresses concern about a lost object, the Christian worker should seize the opportunity for God. Dye encourages the Christian worker to have the person pray, asking God to help him find the lost item. Dye does not attempt to defend GNE theologically, rather he places the onus on doubters to prove God does not favor such an approach.

But does making people happy, healthy, wealthy, safe, economically equal, also make them righteous before God? What happens to the "good news" if the lost object is not located, even after fervent prayer by both parties? If sickness does not go away? If social justice does not prevail? In our passionate desire to make the gospel more palatable, are we in reality redefining it? Has the felt need approach to evangelism, intended "to soften up" people for receiving the gospel, become what Paul calls "another gospel"? What perception of salvation remains in the minds of nationals? Does the felt need approach cloud the sin issue that was so vital to Jesus' and Paul's gospel? Does the felt need approach address a person's supracultural need for a restored relationship with the Creator? Will follow-up, with its emphasis on assurance of salvation, help move the listeners toward Christian maturity?

Jesus' dealings with people never avoided the sin issue. In the case of the paralytic, for example, Jesus not only healed the individual but forgave the man's sins (Matt. 9:1-8). It should probably also be noted that Jesus healed the individual to demonstrate his Messiahship. In any case, it is the person of Jesus Christ that represents the good news of salvation.

When the rich young ruler approached Jesus, Jesus did not address his felt need. Rather, he drew attention to his selfishness, no doubt hoping that he would recognize the need of a Savior (Mark 10:17-22). Both Jesus and Paul moved individuals beyond felt needs to the supracultural need. They sought to rectify a broken relationship due to inherited and practiced sin—to make "enemies" become "friends."

While every Christian worker should endeavor to become involved in meeting people's felt needs (whether through Good News Encounters, or another means), this by itself should not be narrowly defined as "the gospel" as taught by Jesus or Paul. Why? Because felt needs change from generation to generation.

The gospel (Jesus' sacrifice to restore people's broken relationship with God and restore the cosmos), on the other hand, never changes. With its roots based in an historical event that will never be repeated, the gospel message remains constant, and is applicable to any people or generation. The unchanging good news is based solely on the death, burial, resurrection, and ascension of Jesus Christ.

The fruit of the gospel, i.e., addressing felt needs, should not be confused with the root of the gospel, i.e., the substitutionary death of Jesus to provide people access to God. The fruit of the gospel focuses on restoring human needs, while the root of the gospel focuses on restoring supracultural needs. Jesus and Paul, while not neglecting the fruit issues of the gospel, made sure their audiences considered supracultural needs. Table 9 compares felt needs (fruit issue) with the root issue of the gospel.

Presenting An Accurate Gospel

Since only one true gospel exists, church planters must do the homework necessary to assure an accurate presentation. Making a clear presentation of the gospel calls for addressing at least the following: the incorporation of two opposing themes, the limitations of various theories, the distinction between the two mandates, and the conversion process.

Incorporating Two Opposing Themes

From the above discussion of the relationship between felt needs and the gospel, it becomes evident that church planters must coordinate two key opposing themes so that genuine conversion can result, i.e., conformity and contradiction (see Figure 19). Conformity addresses the area of felt needs. As Church planters meet the felt needs of a community, they conform to the community's expectations (maintain equilibrium), thereby gaining a hearing for the gospel.

Contradiction, however, challenges traditional assumptions, thereby bringing disequilibrium within a community. To illustrate, the gospel brings contradiction into people's lives by challenging their allegiance to what is substituted for Lord. For example, Paul challenged the Israelites to accept Jesus Christ as the Messiah, but

Table 9

Contrasting Felt Needs from the Gospel

Felt Needs	*Gospel*
Focuses on people	Focuses on Jesus Christ
Emphasizes present need(s)	Emphasizes ultimate need
Focuses on present (doing)	Focuses on past (done)
Recognizes changeableness	Recognizes unchangeableness
Issue of fruit	Issue of root

the offer was rejected by many because it challenged the spiritual and social presuppositions held for generations. Felt needs has its focus on conformities and commonalties while the gospel's focus is on contradiction and confrontation. The gospel brings bad news as well as good news.

Jesus and Paul utilized both conformity and contradiction in their respective ministries. Both wanted their message understood, but neither was willing to compromise the Scriptures to secure a following. They believed that what they taught should set the agenda for a people, not vice versa. This stand resulted in both of them receiving verbal and physical abuse. Whether they were engaged in evangelism or in the discipling process of believers, both Jesus and Paul presumed that their message transcended all cultures, yet it should be incarnated into each one.

Team members should plan to incorporate both tensions in their evangelistic ministry. Should they focus exclusively on aspects of conformity, syncretism or mediocrity may result. Alternately, should they focus exclusively on areas of contradiction, indifference may result. Focusing on both tensions allows the two to be self-corrective.

Church planters, therefore, should craft an evangelistic strategy that incorporates the creative tension between conformity and contradiction. Such a strategy exemplifies the ministries of the two greatest advocates of Christianity the world has ever seen, Jesus and Paul. In an accurate presentation of the gospel, conformity and contradiction will be integrated so that life-changing conversions result.

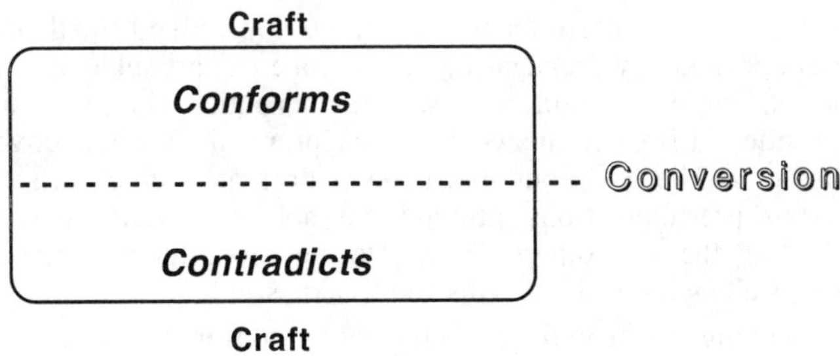

Figure 19. Crafting conformity and contradiction

To identify the components of the gospel that will conform to or contradict the target audience's worldview, it is helpful to conduct a comparative study. Compile a list of every component of the gospel that eventually must be conveyed, and then note how the Bible, team members, and the target audience perceive each component. To illustrate:

	Bible	**Team**	**Ifugao**
God	Personal	Personal	Distant
Satan	Deceiver	Liar	None
Sin	Miss mark	Murder	Stinginess
		Fornication	Anger
Jesus	Savior	Savior	Teacher
Cross	Death	Death	Amulet
Gift	Free	Grace	Reciprocity
Hell	Judgment	Torment	None
Heaven	Worship	Pleasure	None
Others	—	—	—

From this brief list it is apparent there will be more components that contradict the Ifugao's worldview than conform to it. Much foundational teaching will be required if the gospel is to be truely understood. The exercise also points out the need for team members to see how their culture has influenced interpretation of the components, e.g., sin. Taking the time to conduct this study will help assure that God's word is taugth, rather than perception, and allow the church planters to anticipate how the target audience will interpret each component, and strategize accordingly.

Recognizing Limitations of Theories

A theory exists behind every question asked, methodology used, or theology propagated, whether one can articulate the theory or not. For example, in the area of hermeneutics, dispensationalism provides different answers to Scripture than does covenant theology. The questions that investigators ask, which arise from certain presuppositions, provide insights into certain areas while blinding them to others. Each interpretation (theory), therefore, brings along its own strengths and weaknesses.

One anthropological theory, functionalism,[1] has had a profound impact on the first generation of anthropologically trained missiologists, such as Brewster and Brewster (1982), Hiebert (1983a), C. Kraft (1979b), Mayers (1974), Nida (1960), Reed (1985), and Tippett (1987). Functionalism defines a culture system as a number of interrelated parts whose function is to keep a society stable, similar to the way in which various systems of the human body work together to keep it functioning. It focuses primarily on unity, harmony, and balance.

It follows that a number of missiologists trained under the functionalism paradigm place great emphasis on harmony, equilibrium, and unity, as evidenced in the terminology: e.g., bonded relationships, dynamic equivalent translations, dynamic equivalent conversions, dynamic equivalent churches, dynamic equivalent church leadership, functional substitutes, ethnotheologies.

But how does one account for all the cultural variations? Are there dangers inherent in relativism, an obvious outgrowth of functionalism? Is there a better way to handle contradiction and conflict? These, and other related questions, caused anthropologists and others to seek a more inclusive model. Their studies resulted in a conflict paradigm that takes into account both abrupt and progressive change.

Although the conflict paradigm addressed a dimension overlooked by functionalists, it too, like its predecessor, is insufficient by itself.Team members will need to include both paradigms if they are to attain a balanced model.

Functionalism encourages church planters to be sensitive to the culture, which is a necessary element in gaining an audience. Conflict theory, on the other hand, calls attention to the existence of contradiction and conflict within a people group, both of which are necessary components of the gospel and Christian walk. Not only must team members know of the strengths and weaknesses of their theological theories, but they must also be aware of the corresponding anthropological paradigms. Without these insights, an accurate presentation of the gospel, and its ongoing communication by nationals, becomes difficult.

Distinguishing the Two Mandates

Scriptures speak of two mandates under the umbrella of the Kingdom of God, the cultural mandate and the Great Commission mandate. The cultural mandate (Gen. 1:26,28; 2:15) commands believers to care for the social, political, economical, ecological, agricultural, and cultural needs of others. It challenges injustice in every area of life.

The Great Commission mandate (Matt. 28:18-20; Mark 16:15-16; Luke 24:46-47; John 20:22; Acts 1:8) commands believers to proclaim the gospel, and disciple those who respond to be responsible members of the community of faith and the world. The Great Commission mandate deals primarily with the spiritual needs of humanity.

The Bible speaks clearly about both mandates, yet differentiates between the two. To protect the dissemination of the gospel, this distinction must remain clear in the minds of the church planters.

Recognizing the Conversion Process

The Church Growth movement, developed under the creative leadership of the late Donald McGavran, encourages church planters to count responsible church members, rather than "decisions" for Christ. The Engel-Norton (1975) communicational model, one that emphasizes the spiritual journal as a lifetime process, provides another impetus in this direction. Raising a hand, reciting a prayer, or walking an aisle does not necessarily indicate a person has become a believer. Responsible church membership, on the other hand, serves as a much better criteria for determining effective evangelism.

> ...does making people happy, healthy, wealthy, safe, economically equal, also make them righteous before God? In our passionate desire to make the gospel more palatable, are we in reality redefining it?

While appreciating the Engel-Norton model's emphasis on process, Conn (cited in Stott & Coote 1979) correctly offers a critique of the paradigm as western in that it not only isolates certain facets of conversion, but it then proceeds to arrange them in compartmentalized units. Unfortunately, personal growth rarely follows such a manicured sequence.

Before people change their faith-allegiance, most will make multiple decisions that move in that direction. Which decision moves an individual across the line (from an enemy of God to a friend) is very difficult to determine. The Bible seems to offer little help in this area. No record exists of individuals praying to receive Christ, walking an aisle, or asking Christ into their hearts. On the other hand, the Bible does expect all true believers to evidence renewed minds and transformed behavior. (See Appendix M for a chart on the conversion process.)

I agree with the Church Growth movement that the fruit produced by professing believers is of greater importance than knowing the precise moment one comes to believe in Christ. I have a concern, however, that such an emphasis can shift a church planter's focus from accurately presenting the gospel to a focus on shepherding and teaching. While I certainly do not want to minimize Christian training, at least equal emphasis must be given to a clear presentation of the gospel message, the foundation upon which new churches are built.

Comprehension of the Gospel

Some type of measurement is necessary so that team members can determine how well they communicate the gospel. Although no human being can know precisely the heart of another person, a checklist that measures comprehension of the gospel can be helpful.

As I reflected on the early days when many Ifugao professed to turn to the Lord, I remember looking for several indicators that would indicate a faith-allegiance change. One of these pertained to their personal testimony. Did their verbal testimony give evidence of the need for a substitute to solve their broken relationship with God because of sin? I was not looking for any particular words; rather, I wanted to be sure that they comprehended the concept of substitution in regard to the sin issue.

Another indicator of saving faith I looked for concerned some sign of repentance. If an Ifugao turned to God, he or she also turned from some former allegiance (I Thess. 1:9). For the Ifugao at that time, this meant turning from the sacrificial system. Dropping the sacrificial system became a major bench mark in an Ifugao's movement towards Christ. To date, I know of only one person who claimed to be a believer and later, after two of his young children died suddenly, and because of tremendous pressure from unbelieving parents, returned to the sacrificial system. (He later confessed his actions as sin to the believers and they restored fellowship with him.)

Other indicators I looked for related to their obedience to Christ's commands (Matt. 28:20). Were the professing believers interested in knowing and following God's Word (I Pet. 2:2)? How did they describe the gospel when they witnessed to others? Patterson's (1981) materials provide guidance in this area. He argues that all believers should obey Christ's seven commands: repent from sin, be baptized, express practical love, partake of the Lord's supper, pray, give, and witness.

Baptism became a clear bench mark of faith in Christ for the Ifugao. The Ifugao believers considered anyone unwilling to be baptized to be still tied to the sacrificial system.

A reordering of the use of resources served as another indicator of a renewed heart. Did their use of material goods and money demonstrate a new model of servanthood and sharing?

A final area, and one to which I gave tremendous credence, concerned confirmation of their testimony by their peers. Words come easily. Confirmation of one's words by one's peers enhances their validity. So I asked myself continually: Who is it that believes this person changed his or her allegiance to Christ?

If, in evaluating a person's testimony, the church planting team hears the concept of substitution, observes some cultural form of repentance, sees a desire for studying and obeying God's Word, notes a reordering of resources, and receives confirmation of his or her testimony by family and friends, they can be relatively sure of the individual's faith-allegiance change. These six areas (and perhaps others) could be charted on a checklist that moves from "1" (lowest) to "3" (highest). The more checks found in columns two and three, the greater the reason to believe the individual has accepted the gospel (see Table 10).

For the checklist to be highly effective, however, team members must not only know the language well, but must also possess a deep understanding of the culture. Repentance (and all the other areas to be measured) should be defined according to the target people's worldview, not the worldview (or Christian subculture) of the team members. This requires the team members

Table 10

Evaluating Comprehension of the Gospel

	(Low) 1	2	(High) 3
• Personal testimony (substitution)			
• Repentance ("turn to God from...")			
• Desire for the Word			
• Witness			
• Reordering of resources			
• Confirmation by others			
• Others			

take learner roles. In this way, syncretism can be minimized, the understanding of the gospel maximized, and phase-out becomes much more feasible.

Conclusion

The gospel is both good news and bad news. Its is good news because God accepted the death, burial, and resurrection of Jesus Christ as a means of salvation for the human race. Jesus' doing and dying met God's total requirements of love and justice.

The gospel is bad news because it contradicts a people's faith-allegiance. Potential converts must accept the fact that Jesus Christ alone provides the avenue to God, turn to him (away from previous gods), and follow him.

How church planters present the gospel message will determine to a large extent the type of churches that will result. Church planters must present the gospel accurately, as well as shepherd and teach those who respond.

A model that unites evangelism and discipleship will now be explored.

1 The British anthropologist Bronislaw Malinowski first introduced functionalism which defined culture as an integrated whole that functions to meet the needs of individuals. Radcliffe-Brown changed the focus somewhat by emphasizing society rather than the individual. According to Radcliffe-Brown, a culture system is comprised of a number of interrelated parts whose function is to keep a society stable, similar to the way in which various systems of the human body work together to keep it functioning. Even though the fathers of the functionalist theory differed in focus, both agreed that unity, harmony, and balance maintained stability and ultimately life.

Since the individual parts are essential to the whole, removal of any part can easily result in the total disintegration of a society. The functionalist theory therefore contends that since every aspect of a culture benefits the society as a whole, all should therefore be protected.

The functionalist theory, however, can easily result in cultural relativity. By arguing that no culture supersedes another culture, functionalists end up emphasizing their own distinctives. For this reason, cultures should be judged on the basis of their own merits, not by comparing one people with another.

Thirdly, the functionalist theory sees the present essentially as a continual reenactment of the past. Any introduction of change, therefore, can open the door to the breakdown of a society. Change is dangerous because it threatens the stability of a society by altering one or more of its parts. Tampering with one part means tampering with the whole. Functionalists will concede that change occurs in a society, but their theory does not allow for handling the change issue adequately. [See Conn (1984) for an excellent overview and critique of functionalism.]

11

Designing an Evangelistic-Discipleship Model

As my skills in language and culture grew, making public teaching possible, I began to develop a number of lessons following the topical outline received in prefield training. The outline covered the Bible, God, Satan, humanity, sin, judgment, and Jesus Christ. Once listeners were introduced to the authority-base (Bible), I would then move on to the second part of the outline (God), and so forth. A general outline for discipleship followed. It dealt with such topics as the Christian walk, the universal and local church, leadership and a host of other Christian doctrines (e.g., justification, the Holy Spirit, prayer, spiritual gifts, eschatology). I presented the evangelism and discipleship lessons from a systematic theology format.

I believed the lessons would provide an excellent foundation for the gospel, hence avoiding easy-believism. But as I began to teach publicly, I soon realized that the Ifugao found it difficult to follow my topical presentations, and found it even harder to explain them to others. I was astonished and perplexed.

Some changes were necessary so I added a number of stories from the Old Testament to illustrate the abstract concepts in the lessons through concrete examples (e.g., creation, the fall, Cain and Abel, the flood, the escape from Egypt, the giving of the Ten Commandments, the Tabernacle, Elijah and Baal). Because only small portions of the Old Testament existed in the dialect, I bought a number of children's books and had the selected stories translated. The people soon wore these out; they obviously enjoyed them. From then on I integrated stories in all my evangelistic efforts.

As a number of Ifugao began to believe the gospel, they wanted to tell their friends of their new found Savior. As I listened to their witnessing I seldom heard any topical teaching. Moreover, I noticed the same was true as I listened to young believers communicating to other believers the basic elements of key doctrines. So I decided to further revise my teaching approach. While I did not drop topical teaching of foundational doctrines entirely, I now spent the majority of my time teaching believers book studies thematically (whole to part), selecting studies that addressed current needs faced by the young Ifugao believers. With this new approach the teaching times came alive. The young believers loved especially James because of its emphasis on God and on the need to demonstrate one's faith. Hebrews became another favorite book due to their familiarity with the practice of sacrifice. What was more impressive, they could communicate accurately the teachings of these writings to friends.

It was finally occurring to me—different people learn differently and I must therefore adjust my teaching style accordingly. My pedagogical conversion had begun. Not only do different people learn differently, God, reflecting his own diverse ways of thinking, chose to communicate in his Word in a variety of ways.

I will now examine a comprehensive evangelistic and dicipleship model designed to reach concrete relational thinkers living in urban or rural settings. The model, the Chronological Teaching approach, designed by Trevor McIlwain, originated in the Philippines with New Tribes Mission in 1980. I will argue for the need and usability of the model, followed by a critique and suggestions to improve it.[1]

A Comprehensive Model Needed

I will digress briefly to continue my own story. While my teaching approach continued to evolve, I sensed I still lacked a comprehensive teaching strategy, built upon a strong evangelistic foundation. In short, I needed a model that would provide a strong preamble for the gospel and be able to extend their understanding of the "whole will of God" (Acts 20:27, NIV). Yet it had to be reproducible by teams of Ifugao believers. It was at that time I was introduced unceremoniously to what would later become known as the Chronological Teaching approach.

While in Manila to pick up the first published evangelism lessons in the Keley-i Ifugao dialect, my colleague Trevor McIlwain, having just returned from furlough, informed me there was a much better way to lay a firm foundation for the gospel and develop a comprehensive teaching model. Eager to hear any new revelations we headed for a secluded spot. The model Trevor laid out impressed me in that it fulfilled the criteria I had set for a teaching strategy: contextual, confronting, comprehensive, reproducible. After our discussion we met with the Field Leader to discuss the model's implications for the Philippine field. The Chronological Teaching model was born. Seminars were held eventually on the islands of Luzon, Mindanao and Palawan. The Southern Baptists and a host of other agencies picked up the model and are now using it extensively in both rural and urban contexts.[2]

The Chronological Teaching Model

The content and methodology of any evangelistic approach plays a major role in the type of churches planted. One of the best models that exists today for providing a firm foundation for the gospel and an overview of the Bible is McIlwain's (1987; 1988; 1989) Chronological Teaching model. McIlwain designed the model for long-term church planting rather than spot evangelism. He assumes Christian workers will build solid relationships, model Christianity and minister to physical and spiritual needs in tandem.

The model differentiates between felt needs and the gospel, a distinction necessary to keep the focus of the message on Christ's efforts to restore our broken relationship with God. This is pertinent especially today in our pluralistic society when even some evangelicals espouse universalism.

The model addresses clearly the limitations of the anthropological theory of functionalism, i.e., focusing primarily on commonalties while tending to neglect contradiction and confrontation. It recognizes that conversion is a process as well as a point, emphasizing the need for foundation as well as follow-up. It communicates well due to the story format, making listeners become instant storytellers. It provides the big picture before introducing isolated parts, thereby avoiding the piecemeal introduction to Scripture most of us received. It calls for constant repetition. It emphasizes biblical theology, thereby encouraging discovery learning of the cosmic plot as the history of redemption unfolds. And it provides a comprehensive understanding of the entire Bible for believers in a relatively short period of time.

An Overview of the Model

McIlwain urges church planters to begin evangelism with an overview of the history of redemption beginning with Genesis on through the ascension of Jesus Christ (Phase 1). Says McIlwain:

> We must not teach a set of doctrines divorced from their God-given historical setting, but rather, we must teach the story of the acts of God as He has chosen to reveal Himself in history. People may ignore our set of doctrines as our western philosophy of God, but the story of God's actions in history cannot be refuted (1987:81).

To accomplish this, McIlwain developed 68 lessons, 42 from the Old Testament and 26 from the New Testament. These lessons deal with the nature and character of God, Satan, and people. Designed primarily for unbelievers, the lessons are helpful also for believers in that they demonstrate the preparatory role the Old Testament plays in evangelism. Key words for the first phase are separation (from God) and solution (through Jesus Christ). (See Figure 20.)

McIlwain emphasizes four basic themes in the evangelism phase. The first theme emphasizes the character of God. God is supreme and sovereign. He communicates with humanity, is omnipresent, omniscient, omnipotent and holy. In his second theme he emphasizes Satan's role, that he fights against God, holds humanity captive and is characterized by lying and deceiving. The third theme deals with humanity. Because of inherited and practiced sin all people find themselves separated from their Creator. His fourth theme focuses on Jesus Christ who is God, man, holy, righteous and the only Savior. The interweaving of these four themes, argues McIlwain, allows the gospel of Jesus Christ to become the good news that God intends it to be, in that the themes provide sufficient background for basic comprehension. McIlwain fully expects listeners to be ready to receive the gospel at the completion of Phase I teaching, if not before.

Phase II moves forward to demonstrate one's security in Christ, and contrasts this with separation and death that result apart from him (Phase I). To illustrate, in Phase I, due to lack of faith in God, unbelievers find themselves outside the closed door of the ark (separation). Death is inevitable. In Phase II, however, believers find themselves safe within the ark behind the closed door. Faith in God results in safety and security.

By reviewing Genesis through the ascension of Christ, new themes are introduced in the lessons and further foundational material is provided as preparation for Phases III and IV. For example, in that the ministry of the Holy Spirit is emphasized in the Gospels, Phase II highlights certain aspects of that ministry so that when the topic reappears in Acts (in Phase III), the listeners can build easily upon the previous background. Such study will equip them for spiritual battle and the advancement of the Kingdom.

The third phase begins with a brief overview of the book of Acts to introduce new believers to church life: the Power behind

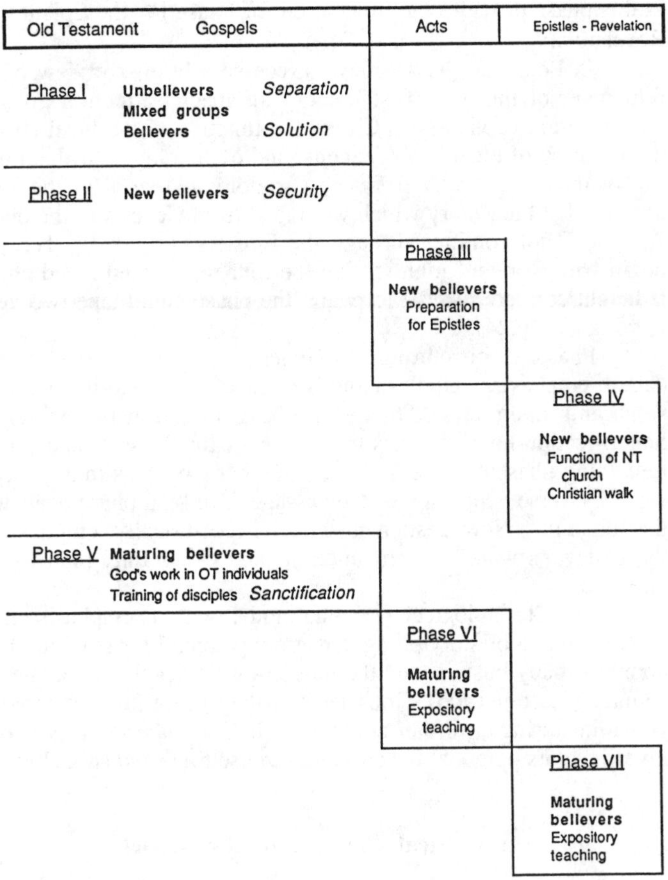

Figure 20. The Chronological teaching outline

(Source: Adapted from McIlwain 1981:12a-12c, 1987:131)

God's kingdom, the conflict with Satan's kingdom, the Christian life, miracles, instruction, worship, food, prayer, giving, conflict resolution, leadership and followership roles, and God's vision for planting and equipping new communities of faith in strategic areas of the world. Other emphases include: the spread of Christianity from Jews to Gentiles, and from Jerusalem to Rome. Subject matter in this phase provides the foundation for Phase IV, the Epistles and Revelation.

In Phase IV, new believers receive a brief overview of the remainder of the New Testament, with special attention given to their position of victory in Christ, the function of the local church, the ministry of elders and deacons, and eschatology. At this point, McIlwain moves away from the chronological story of the Bible arguing that the, "story which we traced from Genesis to the end of Acts does not continue through the Epistles" (1990:19). Teachers begin with Romans, highlighting the four topics mentioned above. If taught correctly, says McIlwain, the phase could take two years to complete (p.24).

Phase V, in returning to Genesis through the ascension of Christ, emphasizes God's methods of sanctifying and maturing his sons and daughters. This phase targets maturing believers. Sanctification now becomes the key word for Phase V and for the remaining phases. Phase VI covers the book of Acts in a detailed, verse-by-verse exposition of the passage. The final phase deals with the remaining New Testament letters expositionally, emphasizing the believer's walk, church functions and God's final plan for the universe.

The Chronological Teaching model, with its emphasis on the concrete mode of storytelling, has great potential for reaching baby boomers, baby busters, and the numerous ethnics that populate this country (Steffen 1996). Don't let its tribal origin turn off those of you ministering in urban contexts. All Christian workers should investigate its potential for cross-cultural settings and subcultures.

A Critical Critique of the Model

As with all evangelistic based teaching models used in urban or rural contexts, the Chronological Teaching model brings with it obvious strengths and weaknesses. Adapting Frackre's (1975) analogy of story I will now examine the strengths and weaknesses of the model and suggest ways to improve it. To accomplish this I will consider the storybook (the Bible), the storyline (the gospel of Jesus Christ), the storyland (the biblical and target cultures), and the storyteller (the witness). In that little field work has been done in the later phases (V-VII), this critique will deal exclusively with

Phases I-IV.

The Storybook

Strengths. A major strength of the Chronological Teaching model is its presentation of the Bible as an integrated story. Many evangelists and church planters, perhaps unknowingly, present a fragmented understanding of the Bible rather than an integrated flow of redemptive history. This is particularly true if the focus is primarily on New Testament teachings.

Many Christian workers prefer the New Testament over the Old. Not surprisingly, they often use one of the Gospels to introduce people to Jesus Christ. This approach should certainly be questioned when attempting to reach those not having a Judeo-Christian heritage. Such a fragmented introduction to the gospel can produce a truncated understanding of the message. It can also produce witnesses who perpetuate an unbalanced and segmented presentation by following the teacher's example, this despite the fact that Old Testament teachings set a necessary foundation for the gospel.

Have you ever picked up a book and began reading it from the middle? If so, you must make a number of assumptions (which may not necessarily be the author's) to try to figure out why things are as they are at that point in the book. Evangelists often cause their listeners to do the same thing when they begin God's message in the middle of the Book. Without having some knowledge of what proceeded the life of Christ, much meaning is sure to be lost, especially for the growing number of our population not having a Judeo-Christian heritage.

What Old Testament background should be presented to the audience before Jesus' story will make sense in the way God intends it? Why did Jesus come to this earth? What events began the Conflict of the Ages between God and Satan? Who are the main protagonists? antagonists? What are the issues at stake between the warring factions? How do these issues relate to the life of Christ? to the target audience? Significant Old Testament background should be provided before presenting the life of Christ. The Chronological Teaching method actually encourages this break from traditional evangelism (including the middle-of-the-book presentation of the "Jesus" film) because its treatment of the gospel allows access to the entire Word to influence and protect the conversion process.

Weaknesses. But how much Old Testament background does an audience need before Jesus' story can be understood? One weakness found in Phases I and II pertains to an overload in both length and content. McIlwain selected Old Testament content based on who and what the Holy Spirit emphasized in the New Testament. He then added pertinent background information or other Old Testament stories to assure continuity of progression (McIlwain 1981:10-11, 20). In that the New Testament alludes to over 100 Old Testament events, some difficult choices must be made to keep the content load manageable.

Even though many audiences neither use or prefer long chronologies, McIlwain's Phase I consists of 68 lessons. To assist the audiences' memory of key individuals and events chronologically, he advocates introducing key characters by placing their names sequentially on a chart. An alternative teaching aid might be the 105 colored pictures covering Phases I - III designed in the Philippines by New Tribes Mission, Philippine Branch together with the Philippine Baptist Mission, Southern Baptist Convention.

Although the above teaching aids can help, for most audiences, Phases I and II contain far too much material. Christian workers using this model in the Philippines noted that faithful attendees usually found it very difficult to master the considerable number of lessons particularly when they were spread out over an extended time period. For those who attended sporadically, it became virtually impossible.

McIlwain (1987) argues that the apostles began their evangelism by using the Old Testament to emphasize God's dealings with such historical people as Abraham, Moses, David, and then linked them to Christ as revealed in Jesus (Acts 2:22-36, 3:13-26; 10:34-43, 13:16-41; 17:2, 3). All of these passages cited, however, deal with Jewish audiences predominately, except Acts 10 which is the account of the god-fearer Cornelius who no doubt knew the Old Testament well. Conspicuously absent in the preceding list of verses are two passages that deal specifically with Gentiles, Acts 14:8-20 and 17:16-34. While these passages may validate the use of the Old Testament for evangelism, they certainly do not adhere to Phase I of the Chronological Teaching approach.

A comparison of the evangelistic messages used with Jewish and Greek audiences in Acts shows that Paul adapted his message to his audience. When Paul addressed Gentiles he contextualized the message, emphasizing a creation-centered theology, judgment, and Lordship. Jewish audiences heard more about their historical ties to the Old Testament and the promised Messiah. For Paul, the audience determined the type of wrapping paper to be used on each evangelism package. Even though the gift never changed, Paul refused a one-wrapping-for-all philosophy (1 Cor. 9:20-22; Gal. 1:8-9).

Improvements. One way to improve the model would be to reduce the content load found in Phases I-II. One may ask, how important is the Old Testament for evangelism, especially for Gentiles? Weber (1957) correctly points out that Jesus must not be de-Judaized to such an extent that he is de-historized. Since approximately 95 percent of the Bible's action takes place within an area of 330-by-110 kilometers, historical Israel should not be ignored in either evangelism or discipleship. In other words, Christian workers can ill afford to neglect Christianity's roots in Israel's history.

However, to introduce everything in the Old Testament in Phases I and II that is emphasized in the New Testament by the Holy Spirit, as McIlwain argues, results in far too much material. It would seem more productive to add much of this information at a later date rather than to overload the listeners in the initial phases.

When the Ifugao taught Phase I, I noticed they drastically condensed a number of lessons into one. They were able to teach the 52 lessons that comprised the Ifugao Phase I in only five or six sessions. And their listeners did very well in grasping the content.

Team members should ask at least three basic questions when considering content load for a lesson or phase: How long a period of time can the people be expected to meet for teaching? How much material can they assimilate realistically at one sitting? What religious background to they have? Answers to these questions, which will differ in urban and rural contexts, can help determine the effective content load of a lesson and the appropriate length of a phase.

The Storyline

As Christian workers attempt to communicate the message of the storybook, it becomes imperative that the story of Jesus Christ be presented accurately (Gal. 1:6-24; II Tim. 2:12). The Chronological Teaching model's design helps assure the delivery of a pure gospel.

Strengths. McIlwain's model offers a plus in guarding the gospel in that it allows ample time for foundational understanding. Western witnesses tend to head for the "bottom line" of the gospel as quickly as possible "to seal the deal." But unfortunately for many people, centuries of spiritual darkness seldom evaporate after just one hearing of the gospel message. The listener's concepts of God, Satan, people, sin, and the world are usually very different from those presented in the Bible. Many will require considerable time before they realize that the God of the Bible is challenging their present worldview. Phase I of the Chronological Teaching helps avoid syncretism by laying a solid foundation for the gospel.

Another strength of the Chronological Teaching model has to do with distinguishing felt needs from the gospel. For many heralds today, the gospel message is synonymous to felt needs. For example, if a person faces health problems, the good news becomes Jesus as Healer. If a person fears the spirit world, the good news becomes Jesus as the most powerful Spirit. If a person experiences financial woes the good news becomes Jesus as Provider. If a person experiences loneliness the good news becomes Jesus as Companion. While all of these are true in and of themselves, they are not the specific message of good news as defined by Paul, rather they are the result of that good news. Fackre captures this thought well when he states:

> To think first and foremost of our own tale is to get into a kind of navel-gazing in which we still are trapped in "I, me and mine." But the goal of God's action remains unreached until his Story becomes our story. Story-telling is, first and foremost, the biography of God, not my autobiography. It is an account of what "he" has done, is doing, and will do. Only in a modest and derivative sense is it concerned about our appropriation of these gracious actions (1973:14, 43-44).

For Paul, the good news meant God has accepted wholeheartedly and irreversibly Jesus Christ's sacrifice on the cross to restore our broken relationship with himself. The heralds of the gospel must focus their message on the redemptive efforts of Jesus Christ.

The Chronological Teaching model avoids another traditional western evangelism trap by refusing to specify a particular form of decision-making to connote transfer of allegiance from a previous god to Jesus Christ. Contemporary evangelism approaches often call for reciting a certain prayer, raising a hand, walking an isle, and so forth. How will the watching audience comprehend these forms of decision-making? Do they prefer to make individual decisions or group decisions (multi-individual, mutually interdependent)? If the latter, how much time will be required before peers or family members have opportunity to discuss the pros and cons of such a decision? Does raising a hand signify a new follower of Christ or an individual that does not wish to offend socially those presenting the message? Does repeating a certain prayer signify a new follower of Christ or serve as a new means of ritual to use in earning favor with a new god? For many people around the world, decision-making is a group event conducted over a period of time. This model advocates function over form when it comes to decision-making.

Weaknesses. One problem that becomes evident in the redemptive history of Jesus Christ is McIlwain's overemphasis on God's justice. The focus in Phase I is primarily on the theme of God's justice and the punishment it demands for sin. This tends to present an unbalanced picture of God. Does not the Old Testament reveal a God who interacts with his creation by means of law and grace? The Law as discussed in Genesis through Deuteronomy speaks of expulsion and promise, of deluge and promise, of dispersion of all nations and yet the calling of one individual to form a new nation, of law and sacrifices. The Prophets (Joshua through Malachi) emphasize not only captivity but restoration. The motifs of judgment and deliverance flow intertwined throughout the entire Old Testament.

A second weakness centers around which redemptive analogies should be used when conveying the story of Jesus Christ. McIlwain (1987:69-71) seems to believe that use of redemptive typologies and analogies found in the Bible rather than those found among a particular people, will assure protection against misunderstanding or syncretism. This he bases on an assumption that God has provided all the necessary biblical redemptive analogies for the entire world through the one nation of Israel.

Improvements. The story aspect of the model could be strengthened by providing a balanced perspective of the character of God. The history of redemption speaks simultaneously of grace and judgment. In that God's justice speaks of tough-love, the content of Phase I should do likewise.

Another way to help secure an accurate presentation of the story would be to conduct two major studies: first, identify the major unifying and antithetical cultural themes within the target audience. Identifying these themes will help the team learn about the people they work among, the social environments, the religion(s) and cult(s) in the area, and the local economical and political influences.

The second major study involves developing general and specific theological objectives. The general objective for the Ifugao Phase I reads: *Upon the completion of this phase the Ifugao should be able to comprehend a personable God who defeated Satan, provided a provisional substitute for their salvation from sin through Jesus Christ and appropriate this provision by faith.* With this aggregate information, a contextualized phase can be produced that will protect the purity of the gospel message, yet remain relevant to the target audience. This leads us to the next analogy: the storyland.

The Storyland

Strengths. When defining the storyland one must address biblical cultures. The Chronological Teaching model introduces the listeners/readers to a host of different Old Testament and New Testament cultures. Through these diverse cultures the audience begins to perceive personal and collective responsibility before the Creator-King of all peoples.

Besides the biblical cultures, the land in which the story will be told must be well understood by the storytellers. Here McIlwain receives mixed reviews. On the positive side of the ledger, albeit not by design, McIlwain presents a biblical theology based model that works well for approximately three-fourths of the world's population. The model incorporates a holistic perspective. The first four phases provide an overview of the entire Bible in a relatively short period of time. Moreover, its global approach to teaching provides a holistic framework for future teaching. It employs the learning style of the majority of world's population, that is, it moves from the whole to the part.

Another helpful feature of this comprehensive model is its teaching design. The model builds from the simple to the complex in spiral fashion, one lesson providing the foundation for the next lesson, one phase providing the foundation for the next phase. McIlwain's model offers continuity to the listener/reader by building from the familiar to the unfamiliar.

A third strength lies in its repetition of key content through review questions that emphasize dialogue. Those appreciating the visual and concrete tend to prefer repetition and participation. The Chronological Teaching model encourages both of these communicative styles.

Weaknesses. Probably the major weakness of McIlwain's theological based model is his failure to recognize the need for a contextualized curriculum for each audience. Socio-economic levels, political persuasions, generational differences, communicative style preferences and the influence of non-Christian religions and cults seem to be overlooked totally by this model. This oversight drives McIlwain to conclude that one evangelistic model (Phase I) can be expected to reach all people groups of the world. We have moved from four spiritual laws to sixty-eight.

Another shortcoming surfaces when one looks for lessons that address the material world. On the one hand, the author develops the relationships between God, Satan, and people, but then fails to show how these relationships apply to the material world considered so important to the daily lives of many. This lack of emphasis presents a bifurcated picture of the spiritual and material world. More emphasis on the Kingdom of God could help remedy this.

A third weakness of the Chronological Teaching model arises from its almost exclusive emphasis on the narrative. Some people groups prefer socialization by means of proverbs, psalms and/or thought-organized content. Phase I-IV tends to by-pass other valid literary styles.

A further weakness lies in the review questions. While they help the listeners/readers review the cognitive content of a lesson, they often fail to take into consideration their traditional use in the storyland, and fail to call for personal or group application.

Improvements. One step toward matching the model with the storyland could be the scripting of phases for each specific people since no curriculum exists that addresses every people group in the world sufficiently. Communicative styles, economical, political and religious influences, and felt needs all differ greatly from one social environment to another as well as from one generation to the next. Every people group should be entitled to its own curriculum.

Another improvement would be to insert an introductory lesson in Phase I that paints in broad strokes, from Genesis to Revelation, God's redemptive plan for humanity and the cosmos (Phases I-IV). (The same would be true for all succeeding phases.) Such a lesson would provide holistic thinkers a global picture from which to hang all subsequent lessons. Connecting the Epistles (Phase IV) with the ongoing story of God should also improve understanding and communication of these lessons.

> Church planters must never minimize the power that resides in the gospel story (Rom. 1:16; I Thes. 1:5). Nor must they overlook the imaginative power unleashed through the communicative style of storytelling.

Teaching whole to part in Phase IV would add another significant improvement to the model. Rather than teaching each book piece-meal, teachers would present the basic message of the book (theme[s]) and tie the text into it. They would also emphasize how the concrete elements of imagery and characters found in the text emphasize the basic theme(s) of the book.

Encouraging the use of other communicative styles could serve as another means to improve the comprehension and circulation of the story. To illustrate, the Ifugao, using a traditional *Salidumay* tune, composed a song of one hundred and forty-six verses to review God's redemptive history from Genesis through Acts 1. While this did not call for a change of chronology in the teaching format, such a change may be necessary for other people groups. For those who have a deep appreciation for poetry, it may be wise to begin with Psalms or wisdom literature, and then skip back to Genesis. A shake up of the chronology may be necessary so that communicative style preference can be maximized.

A further improvement would be to give the material world greater emphasis. Kingdom-based church planting demands such. Not only does Genesis 1:26 speak of an "I-Thou" relationship, it also refers to an "I-It" relationship. The Bible never separates people from their environment. Note, the Trinity placed Adam and Eve in the Garden of Eden, and the descendants of Abraham lived in the promised land of milk and honey (regarded as another Eden). Moreover, believers look forward to new bodies and to life in a new environment. The Bible indicates that people have material bodies, and that they reside in environments appropriate for those bodies. The interrelationships of God, Satan, people and the material world therefore should receive greater attention. Providing more emphasis on the Kingdom of God theme would help wed the spiritual and material worlds.

A fifth way to improve the Chronological Teaching model would be to raise some questions about the use of questions in the storyland. Does the audience find questions confrontive? shame-producers? Should the questions call for response from individuals, families, peers, communities, or some combination of these? Should application of the content be implied in the story or called for through direct questions? How the target audience uses questions (and other discourse features) should impact how the Christian workers use them in oral teaching and written curricula.

A final suggestion for matching the model to the storyland would be to evaluate each team that is using the model in either urban or rural settings. From such an evaluation, other ways to improve each phase would doubtless emerge, especially those features that are readily reproducible by the listeners/readers. Such an evaluation would also facilitate the phase-out process of the Christian workers in that it would be a help in developing more effective lessons and phases, and in developing more effective storytellers.

The Storyteller

Strengths. One of the most positive features of the Chronological Teaching model is its emphasis on the narrative. Since most people love to hear stories, Christian workers would do well to tell stories extensively in both evangelism and discipleship. Miller notes:

> The fundamental mode of Scripture is story. Both Torah and Gospel are stories to tell....Even Romans must not be read as simply an abstract propositional statement of truth. The book is best understood within the story of Paul's missionary journeys (1987:117,128).

The Chronological Teaching model underscores the literary value of stories by allowing the listeners/readers opportunity to experience emotionally the lives of real people and animals living in real places.

Most of the narrative sections of the Chronological Teaching model, when contextualized, are reproducible by the listeners/readers. The ultimate task for any teaching model for phase-out oriented Christian workers must be: Can it be reproduced accurately by those who hear it? While no statistics exist to document the number of phases being reproduced currently by nationals in the Philippines, a number of missionaries have indicated to me that nationals on the islands of Luzon, Palawan and Mindanao can reproduce Phases I-III. Reports from other countries confirm the same. Phases IV-VII, depending upon design, may require different types of communicative styles which may prove much more difficult to reproduce for concrete relational thinkers.

Weakness. McIlwain asserts boldly that the Chronological Teaching model surpasses all other teaching approaches for any people group. He apparently assumes a premise that his chronological model follows "divine guidelines" (1987:8). However, just what McIlwain means by the "divinely revealed order of teaching" (1987:78) is difficult to determine. If this refers to the narrative focus of the Bible, one could claim he is overlooking other valid literary forms. In any case, he obviously means the Old Testament is to be taught prior to the New Testament.

> The Chronological Teaching model, *when contextualized for a specific urban or rural context,* has to be one of the most effective approaches to evangelism and discipleship that exists today.

But how much Old Testament teaching should be considered "basic" or "adequate"? If this includes the 68 lessons of Phase I proposed by McIlwain, and the subsequent phases, one could justifiably be critical because historical and chronological order of the "divinely revealed order of teaching" tends to be highly subjective. For one thing, McIlwain does not always follow his basic premise, i.e., teach the Scriptures chronologically. To illustrate, lesson four of Phase I adds Lucifer, lake of fire, Satan's opposition to God and his abrupt departure from heaven. Phase IV drops the chronological story progression to focus on four major themes pertinent to new believers.

A related problem arises in that it becomes very difficult to follow the chronological order in the Bible. Information is often given without prior explanation, e.g., Abraham and tithing (Gen. 14:20). Sequential problems also arise. Where does Job fit chronologically in the canon? Galatians? James? (Luther's view of justification by faith caused him to want to exclude James from the canon, or at least place it at the end of the Bible.) Not everyone agrees with the chronology of *The Reese Chronological Bible,* nor will all agree with McIlwain's proposed chronology.

Improvements. The storyteller can avoid such pitfalls of claiming to have discovered the exclusive teaching model for the world by remembering that before one becomes a storyteller, one should become a listener of the individual and community stories of the target people. Not only do we have a specific story from the storybook to tell in a specific land, we have stories to learn from those to whom we wish to communicate the greatest story ever told.

Communicators can go a step further. Once one becomes a listener of the stories of others, one often gains the opportunity to tell his/her own story. Having earned the right to be heard, it is only a short jump from his/her story to the storybook. Effective evangelism tends to connect the target audiences' stories with the witnesses' story with the Story-of-stories (Larson 1978; Steffen 1996).

A further step storytellers can take to help assure effective communication is to recognize the complexity of telling the simple gospel message from Genesis through the ascension via a story format. While the gospel remains a simple message, using the Chronological Teaching model cross-culturally requires a great deal of sophistication. Not only must the storyteller have a grasp of discourse features, he/she must also have an in-depth understanding of the target audience's worldview before beginning story-telling. A cursory view of the content covered in Genesis 1-11 demonstrates the vast depth of worldview knowledge necessary for the storyteller: God, Satan, creation, sin, flood, rainbow, death, soul, communication with the spirit world, reconciliation, to name just a few. One way to learn all this is to become a storylistener. (See Appendixes N and O for phase objectives and an evaluation form.)

Conclusion

Because the content and method of evangelism constitutes the foundation for starting a community of faith, just how Christian workers orchestrate its initial steps influences to a great extent the type of churches that result. The Chronological Teaching model, *when contextualized for a specific urban or rural context,* has to be one of the most effective approaches to evangelism and discipleship that exists today.

But the model also brings with it a number of weaknesses that Christian workers will want to adapt or rectify. This requires they take a learner role, i.e., become storylisteners, and include their audience throughout the entire development process. Such an approach should result in teaching and curricula that is not only relevant, but comprehensible and reproducible.

Improving the model should not prove difficult for those willing to become storylisteners. Learning the stories of the target audience will go a long ways in producing a relevant learning experience rather than imposing a program from the outside. Such an approach should produce readers/listeners capable of reproducing the materials in an uncompromising way in that such things as content, communicative styles, chronology, lesson length, and duration of a phase, reflect the needs and communicative style preferences of a specific audience.

Church planters must never minimize the power that resides in the gospel story (Rom. 1:16; I Thes. 1:5). Nor should they overlook the imaginative power unleashed through the communicative style of storytelling. This significant genre, albeit recognized belately, must again come to the forefront. McIlwain's narrative model, when contextualized, will meet one of the major challenges facing the Church in the 21st Century—introducing a rapidly increasing number of concrete relational thinkers who lack a Judeo-Christian heritage to the sacred Storybook, the storylands and the story of Jesus Christ. And more importantly, it should produce a host of new storytellers.

Effective communication of the Story produces believers. These beleivers must be empowered to minister, if phase-out is to result. I will therefore now consider some of the "hows" of releasing empowered church leaders / planters.

1 Two key terms related to this chapter are "narrative" and "story." I will use the term "narrative" to refer "in the broadest sense to the account by a narrator of events and participants moving in some pattern over time and space." The word "story" takes a "narrower literary meaning: an account of characters and events in a plot moving over time and space through conflict toward resolution" (Fackre 1984:5).

2 For an analysis of how different agencies in the Philippines contextualize the Chronological Teaching model see Steffen 1995.

PART 5

Postevangelism

"Since Christ had to suffer physically for you, you must fortify yourselves with the same inner attitude....You should not therefore spend the rest of your time here on earth indulging your physical nature....I left you in Crete to set right matters which needed attention, and gave you instructions to appoint elders in every city."

(I Pet. 4:1-2; Titus 1:5, Phillips)

12

Releasing Empowered Church Leaders / Planters

Church planters have long been accused of being world Christians who, for some reason, fail to communicate that same vision to national believers. Because my wife and I did not want to repeat this mistake with the Ifugao, we took certain steps to ensure the development of national leaders who were willing to and capable of reproducing new churches cross-culturally as well as at home.

When a number of the Ifugao became believers, we asked them where to go to present the gospel. After some discussion, they chose a village to the south. During our evangelistic trips we began to focus their attention on other unchurched areas. We asked, "Who lives over there? Are they believers? How can we reach them?" These 'trail talks' did much to cement in the minds of the young believers a Christianity that focused outward.

Another way we tried to promote world vision came through the use of a map of the Ifugao territory and surrounding areas. Together we pinpointed villages that showed interest in the gospel within and outside the tribe. Our communal prayers focused on the people living in the selected villages, and in time initiated evangelistic trips. Our ultimate goal was not only to witness, but to plant a church that could then plant other churches in the surrounding areas. We used our annual conferences to update our efforts and make plans for the next year. In this way, outreach strategy became a group affair from the very beginning.

But my wife and I wondered if the Ifugao would maintain this vision to reach outward once we became Itinerant and even Absent Advisors? What else could be done to ensure the development of Ifugao church leaders / planters? Would the Ifugao believers accept our programmed absences and eventual withdrawal? We knew their reaction could either promote or impede their world vision. We continued to wonder, worry, and pray.

For ongoing church planting to continue within and outside of a people group, the national leaders must own the vision, be equipped to implement it, and be given the opportunity to accomplish it successfully. For this to happen, the church planters must spend sufficient time during their Resident and Itinerant Advisor roles to create a world vision, see it take root, train nationals to accomplish it, and delegate full responsibility to them to carry it out. The types of responsibilities church planters and nationals must take for this to happen, i.e., nationals capable of leading their own churches in a way that will inspire vision for planting new churches among unreached peoples, will now be discussed.

Chruch Planter Responsibilities

Evangelism works upon the premise of addition. Churches grow by adding new believers to the rolls. Church planting, however, works upon the premise of multiplication! New church plants not only add new believers to the rolls, they launch generations of outreach patterns with the potential of winning multitudes to the Lord. Effective church plants are dynamic in that they effectively evangelize an area, while at the same time establish a base from which to launch new church planters, so that the cycle can begin again in other unchurched areas. Effective Christian workers will seek to church areas, rather than to merely evangelize them.

Church planters cannot expect to complete the Great Commission without the help of nationals (and vice versa). Nor can they do it solely by developing churches whose primary focus is evangelism. Only by planting new churches in unchurched areas, not just facilitating the growth of existing churches, can church planting team and nationals reach the entire world with the gospel. For this to happen, church planters must empower nationals to plant new churches, while at the same time, phase-out of their respective responsibilities to begin the process again elsewhere.

Avoid Extremes

Cross-cultural church planters have several options once they become involved in a church plant. On the one hand, they can decide to remain in the area permanently. Or they can plan to leave. If they choose to remain, they can assume one of three roles:

a partnership role, a subordinate role, or a dominant role of control. If they decide to leave the church plant, they can choose either to pull out abruptly or phase-out over time (see Figure 21).

A decision to pull-out may be determined by any of a number of factors: by the health of the church planter or child, or by subversive elements. Or a catastrophic event may demand an abrupt departure. In some cases, however, church planters abandon their ministry too hastily due to discouragement or burnout.

Perhaps the best exit strategy under normal conditions is a balance between the two extremes. Such a plan would avoid premature abandonment or paternalism. Responsible departure could be attained by programming absences over time of increasing length so that relationships between the church planters and nationals could be built, and the teachers' model emulated and adapted.

Should team members receive a request to work in partnership with the national church, much prayer should go into the decision. Church planters will want to make sure the position offered includes in the job description the necessity for training a national replacement.

Basic assumptions. A number of basic assumptions led me to conclude that programmed absences over a period of time is one of the most effective ways to produce national leaders / church planters. Some of these assumptions include: a) the pilgrim character of most cross-cultural church planting, b) the priesthood of believers and the body principle demand good stewardship of all resources [human and financial], c) the necessity of building and maintaining solid friendships with members of the target community, d) the length of stay for team members involved in community development ministries may be longer than for those involved in church planting primarily, e) the timing for phase-out.

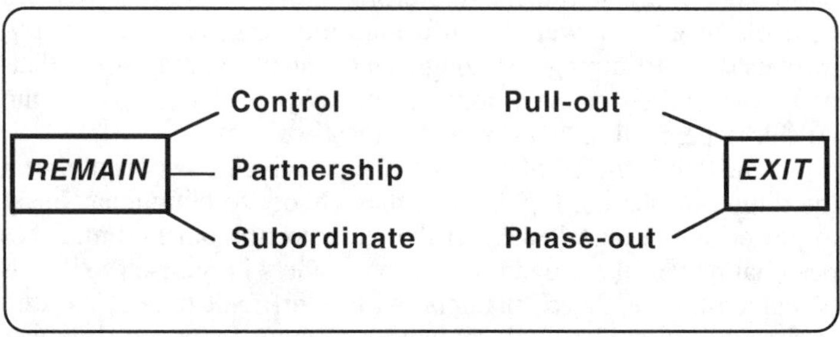

Figure 21. Possible Church Plant Outcomes

differs for every church plant, g) the Holy Spirit can develop *all* his people, h) mistakes should be expected, i) empowering others for ministry multiplies personal power rather than reduces it.

Closure theology. A number of reasons and verses come to mind when thinking of an exit strategy that will avoid staying too long or leaving prematurely. Jesus left his disciples after three years. Paul's stays rarely exceeded three years. Consider the following verses:

> "Now I commit you to God and to the word of his grace, which can build you up" (Acts 20:32).
> "After we had torn ourselves away from them, we put out to sea" (Acts 21:1).
> "I tried to come to you many times so I could have a harvest among you too (Rom. 1:13).
> "It has always been my ambition to preach the gospel where Christ was not known, so that I would not be building on someone else's foundation" (Rom. 15:20).
> "And the things you have heard me say in the presence of many witnesses entrust to reliable men who will also be qualified to teach others" (II Tim. 2:2).
> "Straighten out what was left unfinished and appoint elders in every town" (Titus 1:5).
> "You are a chosen priesthood" (I Pet. 2:5,9; Rev. 1:6).
> "I face daily the pressure of my concern for all the churches" (II Cor. 11:28).
> "Let My people go, that they may serve Me" (Ex. 8:1).

The impact of power. Whoever controls the resources has power. These individuals or groups can reward or punish others by providing or limiting access to resources. Such actions result in creating relationships of inequality.

Church planters often hold tremendous power in the eye's of nationals. Many nationals, therefore, feel the church planters control access to wealth, information, personal availability, influence, and training. Although team members may view their power as limited or even nonexistent, they must realize it is the outsider's perception that carries the most weight.

Just how church planters use the perceived power can impact the timing of phase-out greatly. If they choose to cling tenaciously to power, in the mistaken belief that empowering others diminishes personal power, the growth of national leaders in ministry skills, as perceived by the church planters, will be difficult to see. Turning to the other side of the coin, if church planters choose to empower nationals, the national leaders will gain confidence in using their ministry skills. In that shared power usually results in multiplied power for both parties, discerning church planters will know when to release personal, positional, and spiritual power, and when to keep it. Shared power releases synergistic power—and promotes responsible phase-out within a reasonable amount of time.

Empowering Nationals

Leaving the spiritual family in which one has played a major role in birthing and nurturing is not easy to do. Paul experienced this when he had to literally tear himself away from the Ephesian elders (Acts 21:1). The church planting team must recognize the inevitable, and do all it can to prepare national believers, as well as themselves, for the eventual trauma that accompanies phase-out.

Attitude toward followers. All too often church planters view leadership in isolation from followership. Some even characterize followers as "sheep," as if they were destined always to follow and not worth the effort to train. These individuals make the following assumptions: 1) followers never lead, 2) only leaders have vision, 3) followers know how to follow, 4) leaders are more important than followers, 5) only leaders lead, 6) leaders do not follow.

In reality, it is the followers who bestow power upon their leaders and the leaders who enable followers to become powerful (see Figure 22). Leadership and followership both involve shared power; they are interdependent. Paul recognized this when he told the Romans he would help them, but that they would also influence him (Rom. 1:11-12).

Kouzes and Posner (1987) suggest a simple test to detect if someone is a potential leader—does the person use the word "we"? Leaders who share their power with followers are actually setting the stage for developing new generations of leaders. Followers, by

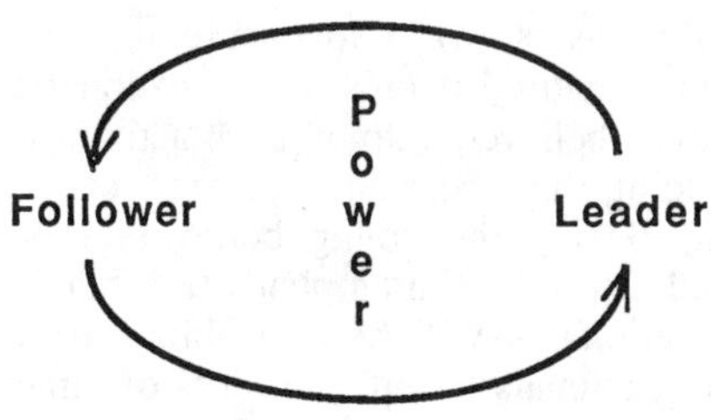

Figure 22. The circular effect of leading and following

accepting a leader's influence will, over time, begin to change roles. That is, they will begin acting more and more like leaders themselves. Soon that follower will become a leader of a new group of followers. As leaders empower their followers the multiplication continues, creating new generations of leaders ready to carry on the vision of reaching a lost world for Christ.

Delegate and evaluate. church planters sometimes fail or hesitate to delegate ministry responsibilities to nationals. They may fear that the nationals' vision and/or methodology will produce results different from their expectations. This attitude may show lack of confidence, which helps explain why church planters tend to remain in charge far too long. There is a familiar axiom that states: *The more church planters become involved in the day-to-day activities of evangelism, church development, and church multiplication, the less delegation that will take place.* Indeed, such an approach to ministry usually impedes the spiritual development of nationals, and ultimately slows or halts the phase-out process.

The sooner the church planters learn to delegate ministry opportunities and provide immediate feedback, the less the above axiom will apply. Moreover, the strategy of delegating and evaluating will demonstrate confidence, provide hands-on experience, offer prompt feedback (if adjustments are necessary), and provide essential encouragement. Like Moses, church planters must not cling jealously to their dominant roles, but rather seek to provide ministry opportunities for all who follow willingly the Holy Spirit (Num. 11:24-30). And they, like Moses, will avoid burnout as they distribute the work load (Ex. 18). If church planters enter with an expanded world vision, help that vision take root, and then release it, their contribution will be the creation of mature national believers ready for phase-out.

National Responsibilities

One of the easiest ways to ensure that ongoing church planting becomes a natural expression of national churches is to incorporate national believers into all such activities from the very beginning. By doing this, the church planters can model ongoing church planting. Seeing the young believers brought together, leaders appointed, and new church plants facilitated—all of which have included nationals—will help establish a model that sets precedent for the nationals to replicate. It is of utmost importance that national believers move beyond mere observation and participation. They must repeat the process on their own, while at the same time avoiding two perils: apathy and nationalism.

Extremes of Apathy and Nationalism

Among the potential barriers to effective implementation of sequential church planting is apathy. One national lamented: "Why should we become involved when the church planters are doing such a good job? Besides, they can spend full-time in ministry because they are supported, but we who have to work all day must do all this during our off time. Ministry tires us out."

Yes, ministering to others does tire one out. Paul (and countless other believers) became tired because they served others. Yet, they continued to give themselves for others. Why? Because of the understanding of God's grace, the grace that changed their standing before God from an "enemy" to a "friend." This became their driving force for carrying the life-changing message to others. An accurate understanding of God's grace as demonstrated through the life of Jesus Christ goes a long way in fighting apathy.

> *The more church planters become involved in the day-to-day activities of evangelism, church development, and church multiplication, the less delegation that will take place.*

A second potential barrier to ongoing church planting by nationals is nationalism. Some national believers feel outsiders have usurped their rightful authority far too long; it is high time they took control of their own destiny. Mission history records all too poignantly the reality of many of these accusations against paternalistic Christian workers.

Nationalism, however, tends to lead to extremes. Some advocates demand all church planters leave immediately, believing they are capable of handling their own affairs without outside help.Others prefer access to their wealth. When these attitudes are applied to the universal Church, church planting can be stifled because a key biblical tenant is neglected, i.e., the body principle.

National believers can benefit from the assistance of the church planters just as the church planters can benefit from the help of national believers. For planting of new churches to continue several questions must be considered: How much assistance is required? When should it be given? Who should provide it?

A case could be made for heavy outside assistance initially, with immediate tapering off as nationals become more adept in their ministry skills. The advantage of this approach is that it allows for immediate feedback, encouragement, correction and growth, while at the same time it eliminates the need for permanent participation by the church planters. In other words, it allows for direction without dominance. In effect, through partnership it fights the deadly affects of both paternalism and nationalism.

Church Planting Activity and Development

Wise church planters concentrate their efforts on faithful national believers. I define faithful believers as those who are "capable" (Ex. 18:21, NIV), who seek to "obey everything I have commanded you" (Matt. 28:20, NIV), and who are "qualified to teach others" (II Tim. 2:2, NIV). They possess character, commitment, a certain degree of competency to handle complex tasks, and a willingness to coordinate efforts. National believers who are serious about developing their character and ministry skills should receive serious attention from the church planters.

Faithful national believers commonly advance through four levels to become effective church leaders / planters: a) they accompany the church planters in their activities; b) they participate according to their comfort zone; c) they expand their comfort zone by taking leadership in unfamiliar areas; and d) they train others who have been observers of their respective ministries. Such a developmental approach allows an advance from one level to the next within the national's own time frame. Moreover, it encourages drawing strength and confidence from the Holy Spirit rather than from the church planters who will soon move on to become Absent Advisors. (See Figure 23.)

As the church planters move through the various roles (i.e., Evangelists, Teachers, and Resident Advisors) they should continually watch for corresponding changes on the part of their national counterparts. For example, as the church planters begin teaching, they should look for faithful nationals who not only will accompany them, but will also participate in teaching, and eventually be willing to take roles as teacher and trainer of other teachers.

To illustrate: in level one, the church planters begin to share with national believers the expectation that this aspect of ministry will eventually be theirs. (Presumably the nationals already know the church planters do not intend to remain permanently in the area (where appropriate) because of the many other people groups who remain without the gospel.) The church planters encourage the nationals to accompany them and participate within their comfort zone.During these activities, nationals should be encouraged to trust the Holy Spirit for boldness and wisdom.

Mapping out a church planting strategy for the surrounding

areas is a great way to encourage national participation. On the way to the outreach point, the younger believers may be asked questions pertaining to those living in the neighborhood so as to identify feltneeds. During evangelistic meetings, team members will encourage the younger believers to answer questions and share their testimony. Debriefing times are designed to hone their evangelistic skills.

At the second level, the national believers are again encouraged to rely on the power of the Holy Spirit by expanding

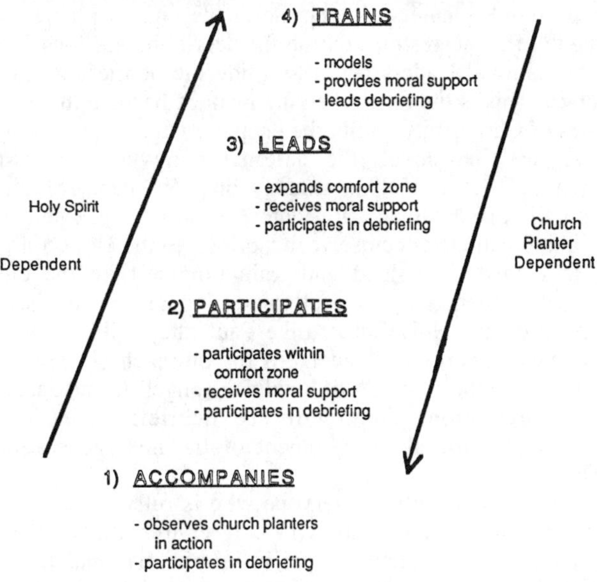

Figure 23. Developing effective church leaders/planters

their comfort zone as they practice their ministry skills. Team members provide opportunities to discuss church planting strategies, share testimonies, answer questions posed by nonbelievers, participate in evangelism, pray for the lost, for laborers, for the sick, and for the release of people from the control of Satan and his cohorts. As nationals step out in faith, God will honor their efforts. During debriefing sessions the participants can be affirmed, corrected, rebuked, and encouraged by patient and discreet church planters. After all, the goal is to build character and maximize the confidence level (II Tim. 4:2).

At level three, it is obvious that the national believers' confidence in the Holy Spirit is growing. Some now can take an active lead in evangelism and encourage fellow believers to join them. They plan the evangelistic trips, the prayer sessions, the visits to the sick. Some will even feel comfortable baptizing those who respond. Phase-out oriented church planters will continue to relinquish control as they also affirm the aspiring new national leaders / church planters. At this point the church planters may continue to offer suggestions during the debriefing sessions, but the emerging national leaders begin to guide the debriefing sessions themselves. This is the time when the insiders become the primary advocates of Christianity within the people group.

At the final level, the national believers are actually implementing the evangelism strategy on their own. The church planters will have assumed a Resident Advisor role in evangelism. Now it is the nationals themselves who look to the Holy Spirit for power and wisdom to lead and train others. Like the church planters before them, they too seek to develop new evangelists who can depend on the Holy Spirit. Like Paul, they will endeavor to develop intergenerational leadership for outreach (II Tim. 2:2). They will affirm the activities of budding evangelists and encourage further participation. They will use debriefing sessions to encourage the spiritual development of the next generation of evangelists.

Jesus commented: "...everyone who is fully trained will be like his teacher" (Luke 6:40, NIV). If church planters model church-planting evangelism properly, faithful national believers will very likely imitate what they have seen modeled. In our case, the Ifugao leaders never asked how to plant a church. They feel very comfortable training church leaders / planters because they themselves participated in church planting *from the beginning*. To the Ifugao, church leadership and church planting had become synonymous.

The book of Judges records a tragic failure, the failure to produce effective successors. Team members can avoid the "Joshua syndrome" by encouraging faithful Christian leaders to own the vision of ongoing church planting and development. As they do this, the Holy Spirit will help them put their vision into action. Having effective successors will assure sustained church planting and phase-out, but this requires that participants take different responsibilities at different times.

Situational Responsibility

Church planters who either suffer burnout or give evidence of paternalism have a tendency to leave congregations prematurely or remain too long. Or they may create unproductive ones. On the other hand, national believers who become apathetic or are overly nationalistic tend to stifle expansion in their churches. (See Figure 24.) For ongoing church planting to be successful, the church planters must release power and nationals must assume power. Both parties must accept the various responsibilities as dictated by the timing and complexity of the situation at hand.

In the Situational Leadership Model, Hersey and Blanchard (1982) posit four basic leadership styles: Telling, Selling, Participating, and Delegating. The model deals with the functions of the leader, the follower, and the situation. The Telling style is characterized by high direction and low relational support, the Selling style by high direction and high relational support, the Participating style by minimum structure and high relational support, and the Delegating style by minimum structure and minimum relational support. Leadership becomes effective as a person is able to match his or her leadership style with the commitment and competency levels of the follower initially, and over time.

It is possible to expand the Situational Leadership Model by giving equal emphasis to followership. The revised model can be achieved by: 1) identifying role changes for the followers (from

	Church planter	*National*
Unsuccessful	burnout paternalism	apathy nationalism
Successful	releases power	assumes power

Figure 24. Hindrances and solutions to church planting

Receiving, to Learning, to Implementing, to Reproducing), and by 2) incorporating eight basic skill areas essential for shepherding and ongoing church-planting evangelism (goal setting, planning, decision-making, motivation, resources, implementation, evaluation and conflict resolution). Use of all eight skills provides opportunity for nationals to evaluate culture-acceptable ways of dealing with issues from a biblical perspective. I call this model Situational Responsibilty (see Figure 25).

The four quadrants illustrate a church planter's change of roles. These include: a) *Directing* (without becoming dictatorial), b) *Coaching* (when commitment and competency are evident), c) *Facilitating* (when well-developed skills are evident but a lack of confidence remains), and d) *Empowering* (so that the developed leaders can reproduce without outside assistance). The model moves from the church planter leading (lower right quadrant) to becoming a follower so nationals can lead (lower left quadrant).

From the national's perspective, the four quadrants emphasize an apprentice role and include: a) Receiving (accepting advice), b) Learning (experimenting with one's abilities), c) Implementing (taking initiative), and d) Reproducing (repeating the process independently). The model moves from following (lower right quadrant) to leading (lower left quadrant).

Since environmental changes can bring about power plays, situational responsibility calls for negotiation between church planters and nationals to determine how much responsibility each will take in a particular situation. Depending on the situation and/or the timing of the event, the church planters may need to take the majority of the responsibility. Other situations (or timing) will dictate that nationals carry the responsibility.

It is helpful to note just what the Situational Responsibility Model does not assume. For example, the model does not assume church planters will always begin in the first quadrant and move toward the fourth quadrant. Many new believers will fit initially in quadrant two, particularly if their commitment level tends to be high but they lack knowledge, e.g., of how to pray or witness. Those raised in Christian homes may find their initial fit in the third quadrant; they may already know how to witness but lack the courage to do so.

The model does not assume that action always proceeds from the first to the fourth quadrant, or advance or digress only one quadrant at a time. Sometimes it moves from the third quadrant to second, or from the second to the first. Alternately, there may be occasions when one particular quadrant is by-passed all together.

The model also does not assume that national believers will necessarily adopt the church planters' culture in any of the eight skill areas. Rather, nationals are challenged to allow biblical

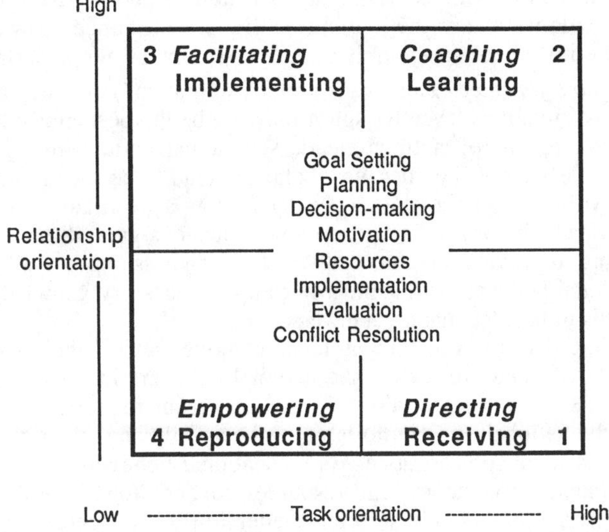

Figure 25. A situational responsibility model

principles to discipline their own culture. Finally, the model does not assume that learning takes place only on the national's side of the ledger. The church planter's role of learner continues through the Postevangelism and Phase-out stages. It matters not which quadrant is the starting point, or which direction is taken. The goal remains unchanged: that nationals eventually take total responsibility for everything related to ongoing church planting and development. For this to transpire effectively, however, the church planters must be as willing to learn as the nationals.

The Church Planter's Style

Church planters must understand leadership style preferences if their role transitions are to be effective. To illustrate, what is their own leadership style preference?[1] What are the leadership style preferences of the emerging national leaders? The success and capability of the next generation of leaders to reproduce leadership will depend to a large extent on how well the church planters can adapt their style of leadership to that of the national believers. (See Table 11.)

The Situational Responsibility Model demonstrates that continual flexibility in leadership styles is needed on the part of the church planters as the young believers advance toward Empowering. Because church planters usually prefer a certain leadership style (many Americans prefer Facilitating[2]) they will use it in most situations, even though it may not be the best choice for the development of national leaders at a particular time. For example, as we noted earlier, new believers tend to be found in the second quadrant. If the church planter acts as a Facilitator rather than a Coach, he or she does the young believers a great disservice by failing to provide them needed structure. The assumption is that the national believers will somehow gain the necessary knowledge and skills to become mature believers.

Initially, effective team leaders move out of their own comfort zone and minister to the national believers in a way that makes them feel comfortable. To do this, team members begin where the nationals are comfortable, and carefully encourage them to expand their comfort zone. As the national believers' level of commitment, competency, and resources advance (or digress), so the church planters adjust their leadership style accordingly. Comfort levels may be expanded by cultivating personal relationships, through words of encouragement, by modeling, and evaluation.

The National's Style

National believers desiring to become effective church leaders / planters will strive to do everything possible to become reproducers. They willingly accept the teams' challenge to grow spiritually, pastor their own people and plant new churches among unreached people, all the while continuing to learn as much as they can from the church planting team who brought them the life-changing message of grace.

Wise national believers begin by placing total confidence in the Holy Spirit, for he will teach, guide, and comfort them. He will also help them determine their competency, commitment, and resource levels relative to the eight skill areas (see Table 12).

Maturing nationals can expand their comfort zone as they seek friendship and advice from the church planters, accompany them, participate with them, take the lead in various activities, and begin to train others. The biblical insights they will gain through these activities will give added insight in ways to transform their culture. Praises from their mentors, together with challenging exhortations, will encourage and challenge them to reach the Reproductive role in all eight areas.

Table 11

Church Planter's Responsibility Styles

CHURCH PLANTER'S RESPONSIBILITY STYLES		
Facilitating		**Coaching**
CP facilitates NAT in ident. prob. & goal set	*Goal Setting*	CP trains NAT in ident. prob. & goal set
CP facilitates NAT in action planning	*Planning*	CP trains NAT in action planning
CP facilitates NAT in decision-making	*Decision-making*	CP trains NAT in decision-making
CP facilitates NAT in self/group motivation	*Motivation*	CP trains NAT in self/group motivation
CP facilitates NAT in securing resources	*Resources*	CP trains NAT in securing resources
CP facilitates NAT in implementing the task	*Implementation*	CP trains NAT in implementing the task
CP facilitates NAT in self/group evaluation	*Evaluation*	CP trains NAT in self/group evaluation
CP facilitates NAT in resolving conflict	*Conflict resolution*	CP trains NAT in resolving conflict
Empowering		**Directing**
CP releases NAT to train others in goal set	*Goal Setting*	CP* ident. prob. & sets goals for NAT**
CP releases NAT to train others in planning	*Planning*	CP develops action plans for NAT
CP releases NAT to train others in decision-making	*Decision-making*	CP makes decisions for NAT
CP releases NAT to stimulate motivation	*Motivation*	CP provides motivation stimulus for NAT
CP releases NAT to train others to secure needed resources	*Resources*	CP judiciously provides needed resources for NAT
CP releases NAT to train others to implement tasks	*Implementation*	CP implements tasks for NAT
CP releases NAT to train others to evaluate	*Evaluation*	CP evaluates NAT
CP releases NAT to train others to resolve conflict	*Conflict resolution*	CP identify problem and initiates resolution for NAT

* CP refers church planter
** NAT refers to national

Setting A Timeline

Westerners tend to believe efficient people set schedules and keep them. Non-westerners, on the other hand, have an entirely different view of time. They tend to believe events are more important and should be completed in their own time, apart from stipulated deadlines. They see support for their view of time in

Table 12

National's Responsibility Styles

NATIONAL'S RESPONSIBILITY STYLES		
Implementing		***Practicing***
NAT initiates problem ident. & goal setting	***Goal Setting***	Nat practices pro.b ident. & goal setting
NAT initiates action planning	***Planning***	NAT practices action planning
NAT initiates decision-making	***Decision-making***	NAT practices decision-making skills
NAT initiates self/group motivation	***Motivation***	NAT practices self/group motivation
NAT initiates securing resources	***Resources***	NAT practices securing resources
NAT initiates implementing the task	***Implementation***	NAT practices implementing the task
NAT initiates self/group evaluation	***Evaluation***	NAT practices self/group evaluation
NAT initiates conflict resolution	***Conflict resolution***	NAT practices resolving conflict
Empowering		***Accepting***
NAT trains others to ident. prob. & set goals	***Goal Setting***	NAT* accepts goals set by CP**
NAT trains others to develop action plans	***Planning***	NAT accepts plans developed by CP
NAT trains others in the art of decision-making	***Decision-making***	NAT accepts decisions made by CP
NAT stimulates others to self-motivation	***Motivation***	NAT's motivation stimulated by CP
NAT trains others to secure needed resources	***Resources***	NAT accepts needed resources
NAT trains others to implement tasks	***Implementation***	NAT accepts CP's advice to implement the task
NAT trains others to evaluate themselves	***Evaluation***	NAT accepts CP's evaluation
NAT trains others to resolve conflict	***Conflict resolution***	NAT accepts CP's evaluation

* NAT refers to national
** CP refers church planter

nature—the calf is born when it is ready; the apple falls when it is ripe. Therefore, if team members announce their projected completion dates to nationals, they may be accused of abandoning their friends, of being task oriented rather than people oriented, or of lacking commitment to continue the ministry.

Does this mean team members should never establish a

completion date? Definitely not. For its own sake, the church planting team should set a date to complete the church plant, and each ministry within the plant. It is only the matter of articulating the date to event-oriented nationals that should be given careful consideration.

Projected departure announcements can be made more palatable to event-oriented believers in several ways. One way would be to state *what* must take place before the team leaves. This places the emphasis on tangible events, e.g., evangelism, discipleship, leadership development, organizing, and finally reproducing a church. Another, and probably the most important way, focuses on *personal relationships*. Church planters must assure national believers that the team members will continue to serve and assist them to reach these ministry levels regardless of how long it takes. By emphasizing tangible events rather than specified time periods, any trauma connected with the team's phase-out can be reduced significantly.

Just as God in the Garden entrusted Adam with the opportunity to name the animals rather than do it himself, so church planters must learn to trust nationals to plant reproducing churches rather than do it themselves.

If building personal relationships has been given high priority among the church planters, departure will most likely result in some level of trauma among national believers. Team members, like Jesus, must do all they can to prepare the nationals for the trauma of separation.

Conclusion

People who feel trusted tend to become trustworthy. Responsible phase-out that results in ongoing church planting is more likely to occur when national believers feel trusted and empowered by the church planters. Just as God in the Garden entrusted Adam with the opportunity to name the animals rather than do it himself, so church planters must learn to trust nationals to plant reproducing churches rather than do it themselves. For this to take place, however, both parties must be willing to move out of their respective comfort zones.

Team members need to listen as well as talk; they should delegate responsibility without withdrawing it abruptly; they need to seek advice as well as give it, follow as well as lead, and to experience losing arguments as well as winning them. They need to learn to draw out the skills and abilities that people may not realize they possess. They need to become excited by the growth of others, and they need to avoid staying too long or leaving prematurely. As team members move in this direction, and national believers respond positively, the phase-out process moves another step closer to completion.

National believers must not only become leaders and church planters, they must also become biblically discerning, culturally relevant leaders. How this can be done will be discussed in the following chapter.

[1] The *Discipling Leadership Profile* available from the Center for Organizational & Ministry Development, 120 E. La Habra Blvd., Suite 107, La Habra, CA 90631, is a helpful tool for determining one's leadership style preference.
Phone: (562) 697-6144; FAX (562) 691-2081

[2] Our testing at the Center for Organizational & Ministry Development indicates the majority of Americans taking the *Discipling Leadership Profile* prefer the Facilitating role.

13

Developing Biblically Discerning, Culturally Relevant Leaders

A large percentage of a particular people group professed Christ as their Savior, the result of numerous years of unselfish ministry by dedicated missionaries. One of the veteran missionaries commented that a number of the believers still participate in the dances and ceremonies that relate to headhunting. Wondering whether these participants were true believers, or if the missionaries had failed somehow in the follow-up teaching, he was not sure how to handle this aberration.

In another people group, families performed extensive sacrifices to remove sickness. Should someone in a family become sick, a family member would call a shaman to the home to discern the nature of the sickness. The shaman performed a preliminary sacrifice to determine what further type of sacrifice was necessary to remove the sickness.

When missionaries entered this people group, and taught the gospel, a number of thriving churches emerged. As I visited with one of the church planters, the matter of how the young believers handle sickness now that they profess Christ as Savior came up. I learned that the believers no longer look to the shamans for help. Rather, they pray to God when sickness strikes their family. I also learned that the missionary had not taught on this issue. He seemed to assume that for those who had become believers, changes in this area would occur automatically.

By the time of our first furlough, in 1975, there were approximately twenty believers among the Ifugao. One of these, a respected Christian leader, asked me what they should do if one of the believers died in our absence. Traditionally, the Ifugao perform elaborate sacrifices over a number of days. The purpose of these sacrifices is to send the spirits of animals and other paraphernalia to the ancestors, hoping they will be appeased, return to earth, and guide the spirit of the dead back to the skyworld *(kabunyan)*. Should this not happen, the deceased may take the life of one of the living. Pablo wanted to know how Christianity would transform traditional Ifugao funerals.

By 1978, the number of Antipolo / Amduntug Ifugao believers had grown to around fifty. At that time they continued a limited participation in sacrifices related to hardships *(keneng)*, but refused to attend sacrifices pertaining to gaining wealth *(keleng)*. They faced a critical question: "If my family cannot expect help from our non-Christian families during times of hardship, can we count on assistance from other believers?"

Customarily, family and village members expected to help those experiencing hardship. Not to offer assistance during such times indicated a lack of concern for others—something considered an abominable sin for the Ifugao. Therefore, the believers continued to participate, to some degree, in sacrifices related to hardships. They provided animals, rice, and rice wine for the family in need; they helped gather firewood, cook meals, and serve food to the many visitors. Some even accepted the sacrificed meat. But all refused to play the gongs, kill the pigs, or participate in any other aspect of the direct sacrifice.

During a seminar held December 1-3, 1978, the attendees, led by respected Ifugao leaders, decided they should no longer participate in any type of sacrifice or receive sacrificed meat. It took hours of discussion, some heated, for them to reach this conclusion. It was apparent that the Ifugao found it difficult to balance Bible teaching with current practices (Rom. 14; I Cor. 8-10).

Some felt that stopping participation in health sacrifices would cause many to reject Christianity. Others felt that the believers were strong enough numerically to care for each other's needs. Moreover, they believed that such a demonstration of unity in the midst of calamity would actually draw many to Christ. The debate continued. Finally, at 1:00 A.M., the leaders summed up the decision; all participation in sacrifices pertaining to health should cease.

The leaders then instructed those present to communicate the decision immediately to their non-Christian family members, before any sickness struck. They also warned against evangelizing only during times of illness, claiming: "The sick will do or accept anything just to get well." They further decided to demonstrate their compassion to sick unbelievers by volunteering to carry the individual to the hospital, and/or assist in meeting the medical bills. Several individuals were appointed to relay the decision to distant communities.

The preceding case studies emphasize the tension national church leaders / planters face when trying to make Christianity culturally relevant, yet guard its purity. Phase-out oriented church planting calls for national church leaders / planters who have spiritual discernment in relation to how Christianity should challenge and conform to traditional culture. The next few pages focus on the development of such leaders through the institution of biblical functional substitutes.

Defining Biblical Functional Substitutes

The term "functional substitute" originated with the anthropological theory of functionalism. It sought to maintain unity and equilibrium between two different entities.

In the search for unity, however, the value of confrontation may be overlooked, and can lead to an uncritical acceptance of cultural practices. Therefore, I prefer to add the word "biblical" to the term to emphasize the role contradiction plays within the community of faith.

Conflict, contradiction, and disequilibrium are necessary for balanced perspectives. God's Word challenges our routine behavior frequently. In that biblical functional substitutes take into account both conformity and contradiction, certain cultural elements will be retained, while others must be deleted, and/or transformed. Biblical functional substitutes call for a "putting off" as well as a "putting on" (Col. 3).

Areas in Need of Biblical Functional Substitutes

Wherever ritual and/or magic fill emotional, physical, sociological or intellectual needs, biblical functional substitutes must be considered. The areas of need, of course, will vary from one people group to another. They may include: recreation, the agricultural cycle, building dedications, hunting and fishing rituals, protection for travel, protection from curses, prowess in warfare, attracting the opposite sex, and events surrounding human life cycles (e.g., preconception, conception, birth, naming, initiation rites into adulthood, marriage, and death.) The institution of biblical functional substitutes can help avoid the precipitation of cultural voids.

In order to discover areas in need of biblical functional

substitutes, team members must assume a learner role. They will have to study the various aspects of the culture such as property, labor and productivity, domestic and community authority, leadership and decision-making, ritual and mythology (see Chap. 7) to determine the key themes that unify and create tension within the community. To illustrate, in my study of the Ifugao culture, I found a number of pertinent themes that required biblical functional substitutes: children, family, land, animals, rice, rice wine, reciprocity, education, unity, and the sacrificial system (see Appendix K). Listed below are some of the biblical functional substitutes applicable for use among the Antipolo / Amduntug Ifugao. How should the themes and biblical functional substitutes differ for your people group?

Children:
1. teaching on sanctity of life of the unborn (abortion issue)
2. prayer during pregnancy for mother and baby
3. dedicating babies

Family:
1. family commitment to Christ
2. elders advise (from the Word) couples during the marraige ceremony
3. elders advise adoption over divorce in cases of bareness
4. elders counsel couples to prevent divorce

Land:
1. thanksgiving to God for fertile land
2. dedicating buildings, e.g., homes, churches, granaries

Animals:
1. thanksgiving to God for fertile animals
2. raising animals for consumption, sale, and contributions to Christianity

Rice:
1. prayer for a good crop
2. thanksgiving ceremony at harvest time
3. sing Christian songs during harvest
4. singspiration time during rice cake celebration

Rice wine:
1. use for communion as a symbol of unity between two factious parties
2. promote social gatherings without drunkenness

Reciprocity:

1. different groups share in hosting social events for believers and unbelievers
2. different groups share in evangelism and teaching roles
3. different groups give their time and finances to meet the needs of others

Education:

1. use of songs for baby dedications, field work, marriage, death, harvest, and what constitutes true wealth
2. use of English, as well as traditional tunes
3. use of genealogies in evangelism
4. use of the apprenticeship model to develop Christian leaders
5. use of certificates and pictures to celebrate the completion of various studies
6. use of inter-, intratribal seminars and conferences

Unity:

1. provide assistance to the sick or those who have lost loved ones
2. provide assistance in work projects
3. in weekly church services
4. provide food for inter-, intratribal seminars and conferences
5. provide food and photo sessions for newly baptized
6. emphasize restoration of fallen believers

Sacrificial system:

1. gather for prayer at the home of sick (James 5)
2. demonstrate from the Bible that true wealth comes from faithfulness to God
3. pray for the living rather than the dead
4. pray for insight to locate lost objects
5. promote the Bible and the Holy Spirit as sources for guidance, rather than the activities of animals
6. pray for protection on long trips
7. provide teaching that emphasizes Christ's sacrifice provides eternal life, not long life
8. provide teaching that shows Christ more powerful than the ancestors, demons, elements, and death
9. use gongs and selected dances for teaching and social entertainment

10. sell loincloths, skirts, and blankets to tourists to perpetuate the weaving skill

Return visits to the Ifugao in 1989 and 1993 provided opportunities to observe the success of some of the biblical functional substitutes instituted. On the frst visit I arrived just as a Christian funeral was in process. A number of the Ifugao mentioned they had instituted a support system for emergencies *(ligat)* such as sickness or death (a partial replacement of the sacrificial system). In this case, each Christian family in the three-village coalition had contributed ten pesos (45¢) to the grieving family.

The contributions (recorded by the grieving family so that appropriate reciprocity can later take place) allow the family of the deceased to provide ample food for all those attending the funeral. This honors both the family, and the corporate group of believers, since a shortage of food would bring shame to both parties. Moreover, it demonstrates to unbelievers that believers love and care for their own. The biblical functional substitutes that address both reciprocity and unity are apparently working well. They help define Christianity and highlight a better way of life.

During the visit, the Ifugao again debated the rice wine issue. Seven years earlier they decided to no longer serve the harvesters the rice wine (required by Ifugao tradition). Instead, they served a reconstituted orange drink purchased in distant stores. A number of the believers, however, continued to brew rice wine *(bubud)* to serve to harvesters. They argued the distance to carry the orange drink created too much of a hardship. Besides, many unbelieving harvesters complained the orange drink was unfair compensation for their work.

As I listened to the debate I was struck by the fact that the issues and solutions differed little from those presented seven years earlier. Some (mainly first generation believers) wanted no rice wine served at all. Others preferred a three-day brew (much must be consumed to cause drunkenness), while a minority lobbied for wine brewed five or six days, but rationed so that drunkenness would not occur. While the majority will probably continue to serve orange drink, other believers will serve rice wine. As of 1993, the debate continues.

Developing Nationals to Institute Biblical Functional Substitutes

The second case study in the introduction discussed the response of new believers to sickness. The missionary seemed to assume Christianity would produce change automatically in the area of healing. It seems the church planters were unaware that the nationals could benefit from instruction as to how to institute biblical functional substitutes. One wonders if secret healing ceremonies, like the secret headhunting ceremonies, were being held. One also wonders how the Ifugao would handle Christian funerals if we had failed to discuss the issue with them?"

Tippett (1967) suggests two key reasons for instituting functional substitutes: a) to retain the relevance of religion in daily life, and b) to meet inherent and felt needs, both of which help eliminate the possibility of creating cultural voids. Moreover, these two factors are fundamental to developing relevant churches capable of reproducing themselves.

Cultural voids result when felt needs remain unmet. Something must fill such voids. Matthew (12:43-45) warns that that something may be worse than the former. For certain of the Colossians, proto-gnosticism filled such a void.

Luzbetak astutely observes: "Syncretism is an evident sign that the missionaries have not succeeded in filling felt-needs" (1970:181). It may also be indicative of a lack of adequate direction for instituting biblical functional substitutes.

Cultural voids may also result in formalism or legalism. Luke writes: "You see, brother, how many thousands of Jews have believed, and all of them are zealous for the law" (Acts 21:20, NIV). Legalism, as well as syncretism, can easily fill cultural voids. Should the church planting team fail to develop leaders who are spiritually discerning, and culturally relevant, syncretism or formalism is sure to result (see Figure 26).

Team members must do all they can to assure that potential cultural voids are identified. Church planters who neglect this vital area, whether through unawareness or lack of conviction, actually

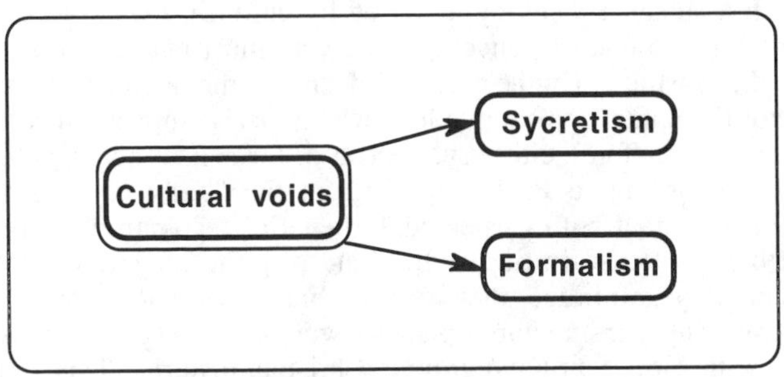

Figure 26. Possible outcomes of cultural voids

create a climate conducive to a split-level Christianity or a cultic movement. Nationals may receive the distinct impression that God is concerned only with their future destination rather than their daily lives. Power encounters may be understood to restore a broken relationship with God to gain future salvation, yet have nothing to do with one's present Christian life.

While I recognize there are inherent dangers in introducing the idea of biblical functional substitutes, to avoid the issue is equally dangerous—perhaps even more so. Willoughby correctly points out: "Repression and ignoring is driving to the background, not destroying. To put something better in its place is the best way of destroying" (cited in Kraemer 1977:347). Where national believers manifest areas of concern, their leaders, together with the church planters, at least initially, should investigate a variety of ways to institute biblical functional substitutes. Such efforts will demonstrate that Christianity impacts not only one's future destination, but also one's daily life.

Instituting Biblical Functional Substitutes

Historically, missiologists and church planters have disagreed as to who should institute biblical functional substitutes. Some argue that expatriate church planters are in a better position to make the major decisions because they possess a broader understanding of the Scriptures. Others feel that the nationals should make the decisions because they understand their own culture best and must live with the outcome. They further argue that this approach promotes ownership, accountability for the decisions, and spiritual maturity—all of which facilitates phase-out.

It seems neither the expatriate team nor the national congregation should act independently of one another in such decisions. Should the church planters take control of the process (which assumes a theology unbiased by culture), their role easily deteriorates to that of police officers, who must maintain the new laws they institute. On the other hand, should the national believers control the entire implementation (which also assumes a theology unbiased by culture), either syncretism or formalism may result.

According to Paul's teaching on the "body of Christ" it would seem that both parties could benefit greatly from working together, at least initially. In fact, a joint adventure could conceivably minimize the cultural biases of each party. To illustrate, input from church planters would challenge nationals to rely on the Holy Spirit and grow in Christian maturity. This would require that team members provide adequate guidance without becoming parentalistic. They must be able to appreciate new expressions of Christianity. Some church planters, like Peter (Acts 10), may need to learn that what God declares clean. Input from national believers would call for moving ahead in faith, yet not compromise biblical principles through syncretism or legalism. This challenges the young believers to take leadership roles without cutting off unnecessarily outside sources of insight.Some national believers may need to realize that certain aspects of their culture must be transformed (e.g., Simon [Acts 8:13-42]).

Transmitting the Goals

Outside assistance can help National church leaders / planters gain biblical discernment. To this end expatriates must transmit the basic goals related to biblical functional substitutes. There are at least two: a) to clarify the gospel and God's Word and b) to introduce a life better than that offered by the traditional religion. Biblical functional substitutes present visual and mental images that attest to the eternal God who revealed himself in history; they promise believers present assistance, and guarantee a hope for the future.

> In that biblical functional substitutes take into account both conformity and contradiction, certain cultural elements will be retained, while others must be deleted, and/or transformed. Biblical functional substitutes call for a "putting off"as well as a "putting on" (Col. 3).

The early Hebrew believers had much to learn about Christianity's distinctives in relation to their daily lives. When the author of Hebrews compared Judaism with Christianity, he pointed out Christ's superiority in a number of areas. He affirmed that Christ was *better* than the angels (1:4), the first covenant (7:22), the high priests (8:6), animal sacrifices (9:23), possessions (10:34), the promised land (11:16), and a trouble-free life.

Respected expatriates can assist national church leaders / planters find a *better* way of life (and vice versa). National leaders with biblical discernment must institute biblical functional substitutes that make clear the eternal Word of God. Moreover, the new institutions must give careful consideration to what conforms or conflicts with the Word of God.

Conveying the Guidelines

In an analysis of the third case study concerning the Ifugaos' decision to stop participation in the sacrificial system, the Ifugao leaders discussed the following four guidelines introduced by us:

1. identify the traditional components and functions,
2. identify areas of compatibility,
3. identify areas in need of change,
4. implement the revision, review and adjust, as needed.

To develop nationals who can discern biblical principles and apply them in a culturally relevant way, they must respect their own culture, yet be willing to evaluate it. The sooner they can begin to employ processes subjected to biblical and cultural scrutiny, the sooner they should become biblically grounded, culturally relevant leaders.

Development begins with self/group-analysis. For the Ifugao it began with asking, *What are the institutions regarding sacrifices for hardship? How do the institutions work?* By isolating the components of an institution and comparing them with biblical principles, it became possible to discover both cultural process and functions. In cases of hardship, the Ifugao identified the following components and functions: the afflicted family and the village's participation by way of food donations, food preparation, and offering the sacrifice. Hardship sacrifices exist to provide the distressed family and community with support during times of difficulty.

Once this was done, the Ifugao could consider the function and components of the particular event in terms of biblical principles. The ingredients of family and community members assisting those in need by supplying and helping prepare food is supported biblically. The function of providing family and community support during times of crisis also can be supported biblically by a number of the "one another" verses. The Ifugao decided to retain the elements of family and community assistance for those experiencing difficulties.

The Ifugao then focused their attention on those functions in conflict with biblical principles. One area in which the Ifugao failed to find biblical support was the whole matter of sacrifice. Related discussions led them to conclude any activity having to do with the sacrifice, i.e., killing the pig, playing the gongs (to summon the spirits), or receiving the sacrificed meat (which creates a debt to the giver requiring repayment) should be considered off limits for Ifugao believers.

The Ifugao also identified components that with some

transformation could be compatible. For example, although they no longer felt comfortable in attending the sacrifices related to health, they recognized some substitute was necessary. As a result, they volunteered to assist the sick by taking them to the hospital, and/or providing financial assistance to help offset medical expenses. They believed such assistance would demonstrate community concern for those in need, thereby relieving them from the responsibility to participate in future sacrifices.

A second decision made by the Ifugao called for implementing a cooperative fund for medical emergencies. Each family would be expected to donate monthly a certain amount of money. They also expressed reluctance about carrying out evangelism activities only during times of sickness because the sick tend to feign belief in Christ just to get well.

After the leaders decided which components and functions should be eliminated, and the transformation necessary for others, like in Acts 15, they implemented the decisions immediately. They sent representatives to the distant villages to inform the other believers of the decision. Shortly thereafter they began the cooperative medical program.

Major decisions such as these should be reevaluated over a period of time. In the case of the Ifugao, discussions continued for at least a year, with most accepting the decision. In fact, the implementation of the cooperative medical fund actually helped draw the believers together. While it demonstrated to the unbelievers the believer's solidarity, more importantly, it validated their love and concern for all community members apart from participation in the sacrifices.

The Ifugao leaders picked up the four guidelines easily. While they may not articulate them in sequence, or answer only one question at a time, they nevertheless can address all the pertinent issues related to instituting biblical functional substitutes. The guidelines helped them clarify God's Word and promote a better way of life. Through discussing which components and functions of a tradition conformed or contradicted biblical principles, biblical discernment and cultural relevancy resulted.

Conclusion

A great many people groups operate holistically. If Christianity is to be relevant to them, it must be viewed as compatible with their holistic worldview. To accomplish this, national church leaders must acquire spiritual discernment, and be capable of instituting biblical functional substitutes in ways that are culturally acceptable. Apart from such leadership, there is the considerable danger of creating cultural voids that open the doors to syncretism or legalism.

Expatriate team members attempting to move to Resident Advisor or Itinerant Advisor roles must give priority to preparing national leaders in ways that emphasize the importance of biblical functional substitutes. Initially, the expatriates and national leaders should discuss together the matter of implementing biblical functional substitutes. This will not only help prevent cultural bias on the part of either party, but it will also contribute to the maturation process of both, particularly if the expatriates back out of the process quickly and willingly. Moreover, it will enable the church planters to move even closer toward their goal of phase-out. Ultimately, the guidelines for establishing biblical functional substitutes proposed above, will greatly assist in developing the next generation of biblical discerning, culturally relevant church planters / leaders.

To help assure that the guidelines, and other important truths, will not be lost to the next generation, the next chapter discusses curriculum development.

14

Life-Changing Curricula

We gathered under one of the Ifugao homes for our bi-weekly evangelistic Bible studies from the book of Genesis. After the lesson, Daniel commented: "If our ancestors had known how to write, our stories (myths) would probably be very similar to those you are telling us. But because they could not write, the stories changed over the years and we no longer know what is true."

Visitors frequently attended the sessions for evangelism and Bible study, often requesting study materials to take home. The same requests came from Ifugao living in close proximity. (Many Ifugao feel written materials lend legitimacy to the spoken word.) Although we had produced a number of lessons, they really required further testing. In fact, we desperately needed an overall strategy to facilitate the development and dissemination of our materials.

At the same time, we asked ourselves a number of questions: How does one involve the target people in the curriculum development and dissemination process? What layouts should be used? How should the publications be distributed? How do curriculum developers know the lessons are accomplishing the stated goals? Can the lessons be designed to facilitate phase-out? I will now set forth fourteen guidelines that emerged from my collective efforts to develop and distribute both written and taped curricula among the Antipolo / Amduntug Ifugao.

Developing Life-Changing Curricula

Since Christianity is a way of life, the curricula should address all areas of life. For our purposes here, I define curricula to include all written or taped materials (videos and cassettes) that are developed to encourage people to experience God—that is, to grow in their love for him, themselves, others and for his creation.

How the curricula is produced and disseminated will impact the team's goal of phase-out in several significant ways. It helps preserve the message of the gospel and other fundamental teachings. It also helps develop astute national teachers who can discover the meaning of a passage and know how to apply it. It encourages ongoing evangelism and church planting. Finally, it can also play a major role in enabling national leaders to look to the Word and the Holy Spirit as their authority, rather than to the church planters.

Focuses on the Whole of God's Word

Just as a good picture frame enhances a painting, so life-changing curricula should elevate and intensify the entire Word of God. Such curricula leads its readers to and through the Bible to find the answers to life's questions.

Curricula that suggests finding answers within its own text, or from expatriate authorities, rather than from God's Word, fails to give credence to the authority of Scripture. It also fails to encourage the spiritual development of national believers, and limits (or inhibits) the disengagement of expatriates. On the other hand, curricula that has been well designed will challenge both readers and listeners by focusing their attention on the Source of all wisdom.

> ...life-changing curricula...leads its readers to and through the Bible to find the answers to life's questions.

Prior to his ascension, Jesus reminded his followers to "obey everything I have commanded you" (Matt. 28:20, NIV). Paul, in his farewell address to the Ephesian elders, declared: "I have not hesitated to proclaim to you the whole will of God" (Acts 20:27, NIV). Thus, both Paul and Jesus emphasized the importance of studying all of Scripture. Wise Christian workers will do likewise by teaching the "whole will of God," which in turn will facilitate the development of curricula with the same emphasis.

Appropriate to Specific People Groups

No one single Bible curricula can address, sufficiently, all people groups of the world. Cognitive learning styles differ, to say nothing of the different political and religious backgrounds, felt needs, and even successive generations within a people group. Beyond that, the materials that aid in the spiritual development of the Christian workers most likely will not have the same impact upon the target people. Every people group, therefore, requires and deserves its own curricula.

Western curriculum developers who write cross-cultural materials tend to receive two major criticisms: 1) they pack in too much content, and/or 2) the materials lack cultural relevancy. Use of western lessons, tapes and textbooks, with verbatim translations into the specified language, is one reason given for such criticisms. Although this approach may save time initially, in the long run the recipients suffer.

Ward suggests six levels of complexity when adapting curricula from one people group to another. These include:

Level 1: Translation (language).
Level 2: Adjusting the vocabulary (to make the reading level of the adapted material match the original).
Level 3: Changing the illustrations to refer to local experiences.
Level 4: Restructuring the instructional procedures implied and/or specified to accommodate pedagogical expectations of the learners.
Level 5: Recasting the content to reflect local world-and-life views.
Level 6: Accommodating the learning styles ("cognitive styles") of the learners.

Curriculum developers who desire to produce life-changing materials should: 1) maintain a learner role themselves, and 2) include nationals in the developing process from the beginning. This attitudinal and participatory approach will make it much easier to design culturally relevant materials (e.g., calendars, a soccer rule book, a daily newspaper, maps, an accounting book, baptismal certificates, Bible studies). This two-dimension approach will also contribute to ownership by the nationals and help develop indigenous writers to replace the team members or work in partnership with them.

To change lives, the curricula must touch lives. People respond to curricula that relates to current experiences. Sadly, most imported curricula fails to do this because it was prepared with another audience in mind.

To be life changing, the curricula should be geared to the needs and learning styles of a specific people. It must wed theology to life and life to theology. It must tie content to context and focus on an in-culture theology rather than an unknown theology of a culture strange to them. It must utilize the familiar learning styles of the people rather than those of team members. Readers and listeners of the curricula should begin to feel that God walks in their garden and lives among them. Effective curricula calls for adapting, not reprinting.

Challenges Individual People Groups

Because the Bible calls for transformed behavior, individually and corporately, the curricula must do likewise. In fact, it should challenge the status quo by urging that God's way be followed in every area of life.

> To change lives, curricula must touch lives.

Derives From Tested Teaching

Published materials that result from time-tested teaching will have taken into account the issues that surface during the preparation of the materials. Cultural, theological, sequential, and applicational weaknesses that inevitably surface over a period of time can be eliminated or altered. Moreover, it allows time for revising so that a finely honed, targeted curricula results. For instance, after a lesson about the Flood, an Ifugao observed that perhaps a more effective way to evangelize would be to begin with the flood (since that is where Ifugao history begins) and then ask them about their origin. When the Ifugao respond that they do not know, present the genealogy from Noah to Adam. (Genealogy demonstrates validity for the Ifugao.) His suggestion now finds itself in print. To be life changing, curricula should be based on extensive input from both listeners and teachers, for no one knows the needs of a people better than those who participate in its daily activities.

Retains a Narrow Focus Yet Broad Application

Bulky libraries have little place among the majority of the world's peoples. As someone once stated: "The church on the march needs a compact theology." The same holds true for a church's curricula. Curriculum developers must become skilled in the fine art of omission.

Life-changing curricula should be narrow in scope, yet broad in application. A narrow focus is intended to assure that basic truths can be reproduced readily by its listeners and readers. Consider, for example, the two basic commandments that tie the entire Bible together: 1) Love God with all one's heart and 2) love others as one's self (Matt. 23:37-38). These two basic themes definitely narrow the focus of the Bible, yet make its root message easy to grasp in any community.

On the other hand, by incorporating a narrow focus, a wide range of application becomes possible. Just how one loves God, his neighbor, and others, will differ greatly from one people group to another. Narrowness in content and breadth in application allows for a quick grasp of the heart of the message and cultural specific application.

Integrates All Aspects of Life

Since many people view life holistically, it is imperative that prepared curricula do the same. To achieve maximum impact, numerous subject matters should be included: the spirit world, health, agriculture, economics, politics, history, theology. Should key areas be neglected, the readers and listeners will look to other sources to fill the voids.

Insiders usually know far better than outsiders what should be included. Therefore, they should be partners in the decision-making process from the very beginning. The problem of syncretism can be minimized by integrating all aspects of life into the curricula.

Graded

Many curriculum developers include every detail possible in a lesson rather than limiting the inclusions to that which an audience can assimilate readily at one setting. Jesus recognized the problem of overload when he commented: "I have much more to say to you, more than you can now bear" (John 16:12, NIV). The writer of Hebrews did the same when he differentiated between the type of instruction required for the immature and the mature (Heb. 5:11-14).

A key word in Jesus' statement in John 16:12 is "now." His audience required "much more" instruction, *but* at a later time. The same was true for some of the Hebrews. This illustrates the need to design the materials in spiral fashion so that the readers progress from the simple to the more complex. In other words, a life-changing curricula begins with an audience's ability to assimilate, and build upon it. This approach not only facilitates learning for the mature, but it also enables more effective communication of the materials to those having less understanding.

Builds Solid Relationships

Many people groups prefer group activities. Life-changing curricula apply this value by specifying in the application sections that groups of people teach, study, and apply the materials together, rather than singling out individuals to take such risks alone. Curricula that encourage team teaching should result in the development of teams of teachers since the responsibility for a lesson is shared by several people.

On an individual lesson level, group studies should be designed to encourage group action. As participants complete a lesson they should be challenged to apply its meaning collectively. Application questions should promote group discussion and require group action. For example, "How can we help Mary while she is recuperating?" "What should the Tayaban family do?" Life-changing curricula build community by bringing people together to teach, study, discuss, and make application. Relationships between God and his people are strengthened, increasing the development of indigenous teachers.

Calls for Immediate Action

The team's educational background, influenced heavily by the Enlightenment, tends to result in an overemphasis on cognitive knowledge. This explains, perhaps, their desire for facts and why they tend to require the same from cross-cultural audiences. This problem becomes acutely apparent when ministry is conducted among people who usually learn through active participation, rather than from internalizing isolated facts.

Determining how learning takes place among a particular people group, whether by an emphasis on knowing, doing, or being, is a key factor in the curriculum development strategy. Although each of these three influences the other, different people groups tend to prefer one over the other. The curricula should reflect this reality. For instance, because the Ifugao prefer to learn by doing, reflective action became central in the design. It also provided tangible benchmarks by which to measure the stated objectives. Figure 27 depicts the interrelatedness of the three aspects, and identifies the appropriate entry point for people who learn customarily through active involvement.

It is interesting to note the emphasis on "doing" in both Old and New Testaments: "give thanks," "sing," "remember," "say," "sell what you have," and "give," "come and see," "go and tell," "watch," "love one another," "pray," "preach," "come down," "follow me," "turn the other cheek," "sin no more," "encourage one another," "forgive," "praise the Lord." Just as Christianity calls for putting one's faith into action, so life-changing curricula goes beyond "mind-training" to emphasize immediate, doable tasks. It goes beyond asking, "Who are you, Lord?," to ask, "What shall I do, Lord?" (Acts 22:8,10, NIV). Christian maturity tends to be produced most readily by practicing one's faith.

Builds Hermeneutic Skills

Basic hermeneutic skills are necessary to understand God's Word accurately. To accomplish this, some suggest courses in hermeneutics. But there may be an easier and more natural way to execute this, at least initially.

How Christian workers design the Bible study curricula is at least as important as the content of the lessons. Use of the same format for each lesson, and each series, helps readers and listeners to learn intuitively how to study the Bible. Continual repetition of the same forms will cement basic hermeneutic principles into the reader's and listener's minds. For example, if those designing a commentary on Philippians include background information about the author, its intended audience and the setting, such inclusions indicate to the readers the importance that background information plays in grasping the author's central message.

Lesson design also underscores hermeneutic principles. To illustrate, the lesson may ask for a passage of Scripture to be read and for prayer that the Holy Spirit will help their understanding. The exercise points to the primacy of the Word, and its Author.

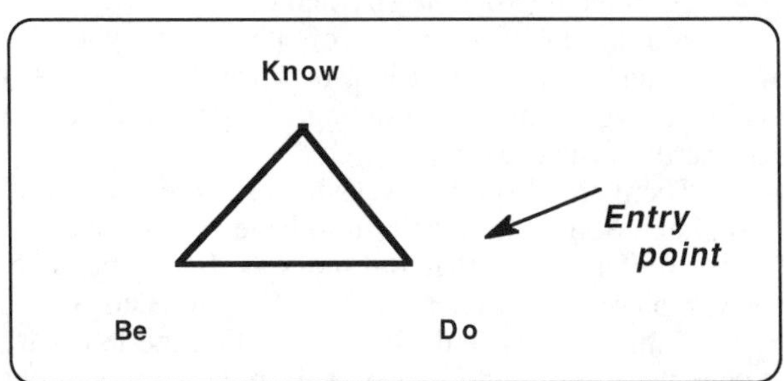

Figure 27. Integrating know, be and do

This could be followed by a short series of culturally relevant questions (when culturally appropriate) to encourage audience discussion of the main thrust of the passage. Such questions will cause participants to think through the passage to discover the writer's intent.

Transformed behavior, of course, is the final goal of the hermeneutic exercise. A number of pertinent questions to conclude the lesson could bring discussion on how the meaning of the passage could be applied immediately to family members, peers, and others.

Curriculum developers should be concerned particularly with whether the study format presents a simple, reproducible, life-changing, yet comprehensive approach to the study of Scripture. If it does, the lessons will teach basic hermeneutic skills implicitly, assist nationals in analyzing and applying the Scriptures (transformed behavior), and expedite the phase-out process.

In relation to Bible studies, curriculum developers should be particularly concerned with whether the study format presents a simple, reproducible, life-changing, yet comprehensive way of studying Scripture. If it does, the lessons will teach basic hermeneutic skills implicitly. The recipients will become proficient in analyzing Scripture and applying the message, bringing about transformed behavior.

Reader's Needs Determine Design

Both the physical design, and the format design of the curricula, affect its acceptance. What size of publication do the people prefer? What colors do they prefer for the cover? Although one of the favorite colors of the Antipolo / Amduntug Ifugao is red, they seem to prefer a darker color for the cover. They reason that the smoke in their houses will soon darken the covers anyway. The team's research should assure that all publications will be produced in the appropriate size and color.

Another factor is the use of space in a layout. Empty space often enhances comprehension, because it minimizes the content load of a page, while maximizing key points. Blank space is not necessarily wasted space.

There are also other ways to ease comprehension within the lesson text: Some find it helpful to have key statements underlined. Others prefer boxes that outline specific sections, e.g., in the application section of a lesson. The "Easy Readers Series,"produced by the Bible Society, indents sentences on the left margin slightly further than the previous one. This breaks the straight line look usually found, and makes it easier to pick up the next line when the eyes return to the left side of the page. (Right margins remain staggered as well.)

Symbols can be utilized to convey information economically. To illustrate, rather than writing out instructions to "discuss the following questions," a question mark (?) could be placed before the section. Another symbol that could be used is an outline of an open Bible that contains a reference. The symbol will alert readers to read the text indicated within the outlined Bible.

Ownship Resides With the Nationals

Expatriates too often consider the curricula as "our" product "for" the target people. This view can certainly impede the development of national writers. The development of the curricula must become integral to, and owned by the national community of faith. It is therefore imperative that a multi-national team of curriculum developers be formed from the start.

While flow charts have certain limitations, e.g., they fail to reflect either the dynamics of interpersonal relationships or potential creativity, they can serve as effective guides. Figure 28 provides a flow chart that focuses on a participatory model for curriculum development. The chart considers: preliminary definitions, identification of needs and interests, objectives, content, resources and methodology, implementation, and evaluation.

Before launching a writing project, outsiders and insiders alike should recognize the potential influence of their worldviews, basic assumptions, and personal/collective agendas on the overall curricula. Team members should also be aware of their agency's agenda, as well as the agenda of the national government. There should be open dialogue between all parties so that a needs consensus may be reached.

Once the needs are identified and prioritized, the group can determine collectively the objectives. The objectives will include at least the materials to be produced and the strategy—the latter having four parts: ongoing evaluation, distribution, funding, and turnover.

After the multi-national team reaches a consensus on the objectives, discussion will turn to decisions regarding content design, resources, and methodology. Content design decisions include: relevant issues and needs, pedagogical expectations, content overload, pictures and illustrations, layout, and application. Resource decisions refer to the choice of size, color, shape, and layout. Methodology deals with the "hows" by taking into consideration the values of outsiders and insiders relative to the stated objectives. After these decisions are made, the multi-national team is ready for implementation.

Evaluation, that is, checking the value outcomes of the curricula, is another step in the participatory model. Effective

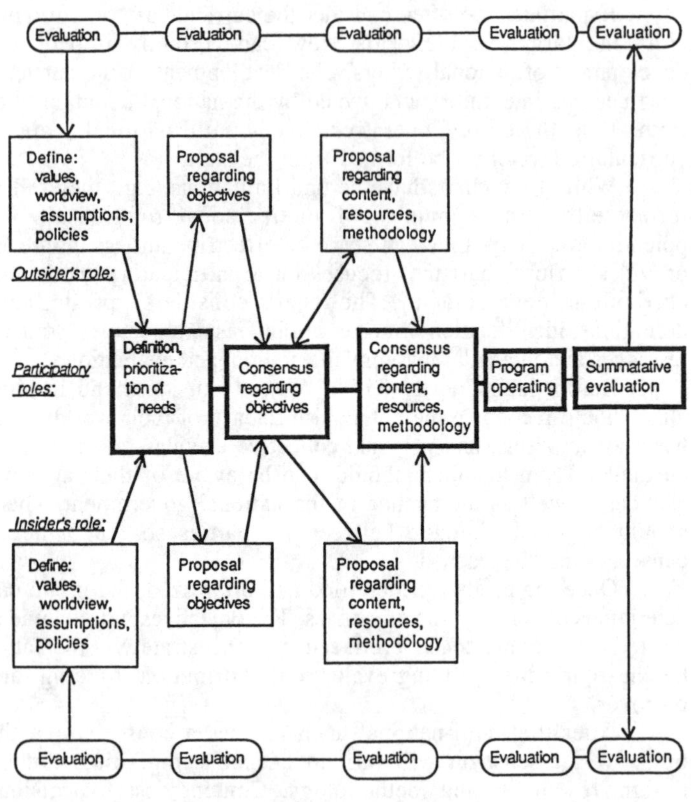

Figure 28. Participatory curriculum development

evaluation takes place on a continual basis (formative) and again at the completion of the project (summative). Such evaluation allows for mid-course correction and gained insights for future projects.

A participatory model for developing curricula takes time and flexibility. Moreover, it should be regarded as a service rendered "among" or "with" people, not "to" or "for." The advantage is that in the long run it produces ownership, accountability, and relevant evangelists and teachers—all of which facilitate the phase-out process.

Has Marketing Visibility

Many cults select highly effective ways to package and disseminate their philosophy. Expatriates and national believers must become more effective.

One goal of the national churches is to reach all of their community with the gospel. The distribution of literature, videos, and tapes is one way to expedite this. The Ifugao believers, for example, make periodic trips to every village to sell literature. As the residents ask questions about Christianity, it becomes culturally appropriate to evangelize. Listed below are a number of methods the Ifugao people use to provide high visibility for their curricula. How would these differ for your people group?

The Ifugao:

1) make literature, videos, and tapes available, for browsing and buying, during social and public activities,
2) give selected materials as a gift to grade school and high school graduates,
3) encourage storekeepers to sell the materials,
4) carry literature, videos, and tapes when traveling,
5) appoint responsible believers to stock and sell the productions,
6) send out teams annually to advertise the curricula in the surrounding areas,
7) give complimentary copies of materials to school teachers and government officials, and
8) give materials, along with wages, to those working for them.

Includes Biblical Examples of Phase-out

Lessons that include biblical examples of those who left ministries in order to share the gospel with other people groups will undoubtedly help local believers understand, and anticipate the phase-out of team members. For instance, Jesus moved from city to city continually so that his message could be heard more widely. Jesus' disciples followed his example. The ministries of Paul's teams provide a later example. The book of Acts captures the idea of the apostles' mobility for Christ, and introduces readers to the problems and successes of those believers left behind. Thus, the New Testament examples of departure can help nationals understand that the disengagement of team members can result in the spread of the gospel as well as maximize opportunities for the development of the spiritual maturity, gifts, and skills of the entire body of Christ.

Conclusion

Life-changing curricula takes its readers to and through the Bible in ways that are culturally appropriate, while at the same time issuing a strong challenge to follow God's universal demands. Curricula that follows the fourteen guidelines, and that is modeled by respected teachers, should produce skilled indigenous writers and perceptive evangelists and Bible teachers. Life-changing curricula will draw the target audience to the Bible and the Holy Spirit, rather than to the transient team members. It will prepare maturing nationals for the departure of team members; the baton is passed.

PART 6

Challenge and Conclusion

"I feel sure that the one who has begun his good work in you will go on developing it until the day of Jesus Christ....it is probably more necessary for you that I should stay here on earth. That is why I feel pretty well convinced that I shall not leave this world yet, but shall be able to stand by you, to help you forward in Christian living and to find increasing joy in your faith...So that whether I come and see you, or merely hear about you from a distance, I may know that you are standing fast"
(Phil. 1:24, 25, Phillips).

Passing the Baton

Kingdom-based church planting can no longer be business as usual. Our journey through the five stages of crosscultural, pioneer church planting has emphasized the need for a comprehensive, phase-out oriented model (Preentry, Preevangelism, Evangelism, Postevangelism, Phase-out). (See Appendixes B, C.) Such a model provides church planters a means by which to gauge their progress, realign their course, and know when to pass the baton. Apart from such, they tend to stay too long, an issue familiar to the Boomer generation, and the generation that preceded it, the Builders. Or they may not stay long enough, an issue facing GenXers. Either way, the national believers will suffer.

The Race to Victory

The U.S.A. 4 x 100-meter track team was expected to win in the 1988 Olympics. Few would be surprised not to see the Americans cross the finish line first during the trial heat. The American team, however, did not go on to win the 4 x 100-meter that year. Because of a late hand-off of the baton by Calvin Smith to Lee McNeel the team was disqualified from reaching the final heat and the gold. Church planters can also find themselves disqualified—and lose the final heat.

Types of Runners

Different types of runners are needed for different times in the relay. Someone quick out of the blocks is needed to grab the lead and establish the pace, while those who receive the baton next must have the stamina and patience to sustain the lead, and the finisher must have that extra kick to break the ribbon in front of the challengers.

Like a good coach, the church planters must be able to

identify those nationals who have the gifts, competencies, and commitment for each of the integrated phases of the race (social concerns, evangelism, discipleship, leadership development, organizing the church, and multiplying churches). And like a good coach, they must know when to exhort, coach, faciliatate, and empower (p.181), so as to get the athletes to perform even beyond personal perceptions of capabilities.

Types of Violations

Race violations can occur in a number of ways. Like John Mark they may refuse to accept the baton, and run outside the exchange area, thereby disqualifying themselves. Or like Phygelus and Hermogenes, character issues may cause them to step outside the lines, thereby disqualifying themselves and never receive the baton (2 Tim. 2:15). Over confident runners, like Peter, may leave the exchange box before receiving the baton. Runners like Timothy, because of timidity, may not leave soon enough and find themselves run over in the exchange (2 Tim. 1:6-7). Runners may also disqualify themselves by taking their eye off of the baton in the exhange and drop it, as did Demas who focused his attention on this present world (2 Tim. 4:10).

To avoid such violations between the church planters and nationals a number of role changes are necessary. The church planters will move from *Evangelists* to *Teachers* to *Resident Advisor* to *Itinerant Advsiors* to *Absent advisors,* all the while being *Learners.* As the nationals *accompany* the church planters, *participate* within their comfort zone, expand their comfort zone to *lead,* and eventually *train* others, the final exchange can take place.

Before that final race, there will be a number of violations in the practice heats, which should be expected. There may also be previously disqualifed runners who now play major roles in the race, such as John Mark (2 Tim. 4:11). Eventually, a clean exchange will be made, making responsible phase-out, and a church-planting movement a reality.

Types of Batons

Batons come in various shapes and sizes. Batons that are too long make it very difficult to exchange from one runner to another. The same is true when the baton is too short, making it difficult to receive. Likewise, weight influences the baton exchange. Heavy batons weigh down the runners, slowing down the race considerably. Or, when the baton is too light, the race speeds up but it becomes difficult for the runners to keep a grip on the baton.

Long batons speak to the excessive requirements placed by

the church planters on the nationals, assuming nationals must reflect their level of competency and commitment before a final exchange can be made. Short batons speak to the lack of modeling and training provided by the church planters, thereby assuming that nationals can conduct ministry just as effectively without it.

Weighty batons reflect the church planters demands for perfection, often resulting in discouragement and lethargy. This helps create the attitude that successful ministry can only be done by outsiders, so let the outsiders do it. Light batons speak of inadequate preparation that covers the entire church multiplication process mono-culturally and cross-culturally. Such lack of preparation can give the nationals a false sense of security which can set them up for the fall once tested in battle.

> Knowing when to leave a church plant is just as important as knowing when to begin it....phase-out establishes the parameters for the entire church-planting movement because it defines a strategy for closure toward which all earlier strategies are directed.

The size and shape of a baton play a tremendous role in responsible phase-out. This demonstrates powerfully the need to locate and analyze the baton *before* the race begins. Appendix F attempts to begin this process by idenifying the key questions and objectives for each of the five stages. This checklist will help assure that apostolic robes do not become replaced with pastoral robes.

Passing the Baton Jesus Style

Jesus spent only three brief years training the disciples. How did the disciples react to his announcements that he would soon be leaving them? How did Jesus attempt to minimize the trama of departure? How did Jesus prepare his followers for his abrupt departure?

Very little time passed before Jesus informed the Twelve that his departure from them was imminent. Some of Jesus' initial announcements about his departure were quite vague. As the time of his death neared, Jesus became much more explicit in announcing his departure plans to the disciples. The shocking realization that Jesus may soon leave them began to set in.

Reactions to Departure

Reactions to Jesus' announcements regarding departure ranged from uncertainty to anger to grief. Initially the disciples did not understand Jesus' comments and were too afraid to inquire (Luke 9:45). As they gained courage to ask questions, Jesus dialogued with them openly (John 16:17-18).

Whether Jesus informed his disciples about his departure implicitly or explicitly, he often tried to soften the jolting announcements. He promised the disciples he would not leave them as orphans (John 14:18). He reassured them that the separation would not be permanent. He promised not to forget them, and that he would see them again. In fact, he would prepare special homes for them in heaven during his absence (John 14:1-3; 16:16).

Jesus tried other ways to lower their stress level. He promised to send the disciples a Comforter/Helper who would teach them whatever they needed to know, enable them to witness, and encourage them along the journey (John 14:16, 26; 15:26). This Comforter/Helper would take them further in their understanding of Christianity than Jesus could (John 16:12-13). Therefore, the disciples should be glad Jesus would soon leave them; it was to their advantage the Mentor would be replaced (John 14:29; 16:7).

The world came to an abrupt end for the disciples when their Mentor was pronounced dead. Enter the scene a resurrected Jesus! He surprised the two Marys as they returned from an empty tomb. Later, he joined two despondent disciples traveling the Emmaus Road, reviewing for them Old Testament prophecies and present realities (Luke 24). He challenged their unbelief, calling them foolish. When Jesus ate with the disciples they remembered his predictions.

Behind locked doors the disciples huddled together trying to decipher the startling events of the past few days. Fear, loneliness, disbelief and disorientation set in. They felt abandoned. Suddenly, Jesus appeared in the midst of the cowering disciples. Some thought he was a spirit. The risen Mentor challenged their skepticism by asking them to touch his wounds. He then joined them for a meal, blessed them, and departed again.

It soon became time for his final departure. The disciples began to experience the power of the promised Comforter/Helper (Acts 2). So did the rest of the known world—people of "the way" turned the world upside down (Acts 17:6). Christ's followers took Christianity to much greater depths and lengths in Jesus' absence then in his presence.

Principles for Passing the Baton

Build deep relationships. Jesus spent significant time getting to know his disciples. They lived, ate, prayed, learned, laughed, traveled, and ministered together. Jesus built solid, ongoing relationships with his disciples.

Building deep relationships requires a certain type of person and specific tools to exegete the target audience. When I left for the Philippines, I took with me a typical Bible College tool kit to plant churches, however, before very long it became apparent that many of the tools were inadequate for the tasks assigned. I realized that by using the wrong tool I could not only hurt myself, but could also hurt those I came to reach with the gospel. Somehow I needed to acquire some better tools, tools that would assist in a better understanding of myself, the team, early Bible cultures, and the target people.

Make sure the national believers own the vision. National believes must not only know the purpose for their existence, they must also know how their gifts and skills can contribute to it's completion. Ownership of a world vision sets the foundation for a church-planting movement.

Model ministry before requiring it. Church planters should never require the nationals to participate in activities they do not wish to model. Rather, they should provide the nationals with examples of effective ministry, and provide adequate debriefing time.

Organize to disperse power. Organize the roles and ministry activities of the nationals in such a way that the power to minister moves immediately from the church planters to them. Such disbursement of power will encourage personal/group development. It will allow a generation of new teachers to teach from their own experiences rather than from the experiences of others. The church planters must never forget that in the spiritual domain, shared power results in multiplied power.

Call for ministry involvement immediately. Once the nationals have observed the church planters in some aspect of ministry, the church planters should challenge them to immediate involvement in the same, and then debrief the outcome. Genuine growth comes best through responsibility, participation, repetition, and dialogue.

Expect mistakes. Church planting is not an exact science, for the church planters nor for the nationals. Genuine growth also comes through making mistakes. People who take risks tend to make mistakes. Developmental growth involves multiple mistakes over time.

Believe in the nationals. In spite of the mistakes the nationals will inevitably make as they grow towards spiritual and ministry adulthood, the nationals must recognize that the church planters believe in them. They must believe they can afford to take risks, even make mistakes, without the church planters losing confidence in them.

Announce departure plans discreetely. Church planters should inform the nationals about their departure plans in a judicious manner. Like Jesus, they must inform them at appropriate times, revealing only what is necesssary for the moment. Church planters must also convince them that the departure will be to their advantage. To overextend the stay would be to steal the nationals' rightful power to grow and reproduce on their own.

Plan programmed absences. In the majority of cross-cultural church plants, an abrupt pull-out will not be the most appropriate response to reactions regarding the departure announcement. Following Jesus' post-resurrection example, church planters should return periodically to visit the nationals. They should bring encouragement, answer questions, review basic biblical truths, and have some meals together. This will rekindle the nationals' enthusiasm as they assist a second generation of disciples to mature in Christ and ministry, and reach out to the world. Programmed absences will help the disciples overcome the feeling of abandonment.

> The church planters must never forget that in the spiritual domain, shared power results in multiplied power.

Jesus' post-resurrection revists to the disciples did not continue indefinitely. *While Jesus left the disciples geographically, he did not leave them relationally (John 16:16).* Today's church planters can keep their relationships intact through periodic letters, phone calls, video tapes, e-mail, prayer, and an occasional visit.

Expect ministy to increase after the church planters' departure. The disciples made both qualitative and quantitative advances after Jesus left them, just as prophesied. The same will be true of believers today. It is realistic to believe that the nationals will surpass their mentors after their departure (John 14:12).

These ten principles will enable the church planters to minimize the trauma of departure. They will also maximize the potiential of all the gifts and skills given by the Holy Spirit to the entire body of Christ.

Conclusion

Knowing when to leave a church plant is just as important as knowing when to begin it. A comprehensive model that will systematically move church planters from phase-in to phase-out will help make disengagement timely.

Because *phase-out,* the final stage of the model, necessitates establishing an agenda for all previous stages, just how a mission agency and church planting team defines this stage will determine what must take place in each of the previous stages. In other words, phase-out establishes the parameters for the entire church-planting movement because it defines a strategy for closure toward which all earlier strategies are directed.

This book has addressed four major phase-out oriented components of church planting. These include: a) committing to and preparing for necessary role changes, b) empowering national believers for responsible leadership, c) expanding the tool kit for the task, and d) implementing a comprehensive plan that ties together all aspects of church planting.

The five-stage comprehensive model provides cross-cultural church planting teams with a guide to measure their progress so that the baton can be passed to nationals within the designated exchange area at the appropriate time. The model proposes six role changes for the transition process. It raises questions, lists objectives, provides a checklist for each stage and a tool to develop action plans (see Appendixes C, F, and G). It encourages mission agencies to move beyond their espoused exit values to established criteria for responsible departures. It also motivates church planters to plan beyond phase-in to phase-out by empowering national leaders to *act immediately* on their faith. Successful church planting teams work themselves out of a job by continually reassessing their plans, and by taking immediate steps to empower the newly formed national community of faith. In this way, the baton is passed at the correct time, making God's team a winner!

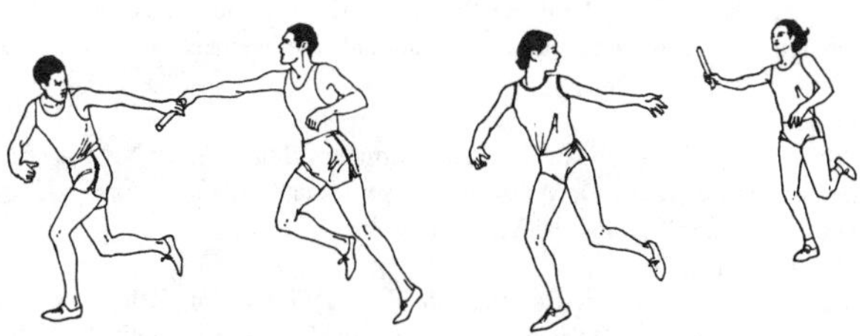

Bibliography

Allen, Roland
1962 The Spontaneous Expansion of the Church. Grand Rapids, MI: William B. Eerdmans.

Anderson, Leith
1992 A Church for the 21st Century: Bringing Change to Your Church to Meet the Challenges of a Changing Society. Minneapolis, MN: Bethany House Publishers.

Apeh, John Enejo
1988 Igala World Views and Contextualization: A Diachronic and Holistic Study of Cultural Themes as a Vehicle for Evangelizing and Theologizing. D. Missiology dissertation, School of Intercultural Studies, Biola University.

Barrett, David B.
1997 Annual Statistical Table on Global Mission: 1997. International Bulletin of Missionary Research 21 (1): 24-25.

Bavinck, J.H.
1960 An Introduction to the Science of Missions. Grand Rapids, MI: Baker.

Bemis, Stephen E., Ann Holt Belenky, and Dee Ann Soder
1983 Job Analysis: An Effective Management Tool. Washington, DC: The Bureau of National Affairs.

Bendor-Samuel, Margaret and David Bendor-Samuel
1987 A Manual for Strategic Planning and Review for Language Programs. Dallas: Summer Institute of Linguistics.

Blanchard, Kenneth
1985 A Situational Approach to Managing People. Escondido, CA: Blanchard Training and Development.

Brewster, Thomas E. and Elizabeth S. Brewster
1976 Language Acquisition Made Practical. Pasadena, CA: Lingua House.

Bryson, John M.
1988 Strategic Planning for Public and Nonprofit Organizations: A Guide to Strengthening and Sustaining Organizational Achievement. San Francisco: Jossey-Bass Publishers.

Buckman, Allan Roger
1978 Cross Cultural Evangelism: The Yala People of Southeastern Nigeria (A Design for Outreach). D. Missiology dissertation, School of World Mission, Fuller Theological Seminary.

Congdon, Garth
1984 An Investigation into the Current Zulu World View and its Relevance to Missionary Work. D. Missiology dissertation, Trinity Evangelical Divinity School.

Bibliography

Conn, Harvie
1984 Eternal Word and Changing Worlds: Theology, Anthropology, and Mission in Trialogue. Grand Rapids, MI: Zondervan.
1985 The Depersonalization Misunderstanding. Urban Mission 2(5): 6-19.

Crofts, Marje
1985 Old Testament Translation. Technical Memo. pp. 19-20. SIL, Philippine Branch.

Davidson, Richard D.
1988 Learning a New Language: A Creative Guide. Berrien Springs, MD: Center for Intercultural Relations.

Davis, Linnel E.
1968 The Use of the Bible in the Kamba Tribal Setting. M.A. thesis, School of World Mission, Fuller Theological Seminary.

Drati, Enock Lee
1987 Using Traditional Media to Communicate the Gospel to Lugbara of Uganda. D. Missiology dissertation, School of World Mission, Fuller Theological Seminary.

Dye, T. Wayne
1980 The Bible Translation Strategy: An Analysis of its Spiritual Impact. Dallas: Wycliffe Bible Translators.

Engel, James F. and Wilbert H. Norton
1975 What's Gone Wrong With the Harvest? Grand Rapids, MI: Zondervan.

Fackre, Gabriel
1973 Do and Tell: Engagement Evangelism in the '70s. Grand Rapids, MI: Wm. B. Eerdmans.
1975 Word in Deed: Theological Themes in Evangelism. Grand Rapids, MI: Wm. B. Eerdmans.
1984 The Christian Story: A Narrative Interpretation of Basic Christian Doctrines. Grand Rapids, MI: Wm. B. Eerdmans.

Faircloth, Samuel D.
1991 Church Planting for Reproduction. Grand Rapids, MI: Baker Book House.

Fowler, Joseph Andrew
1976 Communicating the Gospel Among the Iban: A Resource Manual for New Cross-Cultural Missionaries. D. Ministry dissertation, Perkins School of Theology, Southern Methodist University.

Francis, Dave and Don Young
1979 Improving Work Groups: A Practical Manual for Team Building. San Diego, CA: University Associates.

Freire, Paulo
1970 Pedagogy of the Oppressed. New York: Seabury.
1980 Education for Critical Consciousness. New York: Continuum.

Fuller, Harold W.
1980 Mission-Church Dynamics: How to Change Bicultural Tensions into Dynamic Missionary Outreach. Pasadena, CA: William Carey Library.

Gail, Sydney
1983 Job Analysis: A Guide to Assessing Work Activities. San Francisco: Jossy-Bass Publishers.

Goody, Jack
1987 The Interface Between the Written and the Oral. Cambridge, MA: Cambridge University Press.

Graham, Thomas
1987 How to Select the Best Church Planters. Evangelical Missions Quarterly 23 (1): 70-79.

1988 Strategies for Team Development. La Habra, CA: Center for Organizational & Ministry Development.
1989 Assessor's Manual for Cross Cultural Church Planters. La Habra, CA: Center for Organizational and Ministry Development.

Hansen, Carl Edward
1985 Planting the Church in the Islamic Horn: A Strategy for Penetration. M.A. thesis, School of World Mission, Fuller Theological Seminary.

Harrison, Myron S.
1984 Developing Multinational Teams. Singapore: Overseas Missionary Fellowship.

Hatton, Howard A.
1985 Translating Scripture in the Comic Medium. The Bible Translator 36 (2): 430-437.

Hersey, Paul and Kenneth Blanchard
1982 Management of Organizational Behavior: Utilizing Human Resources. Engelwood Cliffs, NJ: Prentice-Hall.

Hesselgrave, David J.
1980 Planting Churches Cross-Culturally: A Guide for Home and Foreign Missions. Grand Rapids, MI: Baker Publishing House.

Hiebert, Paul G. and Eloise Hiebert Meneses
1995 Incarnational Ministry: Planting Churches in Band, Tribal, Peasant, and Urban Socieites. Grand Rapids, MI: Baker Publishing House.

Hile, Pat
1977 Communicating the Gospel in Terms of Felt Needs. Missiology: An International Review 5 (4): 499-506.

Hminga, Chhangte Lal
1976 The Life and Witness of Churches in Mizoram. D. Missiology dissertation, School of World Mission, Fuller Theological Seminary.

Hohensee, Donald W.
1980 Rundi Worldview and Contextualization of the Gospel - A Study in Theologizing in Terms of Worldview Themes. D. Missiology dissertation, School of World Mission, Fuller Theological Seminary.

Iroezi, Chukwuma Jude
1981 Igbo Worldview and the Communication of the Gospel - A Study in Theologizing in Terms of Worldview Themes. D. Missiology dissertation, School of World Mission, Fuller Theological Seminary.

Kelber, Werner H.
1983 The Oral and the Written Gospel. Philadelphia: Fortress Press.

Kelly, Daniel Paul
1982 A Missiological Guide for Missionaries to North American Indians. D. Missiology dissertation, School of World Mission, Fuller Theological Seminary.

Kingsbury, Jack Dean
1988 Matthew as Story. Philadelphia: Fortress Press.

Klem, Herbert V.
1982 Oral Communication of the Scripture: Insights From African Oral Art. Pasadena, CA: William Carey Library.

Koller, Charles W.
1962 Expository Preaching Without Notes. Grand Rapids, MI: Baker Book House.

Kouzes, James M. and Barry Z. Posner
1987 The Leadership Challenge: How to Get Extraordinary Things Done in Organizations. San Francisco: Jossey-Bass Publishers.

Kraft, Charles H.
1979 Christianity in Culture: A Study in Dynamic Biblical Theologizing in Cross-Cultural Perspective. Maryknoll, N.Y: Orbis Books.
Kraft, Marguerite G.
1978 Worldview and the Communication of the Gospel: A Nigerian Case Study. Pasadena, CA: William Carey Library.
Kurian, George Thomas
1979 The New Book of World Rankings. N.Y: Facts on File.
Larson, Donald N.
1978 The Viable Missionary: Learner, Trader, Story Teller. Missiology: An International Review. 6 (2): 155-163
1984 Guidelines for Barefoot Language Learning. St. Paul, MN: CMS Publishing.
Lawrence, Paul
1981 Contextualizing Theological Education Efforts Among Non-Literates. D. Missiology dissertation, Trinity Evangelical Divinity School.
Lingenfelter, Sherwood G.
1990 Economy and Social Relations for Mission. Course Syllabus, Biola University. La Mirada, CA.
1992 Transforming Culture. Grand Rapids, MI: Baker Book House.
Lingenfelter, Sherwood G. and Marvin K. Mayers
1986 Ministering Cross-Culturally: An Incarnational Model for Personal Relationships. Grand Rapids, MI: Baker Book House.
Livingstone, Greg
1993 Planting Churches in Muslim Cities: A Team Approach. Grand Rapids, MI: Baker Book House.
Loewen, Jacob A.
1964 Bible Stories: Message and Matrix. Practical Anthropology 11 (2): 49-54.
Logan, Robert E.
1989 Beyond Church Growth: Action Plans for Developing A Dynamic Church. Old Tapan, N.J: Fleming H. Revell Company.
Love, Rick
1995 Peacemaking: A Study Guide. Meza, AZ: Frontiers.
MacDonald, George
1978 In Defense of the Genesis Abridgement. Notes on Translation 69 (6): 17-22.
Maslow, Abraham H.
1968 Toward a Psychology of Being. New York: D. Van Nostrand.
Mayers, Marvin K.
1987 Christianity Confronts Culture: A Strategy for Crosscultural Evangelism. Grand Rapids, MI: Zondervan Publishing House.
McIlwain, Trevor
1981 Notes on the Chronological Approach to Evangelism & Church Planting, Vol.1. Sanford, FL: New Tribes Mission.
1985 Notes on the Chronological Approach to Evangelism & Church Planting, Vol. 2. Sanford, FL: New Tribes Mission.
1987 Building on Firm Foundations: Guidelines for Evangelism and Teaching Believers, Vol. 1. Sanford, FL: New Tribes Mission.
1988 Building on Firm Foundations: Guidelines for Evangelism and Teaching Believers, Vols. 2-5. Sanford, FL: New Tribes Mission.
1989 Teaching New Believers, Vols. 6-7. Sanford, FL: New Tribes Mission.
1991 Teaching New Believers, Vol. 8. Sanford, FL: New Tribes Mission.
1991 Firm Foundations: Creation to Christ. Sanford, FL: New Tribes Mission.
1992 Teaching New Believers, Vol. 9. Sanford, FL: New Tribes Mission.

Middleton, Vernon J.
1972 A Pattern of Church Growth for Tribal India People Movements. M.A. thesis, School of World Mission, Fuller Theological Seminary.
Miller, Donald
1987 Story and Context: An Introduction to Christian Education. Nashville: Abingdon Press.
Murdock, George
1961 Outline of Cultural Materials. New Haven, CT: HRAF.
Murikwa, Julius Kaburu
1985 American and Kikuyu Worldview Contrasts and Communication of the Gospel. Th.M. thesis, School of World Mission, Fuller Theological Seminary.
Neighbour, Ralph W.
1990 Where Do We Go From Here? A Guidebook for the Cell Group Churches. Houston, TX: Touch Publications.
Nevius, John
1958 Planting and Development of Missionary Churches. Philadelphia: Presbyterian and Reformed.
New International Version of the Holy Bible
1984 East Brunswick, N.J: International Bible Society.
Nida, Eugene A.
1950 Learning a Foreign Language: A Handbook for Missionaries. N.Y: Committee on Missionary Personnel of the Foreign Missions Conference of North America.
Olson, David R., Nancy Torrance, and Angela Hildyard, eds.
1985 Literacy, Language, and Learning: The Nature and Consequences of Reading and Writing. Cambridge, MA: Cambridge University Press.
Opler, Morris E.
1945 Themes as Dynamic Forces in Culture. American Journal of Sociology 51: 198-206.
Orr, J. Edwin
1982 Playing the Good News Melody Off-key. Christianity Today 26 (1): 24-27.
Patterson, George
1981 Church Planting Through Obedience Oriented Teaching, a Manual. Pasadena, CA: William Carey Library.
Patterson, George and Richard Scoggins
1993 Church Multiplication Guide: Helping Churches to Reproduce Locally and Abroad. Pasadena, CA: William Carey Library.
Phillips, J.B.
1958 The New Testament in Modern English. New York: Macmillan.
Read, William R., Victor M. Monterroso, and Harmon A. Johnson
1969 Latin American Church Growth. Grand Rapids, MI: William B. Eerdmans.
The Reese Chronological Bible: King James Version.
1980 Minneapolis, MN: Bethany Fellowship.
Richardson, Don
1974 Peace Child. Ventura, CA: Regal Books.
1981 Eternity in Their Hearts. Ventura, CA: Regal Books.
Ryken, Leland
1979 The Bible: God's Storybook. Christianity Today 23: 34-38.
1984 How to Read the Bible as Literature. Grand Rapids, MI: Academia Books.
Ryken, Leland, ed.
1984 The New Testament in Literary Criticism. N.Y: F. Unger Publications Co.
Shapiro, Howard B.
1975 Crisis Management: Psychological and Sociological Factors in Decision Making. McLean, VA: Human Sciences Research.

Silvoso, Ed
1994 That None Should Perish: How to Reach Entire Cities for Christ Through Prayer Evangelism. Ventura, CA: Regal Books.

Spruth, Erwin L.
1981 The Mission of God in the Wabag Area of New Guinea. D. Missiology dissertation, School of World Mission, Fuller Theological Seminary.

Steffen, Tom A.
1993 Planned Phase-out: A Checklist for Cross-Cultural Church Planter. San Francisco, CA: Austin & Winfield.
1993 Urban-Rural Networks and Strategies. Urban Mission. 10 (3): 37-42.
1993 Don't Show the Jesus Film... Evangelical Missions Quarterly. 29 (3): 272-275.
1995 Storying the Storybook to Tribals: A Philippine Perspective of the Chronological Teaching Model. International Journal of Frontiers Mission. 12(2): 99-104.
1996 Reconnecting God's Story to Ministry: Crosscultural Storytelling at Home and Abroad. La Habra, CA: Center for Organizational & Ministry Development.

Stott, John and Robert T.Coote, eds.
1979 Gospel & Culture. Pasadena, CA: Regal Books.

Tippett, Alan R.
1967 Solomon Island Christianity: A Study in Growth and Obstruction. Pasadena, CA: William Carey Library.
1969 Verdict Theology in Missionary Theory. Lincoln, IL: Lincoln Christian College Press.
1987 Introduction to Missiology. Pasadena, CA: William Carey Library.

Today's English Version of the New Testament.
1966 New York: Macmillan.

Tregoe, Benjamin B., John W. Zimmerman, Ronald A. Smith and Peter M. Tobia
1989 Vision In Action: Putting A Winning Strategy to Work. N.Y: Simon and Schuster Inc.

Wagner, C. Peter
1971 Frontiers in Missionary Strategy. Chicago: Moody.

Walker, George
1988 Drama in Chronological Teaching: The Use of Skits. Outreach 32: 1-3.

Ward, Ted
1973 Cognitive Processes and Learning: Reflections on a Comparative Study of "Cognitive Style" (Witkin) In Fourteen African Societies. Comparative Education Review 17 (1): 1-10.

Weber, H.R.
1957 The Communication of the Gospel to Illiterates. London: SCM.

Weerstra, Hans
1972 Maya Peasant Evangelism: Communication, Receptivity and Acceptance Factors among Maya Campesinos. D. Missiology dissertation, School of World Mission, Fuller Theological Seminary.

Williams, C. Peter
1990 The Ideal of the Self-Governing Church: A Study in Victorian Missionary Strategy. N.Y: E. J. Brill.

Wiseman, D.
1982 They Can't See the Point. UNICEF NEWS 4: 26-27.

Appendix A

Evidence Why Church Planters Often Fail to Empower Nationals

This article evaluates the contributions and limitations of a number of missiological writings pertaining primarily to tribal and peasant peoples. It searches for reasons why many mission agencies have failed to release churches to nationals. The literature review brakes down into four categories: contextualization, communication, strategy, and theology.

Contributions and Limitations of the Contextualization Emphasis

The first emphasis of literature evaluated lies in the area of worldview and cultural themes (Apeh 1988; Congdon 1984; Conley 1976; Davis 1968; Iroezi 1981; M. Kraft 1978; Murikwa 1985). The basic idea behind each of these contributions is that evangelism and church planting based on the target people's worldview (belief system) results in more effective communication.

Davis' (1968) study of the Kamba people of Kenya investigates their religion and reaction to social change. He advocates discovering cultural themes, and then using biblical correspondents, that is, corresponding Old Testament stories, to enhance communication. Davis believes the Bible should be central to evangelism and church planting. His emphasis on finding worldview themes, and matching these with Old Testament stories to enhance communication, provides a significant contribution to missiological literature.

Iroezi (1981) investigates the existing church of Igbo that is facing problems of secularization and urbanization. He calls for the use of redemptive analogies and a theology of demons for a church facing a fast changing environment. Iroezi's major contribution to missiology is his emphasis that a people's worldview does not remain static; therefore, ethnotheologies which address people's *current* concerns must receive primary attention.

M. Kraft (1978) sought to find the cultural themes of the Kamwe people through componential analysis. The ethnoscience approach assumes people conceptualize objects and events through semantic categories which in turn suggest cultural themes. Once one discovers these worldview themes through emic semantic categories, the potential for enhancing the communication process in presenting the gospel, expressing worship, and leadership development, increases. M. Kraft's major contribution to missiology is her emphasis that each people be approached from *their* own frame of reference.

Apeh (1988) critiques the functionalist theoretical paradigm used in many missiological studies and finds it wanting. He argues the synchronic approach minimizes the impact of culture change actually taking place within a society. Apeh believes societies find themselves in a continual state of tension rather than a constant state of equilibrium. Lastly, he finds the functionalist theoretical paradigm leading to uncritical acceptance of cultural practices.

Apeh prefers a conflict paradigm that analysizes a society, in this case his own Igala people, from a diachronic perspective. This paradigm leads him to conclude that a single Igala worldview does not exist, but rather there are numerous Igala *worldviews,* each having its own specific needs vying for attention. Apeh, following M. Kraft (1978), proposes effective communication is enhanced when Igala worldviews are used as frames of reference for contextualization in evangelism and theologizing. Apeh makes a significant contribution to missiology in recognizing the value of diachonic community studies, and that societies experience constant internal and external tension resulting in the formation of a number of worldviews, each demanding its own theological answers.

While Apeh recognizes the need for differing ethnotheologies among the Igala people, his systematic teaching approach to communicate these truths seems quite Western. Apeh could improve theological education through the use of a more global, concrete approach to teaching rather than abstract, systematic theology.

Conley (1976) conducts extensive study on the conversion process among the Kalimantan Kenya of Indonesia. Following Opler's (1945) model the author identifies the dynamic cultural themes of the Kenyah people. He then considers the themes in a study of socio-religious change, looking at conditions before and after the people movement.

Conley's use of themes as a means of studying pre- and postconversions provides a significant addition to missiological research. Opler's functionalist approach to culture results in a search for themes that maintain a unified worldview. Conley could improve his study by including the opposing themes as well.

In sum, the above authors make significant contributions to missiology by advancing our thinking in evangelism and the local church through emphasizing worldview and cultural themes, communication, and receptivity. Gaps, however, remain. One is the influence of economics and social organization on worldview. Belief systems (ideas) and the material world are intricately interrelated. Apeh (1988) comes closest in integrating these.

Another major gap is that the authors tend to focus on *phase-in* issues (activities related to evangelism and church maintenance) rather than "phase-out" issues (activities that empower nationals to develop leadership among themselves with an eye toward ministry that reproduces). While the authors provide significant contributions for contextualized evangelism, they virtually overlook the areas of discipling, equipping and reproduction (Matt. 28:19-20; Eph. 4:12; II Tim. 2:2). For a complete church planting strategy, phase-out issues must also be addressed.

Contributions and Limitations of the Communication Emphasis

Klem (1982) estimates approximately seventy percent of the world's population cannot be reached for Christ by means of written media. Nor does he see this percentage decreasing in the near future. Klem proposes reaching this significant number of people through use of their own means of oral communication.

To test the validity of his hypothesis, i.e., people of an oral society are reached best through ethno-oral means, Klem conducted a number of different types of Bible studies from the book of Hebrews. He tested four different teaching approaches: (a) a teacher with a written copy of the text; (b) a teacher and a copy of the text on cassette tape; (c) a teacher using the written text, a cassette copy of the text set to music; and (d) a teacher with only the text set to music on a cassette tape.

Klem's study concludes: (a) the schooled and unschooled perform better when oral teaching methods are used, and (b) oral communication methods help break down social distances between the schooled and unschooled. Klem's major contribution to the discipline of missiology is his emphasis that the oral means of communication is the most effective form of communication for an oral society.

Drati (1987) also calls for the use of traditional media to communicate the gospel to the Lugbara of Uganda. He advocates the use of music, dance, and drama, all at the people's worldview level.

D.P. Kelly (1982) provides a missiological guide for missionaries working among North American Indians. He advocates communication within the realm of the experiential and worldview. He emphasizes the use of the concept of power: with power the Indians were successful, without it they were defeated. Kelly's focus on the experiential aspect of communication adds a key dimension to the all too often dominant cognitive thrust.

Weber (1957) calls for reexamination of missionary teaching methods used among tribals. He views the Bible as "God's great *picture book*" which includes *"great drama"* and *"great symbol."* This should translate, argues Weber, into missionaries using teaching approaches that emphasize concrete dimensions.

Weber advocates tribal evangelism that incorporates storytelling accompanied with simple drawings which he calls "chalk and talk." In an appendix (pp. 114-115) Weber includes a chart of pictures used along with the various covenants emphasized: all creatures, Abraham, Israel, and the New Covenant. Each covenant considers God's promises, demands, and the sign associated with it, e.g., the rainbow, circumcision, and the cross. He uses the same simple approach for presenting the history of the Israelites (pp. 116-117). Weber also advocates the use of drama and dance.

Weber makes several significant missiological contributions. The first is his recognition of the need to communicate to concrete relational thinkers through concrete avenues. Secondly, he emphasizes the need to keep things simple, e.g., the drawings, and his approach to evangelism. Weber's objectives do not include a phase-out strategy.

Klem (1982), Drati (1987), D.P. Kelly (1982), and Weber (1957) focus primarily on the mechanics and medium of communication with particular emphasis on evangelism (phase-in). The concept of church, leadership development, and phase-out strategy receives little attention.

Contributions and Limitations of the Strategy Emphasis

Richardson (1974) contends God's keys to unlocking societies for the gospel are redemptive analogies. God designed these natural stepping stones to facilitate the reception of the gospel. Investigators can find a people's redemptive analogies in their oral history and/or present practice. For the Sawi people of Papua New Guinea, the peace child provided the key redemptive analogy for a people that elevates treachery and deceit. Richardson sees redemptive analogies as the "New Testament approved approach to cross-cultural evangelism" (p. 288).

In a later book, Richardson (1981), following Wilhelm Schmidt's now defunct diffusionist paradigm, continues his search for redemptive analogies in other cultures. Even so, Richardson does not believe redemptive analogies redeem people, for there would then be no need of the Word. Rather, he concludes, redemptive analogies contribute to the redeeming of people by helping them comprehend God's truth; they do not culminate it (p. 61).

Richardson's key contribution to missiological literature is his call for church planters to actively search for redemptive analogies, and utilize the emic means of communication in evangelism. His emphasis, in some cases, however, leads church planters to look exclusively for *the* key redemptive analogy, as if only one analogy exists within each society. It seems more probable, however, that a number of redemptive analogies exist within any people group that are appropriate not only for evangelism, but also discipleship. Nor, should the church planter overlook relevant redemptive analogies found in the Bible, e.g., the sacrificial system or the mediator role of priests.

Nida (1952) believes church planters working among aboriginal peoples must incarnate the character of Christ and the gospel message. He does not, however, elaborate how this should be accomplished. (Nida's significant emphasis on incarnating the character of Christ and the gospel message planted a seed later cultivated by C. Kraft [1979:173-178]). Nida's emphasis lies in one's character and ability to communicate the gospel.

Donovan (1978), a Catholic priest ministering among the Masai in Kenya and Tanzania, takes a significantly different approach to ministry than did his colleagues. Rather than follow the traditional institutional approach to missions through hospitals and schools, which he believes leads to dependence upon the West, Donovan chose to go to the Masai rather than have them come to his mission station. He visited various areas, dialogued with family heads, sought bridges to teach about God and sin, and allowed time for families to make decisions. Donavan believes the personal approach far surpasses the institutional approach in gaining converts and promoting independence.

Donavan makes several key contributions. The first is his focus on people rather than institutions. Secondly, Donavan challenges us to consider whether our approach causes dependence on the outside world, or creates independence.

Fowler (1976) designed a strategy manual for new cross-cultural workers working among the Iban people. The writer advocates evangelism without imperialism so that an autonomous church emerges. Fowler offers no blueprint for evangelism but rather calls for listening, acting, and reflecting in the various contexts the missionaries find themselves. He seeks a church that expresses love to outsiders, who in turn respond to Christ in repentance, join the covenanted community in fellowship and praise, and reach out themselves to needy neighbors.

While Fowler's work is microscopic in nature it does offer several contributions for the macro level. The first is each social context is unique, and therefore must be addressed individually. The second is his call for servant minded church planters who seek to establish indigenous churches.

Spruth (1981) sketches a history of mission work in the Wabag area of Papua New Guinea. He mentions briefly the use of seventy Bible stories and Luther's Catechism in bringing people to "full discipleship." Missionaries required each convert to learn eighteen major Bible stories and Luther's Catechism. Spruth does not list the stories chosen, mention the criteria used to select them, or suggest church planting strategies.

McIlwain's multi-volume series entitled *Building on Firm Foundations* (1987, 1988, 1989, 1991, 1992) provides a comprehensive strategy for evangelism and discipleship. In this series the author focuses on an overall teaching program which derives out of his church renewal experiences among the Palawano people of the Philippines.

McIlwain followed up the work of previous missionaries who believed they left behind numerous believers. As he taught the Palawanos basic fundamentals of the Christian life, a lack of response to biblical truth resulted. McIlwain soon discovered he was teaching Christian principles to non-Christians. As he realized what was happening he stopped addressing his audience as believers and began teaching from Genesis through the ascension of Christ, emphasizing the holiness of God, and the separation of all people from God because of sin. When the Palawanos grasped these truths he proceeded to reveal the reconcilitory work of Jesus Christ. In time, a number of Palawanos responded to the gospel.

McIlwain's experience among the Palawanos led him to design a teaching strategy that sets a solid foundation for the gospel, and then proceeds to cover the entire Bible. He calls this approach Chronological Teaching and divides it into seven phases: (a) Genesis through the ascension for non-believers, emphasizing their *separation* from a Holy God and the *solution* provided through Christ; (b) Genesis through the ascension for believers, emphasizing their *security* in Christ; (c) a brief survey of Acts to serve as an introduction to the epistles; (d) a brief overview of each of the epistles and Revelation; (e) Genesis through the ascension for mature believers; (f) Acts for mature believers; and (g) Romans through Revelation for mature believers.

McIlwain's major thesis is found in the title of the series, *Building on Firm Foundations:* healthy churches result from a correct understanding of the gospel; a church built on an unclear gospel will not stand. Two other key theses include: (a) Scripture should be taught chronologically and panoramically because this is God's method of teaching (progressive revelation), and (b) the New Testament can not be understood in isolation from the Old Testament.

The discipline of missiology is indebted to McIlwain in two key areas. The first is his emphasis on the need for building a firm foundation for the local church through the presention of an accurate gospel. The second is the provision of an overall teaching program that incorporates the entire Bible, much of which listeners can easily reproduce. A major lack in McIlwain's model, however, is its shallow sensitivity to the local culture; it tends more towards program than people.

The above authors address strategy from three discernible persectives. Group one, Nida (1952) and Fowler (1976), emphasizes contextualization of one's character and the gospel message. But no equipping strategy emerges. The second group, Spruth (1981) and McIlwain (1987), focus on a holistic strategy that emphasizes both evangelism and equipping. But in this case, contexualization becomes the missing ingredient. The last group, Richardson (1974) and Donovan (1978), also focuses on a contextualized phase-in strategy. While not articulated, an equipping strategy is present within each of their works. The need for an articulated, phase-out oriented, church planting strategy remains.

Contributions and Limitations of the Theological Emphasis

Warneck (1954) believes only the gospel message has the power to deliver sinful, animistic tribal people from eternal hell. Warneck notes church planters must gain a thorough knowledge of "animistic heathenism" before beginning evangelism. He characterizes animistic heathens as ignorant, liars, estranged from God, bound, selfish, immoral, and worldly (p. 133).

Warneck argues the best way to communicate the gospel message is by proclaiming the *deeds* of God, not delivering intellectual lectures on his existence and character. He believes the choice way to accomplish this is through the use of stories. Tribal people, assigned to a "lower stage of human development" (p. 227), can easily comprehended stories. He begins in the Old Testament and moves to the New Testament, allowing the needs of different peoples to dictate which stories receive emphasis.

Despite Warneck's ethnocentrism his perception of tribal animism from a theological perspective is insightful. His emphasis on communicating the deeds of God through the use of Old and New Testament stories that speak to the specific needs of a people is also significant.

Dillon (1972) defines in outline form the purpose, function, and government (always plurality), of a New Testament church. His basic thesis is God not only tells us *what* to do to establish a New Testament church. He also demonstrates *how* to accomplish it through concrete examples provided within the New Testament. If one follows these patterns, argues Dillon, one can expect New Testament results.

Dillon argues the Word must be rightly divided. He believes the Epistles provide God's final revelation for the Church age, and therefore contends the patterns found in the Epistles pertaining to every area of the local church supersede all previous ones.

Dillon advocates founding churches build upon the three selfs: self-supporting, self-governing, and self-propagating. This approach allows local churches to become autonomous. He places great emphasis on the role of the Holy Spirit in the lives of the missionaries and the target people as they follow the Word. (Strong traces of Roland Allen [1962a; 1962b] become evident in these two emphases.)

Dillon believes the most effective strategy for reaching the tribal world is by planting one church in every tribe. In that Christ cannot return until there is a representative from every tribe, reasons Dillon theologically, this strategy is the most pragmatic given the number of missionaries the Church has to allocate.

Dillon makes several significant contributions to missiology. First, he emphasizes the need of the church planter to rely on the Holy Spirit and the Word, for his or her own life, and the lives of the people they hope to reach with the gospel. Secondly, he challenges church planters to indigenize the national church as quickly as possible.

Hesselgrave (1980) designed "The Pauline Cycle," a step-by-step church planting model applicable both at home and abroad. He addresses ten headings in the model from a theological, scientific, and practical perspective: (a) Missionaries Commissioned, (b) Audience Contacted, (c) Gospel Communicated, (d) Hearers Converted, (e) Believers Congregated, (f) Faith Confirmed, (g) Leaders Consecrated, (h) Believers Commended, (i) Relationships Continued, and (j) Sending Churches Convened. Hesselgrave contributes to missiological literature by providing a theologically sound, broad-based church planting model that is followed easily.

Patterson (1978; 1981), a Conservative Baptist, ministered among semi-literate peasants in Honduras where he saw over one hundred churches planted. He accomplished this by forming a Bible institute that combines education, evangelism, and obedient action. Patterson's distinctives for the institute include: (a) Only mature men are enrolled; (b) The total numbers of students in a class are kept small (maximum of 5) to ensure discussion rather than lecture; (c) Lessons are designed according to the needs experienced by the student in his arena of ministry; (d) Curriculum is designed in comic format; (e) Application of the lesson is immediate; and (f) Debriefing with the teacher follows application. Patterson believes theory and practice should always be combined.

Patterson's central thesis calls for obedience to Christ's commands. He supports this theme from the following verses: Jas. 1:22, John 14:15, and Matt. 28:18-20. Patterson believes Christ asks obedience from people in seven key areas: (a) repentance from sin, (b) baptism, (c) practical love, (d) communion, (e) prayer, (f) giving, and (g) witnessing.

Patterson makes several key contributions to missiological thought. First, he emphasizes obedience to Christ's commands; true learning of biblical truth results in appropriate action. He further argues, Scripture has an inherent simplicity that church planters must keep in their teaching content and curriculum design. Thirdly, he insists teaching relate to the current needs and activities of the audience. Lastly, he advocates a leadership training model through extension education which produces reproducing churches.

Summarizing this section, the progress of missiological thinking sharpens through time. Warneck (1954) tends to focus on theological issues yet realizes the importance of knowing one's audience and using appropriate biblical stories. Dillon (1972) calls for plurality of leadership in every church yet does not address how this works, e.g., with the "big man" complex of New Guinea, the *datu* hierarchy found in the Philippines or the "strong man" complex of South America. His emphasis on the "three selfs" moves us in the general direction of contextualization.

Hesselgrave (1980), the strategist, provides a theological based church planting model that results in an abstract, broad-based model designed to be applicable for all types of cross-cultural church planting. Concrete living examples, as well as the lack of cultural tools, are the model's major weaknesses. While Hesselgrave's insightful model is helpful for a variety of different types of church plants, it is not specific enough, nor does it address pertinent cultural areas. The model's sequence is also suspect in relation to empowering nationals, e.g., leadership training begins in the seventh cycle rather than the moment church planters enter an area.

Patterson (1978), the field practitioner, tries to simplify his obedience oriented model for the common person. Yet it seems simplicity for multiplication sake may sometimes be substituted for contextualization. For example, he challenges mature "student-workers" to multiply themselves in others but does not address how this works in a society controlled by the *caudillo* (strong man).

All the above writers make significant theological contributions to the discipline of missiology in the areas of the concept of the church, doctrine, obedience oriented discipleship, and reproduction of new communities of faith. With the possible exception of Hesselgrave, however, the above writers spend little time addressing cultural issues, either those of the church planter, his or her agency, or the target people. While this is no doubt by design, if these key theological contributions are to become **more** significant, the cultural, contextual, communicational and strategical dimensions, must receive greater emphasis.

Conclusion

Various individuals make significant contributions to missiological research in relation to church planting. Some focus on contextualization through emphasis on worldview and cultural themes. Others concentrate on strategies and communication techniques for evangelism. Some take a theological perspective. But no one integrates the perspectives of theology, anthropology, linguistics, strategy, worldview, management principles, and communication, for a comprehensive, phase-out oriented model that empowers nationals immediately. Consequently, church planters tend to remain evangelists and/or teachers, rather than taking partnership roles; they tend to focus on phase-in activities that bring in new members and maintain existing programs rather than activities that lead to responsible phase-out.

This brief review of a number of missiological writings points out at least one major reason why church planters often fail to empower nationals for ministry. Because our church planting strategies tend to focus on phase-in activities rather than those that facilitate phase-out, church planters all too often spawn national churches full of crippled infants. A comprehensive church planting model that promotes the immediate empowerment of nationals in all aspects of ministry is desperately needed.

Appendix B

A Five Stage Phase-out Oriented Church Planting Model

Preentry	*Preevangelism*	*Evangelism*	*Postevangelism*	*Phase-out*
<u>Key Verses:</u>	<u>Key Verses:</u>	<u>Key Verses:</u>	<u>Key Verses:</u>	<u>Key Verses:</u>
Prov. 19:2, 16:3 Josh. 18:8	Prov. 18:13 I Cor. 9:19 I Chron. 12:32	Acts 26:28-29	I Pet. 4:1-2 Titus1:5	Rom. 15:23 Mark 1:38 Phil. 2:12
<u>Key Word:</u>	<u>Key Word:</u>	<u>Key Word:</u>	<u>Key Word:</u>	<u>Key Word:</u>
Preparing	Perceiving	Presenting	Perfecting	Parting
<u>Description</u>:	<u>Description:</u>	<u>Description:</u>	<u>Description:</u>	<u>Description:</u>
Intellectual and experiencial preparation in Bible, the sciences, and technical areas are completed. Financial support is raised, a team formed, the national language learned, and the surveys completed.	Team(s) move into location(s), language and culture studies reach level four, relationships with key individuals are built, felt needs are addressed, penetrating questions provide ground work for the evangelism stage.	Felt needs are met. Key terms and topics are utilized, relevant modes of communication are followed, and key individuals are targeted. A contextualized, confrontational gospel is presented.	Worship, leadership, functional substitutes, outreach strategies, literature production and dissemination, and church associations are instituted in culturally relevant, yet biblical acceptable ways. Avenues to meet social needs are indigenized.	The team begins programed absences until the entire team is eventually withdrawn physically. Relationships are maintained through letters, visits, tapes, and other means.

Appendix C

A Comprehensive Phase Out Oriented Church Planting Model

Church Planting Team
PREENTRY
Church Planting Team
KINGDOM of GOD
KINGDOM of SATAN
Absent Advisor
Itinerant Advisor
Resident Advisor
Roles: Learner
Ministry
Spirituality
Self Improvement
Evangelist
Teacher
Feedback
Securing
Language
Culture
3 Level
4 Level
PREEVANGELISM
EVANGELISM
PHASE OUT
POST EVANGELISM
PHASE I
PHASE II
PHASE III
PHASE IV
BOOKS LETTERS V
Holy Spirit
Curriculum Development
Leadership Development
Topical Development

Appendix D

CANDIDATE RATING SCALE

Please use the following 5-point scale when using the rating categories:
5 = Outstanding 4 = Very good 3 = Developing 2 = Needs work 1 = Very weak

1. CHURCH PLANTING COMPETENCY Superbly qualified in both training and experience; extremely knowledgeable and competent. A leader in the field.

2. COMMUNICATION SKILLS An outstanding ability to communicate with others; demonstrates unusual clarity of thought; highly articulate; uses innovative methods to present material.

3. VISIONARY PLANNING SKILLS Visionary; actively engages in goal setting; self-directed; develops realistic action plans with measurable objectives.

4. LEADERSHIP/FOLLOWERSHIP. Clearly defines responsibilities and tasks; seeks to develop others into autonomous leaders; celebrates accomplishments of others. Enthusiastically and willingly works with others when they are in leadership; always a constructive team contributor.

5. SENSE OF CALL Unquestioned belief that God has called him/her into ministry; strongly impelled to take the gospel to other people groups; prays avidly for the salvation of the lost of the world.

6 SPIRITUAL MATURITY Restingly available, instantly obedient; always rejoicing/full of praise; fully understands and accepts God's sovereign role in all things. · Unwaivering faith in God; expects God to do great things; fervent in prayer.

7. EVANGELISM/DISCIPLING SKILLS Gifted evangelist; greatly used by the Holy Spirit to bring souls into the Kingdom. A consistent, committed and highly successful discipler of others.

8. PSYCHOLOGICAL MATURITY Confident in the use of God given gifts/abilities; well integrated personality; copes with stress effectively; not anxious or depressed.

9. INTERPERSONAL RELATIONS Consistently is aware of others' feelings and needs; effective pastoral intervention is his/her hallmark. An active listener; others seek him/her out.

10. CROSS-CULTURE ADAPTABILITY Exceptionally creative and culturally insightful; willing to take calculated personal risks; exhilarated by ambiguity; has a sense of humor; resilient; goes as a learner.

11a. SINGLE RELATIONSHIPS Has found ways to be fulfilled in singleness; accepts God's sovereign plan for his/her life; sexual relationships are above reproach.

11b. MARITAL RELATIONSHIPS Marriage exhibits Godliness/fruits of the Spirit; partners are completely fulfilled in each other and seek to build each other up; they are physically affectionate.

12. PARENT/CHILD RELATIONS Children are warm-hearted and growing; unconditional love and acceptance consistently expressed by parents.

Appendix E

Job Description Form

JOB TITLE:

JOB SUMMARY:

DUTIES AND RESPONSIBILITIES:

MINIMUM QUALIFICATIONS:

GIFTS -

EDUCATION -

EXPERIENCE -

GOALS FOR PERSONAL IMPROVEMENT:

TERM OF SERVICE:

ACCOUNTABILITY RELATIONSHIPS:

MENTOR:

REVIEW DATE:

Appendix F

A CHECKLIST FOR CHURCH PLANTERS

The Preentry Stage Checklist
(Learner Role)

I. Some Key Questions

A. *Preparing One's Personal Life*

1. How do I know God has called me to be a cross-cultural church planter?
2. What are the minimal qualifications for Kingdom-based, cross-cultural, pioneer church planting?
3. How do I prepare myself for spiritual warfare? Spiritual development?
4. Do I have the discipline to remain pure spiritually?
5. Who could serve as my mentor?
6. What is my strategy for prayer? Bible reading? Times for meditation?
7. Others?

B. *Participating in Local Church Life*

1. How can I serve the local church?
2. How can I gain experience working with a team? With small groups?
3. What experience do I need to gain in evangelism and church planting?
4. Who could serve as my mentor?
5. In what roles should I become active in the church?
6. Will people from my home church vouch for my Christian character?
7. Do others catch my spiritual fervor?
8. Do others follow my example?
9. Do you focus your spiritual gifts and time on the types of ministries that promote the planting and developing of churches?
10. Others?

C. *Preparing in Biblical/Theological/Missiological Studies*

1. What do I need to know theologically? Politically? Missiologically?
2. How do you plan to address spiritual forces?
3. What key books should be added to my library?
4. Who could serve as my mentor?
5. What courses could be taken on the field?
6. What is my strategy to keep myself current in these areas?
7. What do I need to know about developing a church planting strategy? A philosophy of ministry? A job description?
8. Which church planting models will work well cross-culturally?

What assumptions drive them?
9. What role changes should church planters pass through?
10. What role changes do nationals experience?
11. Do I have an insatiable desire to learn?
12. Others?

D. ***Preparing in Cross-cultural Studies***

1. What do I need to learn about language acquisition?
2. What do I need to learn about culture acquisition?
3. What anthropological, historical, political, economic and religious studies have been done on the target people?
4. Who would serve as my mentor?
5. Others?

E. ***Agency Interaction***

1. Which agencies focus on the type of church planting I'd like to do?
2. What questions should I ask before joining an agency?
3. What questions should I ask before becoming a member of a church-planting team?
4. What type of personnel is needed to build a well-balanced team?
5. Who should lead the team?
6. What type of people will the team target?
7. What religious groups (national and expatriates) presently work with this people group?
8. What is the team's Vision Statement?
9. Is there gmeone who can sponsor the team into the community?
10. What does the government require of expatriates working in that country?
11. What type of supply line will the team need to establish?
12. How much will it cost to prepare for church planting? To move to the host country? To live in the host country?
13. Others?

F. ***Evaluating the Stage***

1. How could the team have better prepared for the Preentry Stage?
2. Do team members keep their eyes open for routine that stifles personal growth?
3. Others?

II. PREENTRY Faith Objectives

A. ***Preparing One's Personal Life***

1. Devise a spiritual warfare strategy.
2. Devise a spiritual development strategy.
3. Establish a mentor relationship.
4. Others?

B. ***Participating in Local Church Life***

1. Gain home and cross-cultural ministry experience.

2. Secure character confirmation from your home church.
3. Secure a prayer and financial support base.
4. Establish a mentor relationship.
5. Solicit prayer for a sovereignly prepared sponsor among the target audience.
6. Solicit prayer for team unity.
7. Solicit prayer for target people.
8. Others?

C. *Preparing in Biblical/Theological/Missiological Studies*

1. Acquire an experiential knowledge of the Bible.
2. Acquire an experiential knowledge of missiology.
3. Acquire an experiential knowledge of vocational skills.
4. Acquire a working knowledge of animism.
5. Acquire a working knowledge of the economic and political philosophies of the target country and people group.
6. Establish a mentor relationship.
7. Others?

D. *Preparing in Cross-Cultural Studies*

1. Acquire an experiential knowledge of language acquisition.
2. Acquire an experiential knowledge of culture acquisition.
3. Gain cross-cultural experience in ministry.
4. Establish a mentor relationship.
5. Others?

E. *Interacting with an Agency*

1. Select a sending agency.
2. Build a team.

   a. Pray for a team.
   b. Take test instruments to determine work style preference, leadership style preference, learning style preference and spiritual gifts.
   c. Form a balanced team.
   d. Choose a team leader.
   e. Establish a sense of community and loyalty.
   f. Establish a plan for resolving conflict.[1]
   g. Others?

3. Strategize to accomplish the task.

   a. Gather historical data on the targeted people group.
   b. Agree on a team Vision Statement.
   c. Agree on a Translation Strategy.
   d. Agree on a Community Development Strategy.
   e. Agree on a Church Planting Strategy.
   f. Define the gospel.
   g. Define the Chronological Teaching approach.
   h. Distinguish the changing roles of a church planter.

i. Agree on a Philosophy of Ministry.
j. Write job descriptions for each team member.
k. Agree to adapt all strategies as necessary.
l. Others?

4. Allocate the team(s) in the selected country.

a. Build relationships with key members of the community.
b. Gain a working knowledge of the host country's language and culture.
c. Complete demographics of the targeted people.
d. Revise the team Vision Statement and all strategies.
e. Choose future locations of team members.
f. Others?

5. Allocate the team(s) among the target people.

a. Establish a support base.
b. Find a sponsor to introduce team members into the community.
c. Allocate the team(s) to the designated areas.
d. Build relationships with key members of the community.
e. Others?

F. ***Evaluating the Stage***

1. Evaluate the Preentry Stage formatively and summatively.
2. Publish relevant findings.
3. Revise the team's Vision Statement and all strategies.
4. Identify routine activities that stifle individual growth.
5. Others?

III. PREENTRY Checklist

1. *Warfare strategy*
   Date begun ______ Date completed ______
2. *Biblical studies*
   Date begun ______ Date completed ______
3. *Missiological studies*
   Date begun ______ Date completed ______
4. *Character confirmation*
   Date begun ______ Date completed ______
5. *Select agency*
   Date begun ______ Date completed ______
6. *Locate supporters*
   Date begun ______ Date completed ______
7. *Form team*
   Date begun ______ Date completed ______
8. *Gather historical data*
   Date begun ______ Date completed ______
9. *Design strategies*
   Date begun ______ Date completed ______
10. *Write job descriptions*
    Date begun ______ Date completed ______

11. *Move to host country*
    Date begun _______ Date completed _______
12. *Build relationships*
    Date begun _______ Date completed _______
13. *Study language/culture (host country)*
    Date begun _______ Date completed _______
14. *Demographics*
    Date begun _______ Date completed _______
15. *Craft strategies*
    Date begun _______ Date completed _______
16. *Establish support base*
    Date begun _______ Date completed _______
17. *Locate sponsor*
    Date begun _______ Date completed _______
18. *Allocate team*
    Date begun _______ Date completed _______
19. *Build relationships*
    Date begun _______ Date completed _______
20. *Publish findings*
    Date begun _______ Date completed _______
21. *Evaluate Preentry stage*
    Date begun _______ Date completed _______

The Preevangelism Stage Checklist (Learner Role)

I. Some Key Questions

A. *Earning the Right to Be Heard*

1. How can team members win the target people's confidence?
2. How does data collected previously compare with present experience?
3. How should linguistic and cultural information be gathered and stored for team retrieval? For field retrieval?
4. How do the people resolve conflict?
5. What are the people's felt needs?
6. How do the people socialize their young?
7. How has the international scene influenced local economics? Politics? Education? Religion?
8. Others?

B. *Being Heard By the Right People*

1. What roles will team members take in the community? What roles will be assigned by the people?
2. Who are the key decision-makers of the community that should be targeted for friendship and evangelism? Who are the people of peace?
3. Who from the community should serve as language and culture assistants?
4. How can your circle of friends be expanded?

5. How can the team prepare the people for the evangelism stage?
6. What social programs should be initiated? Who decides?
7. Others?

C. *Preparing for Oral Teaching*

1. Where are the natural people flows?
2. What are possible bridges for the gospel? Possible barriers?
3. Is there more than one world view represented within the people group?
4. What should team members do to prepare themselves for the Evangelism Stage?
5. How do you plan to address spiritual forces?
6. How does the new information gathered challenge the existing strategies?
7. When should verbal evangelism begin?
8. Others?

D. *Preparing for Curriculum Development*

1. Which nationals should be involved in curriculum development?
2. What materials presently exist? How effective are they?
3. What types of materials are needed?
4. What delivery systems exist? Should be developed?
4. What should be included in the evangelism curricula?
5. How will the publications be funded?
6. How will you assure materials are culturally relevant?
7. Others?

E. *Evaluating the Stage*

1. How could the team have prepared better for the Preevangelism Stage?
2. How does the team keep from routine activities that stifle personal growth and the development of nationals?
3. Others?

II. PREEVANGELISM Faith Objectives

A. *Earning the Right to Be Heard*

1. Devise a spiritual warfare strategy.
2. Incarnate the character of Christ.
3. Reach level four in language acquisition.
4. Reach level four in culture acquisition.
5. Identify existing churches and their effectiveness.
6. Build relationships with national Christians.
7. Build relationships with key members of the community.
8. Establish times for prayer.
9. Address felt needs in a culturally relevant way.
10. Others?

B. ***Being Heard By the Right People***

1. Identify key decision-makers of the community.
2. Develop quality "redemptive relationships" with key decision-makers.
3. Challenge your friends to seek truth through the use of perceptive questions related to the spirit world.
4. Communicate the team's nonpermanency (where applicable).
5. Others?

C. ***Preparing for Oral Teaching***

1. Define culturally acceptable modes of communication.
2. Identify gathering places.
3. Identify bridges and barriers to the gospel through collecting key terms and topics (myths).
4. Identify a neutral time and place for conducting evangelism.
5. Establish a means of gaining reliable feedback.
6. How do they tell stories? When? What types? How long?
7. Revise all the team's strategies.
8. Others?

D. ***Preparing for Curriculum Development***

1. Evaluate the strengths and weaknesses of written materials.
2. Gather a group of nationals to assist in the production of curricula.
3. Develop criteria for written and taped materials.
4. Contextualize Phase I of the Chronological Teaching approach.
5. Prepare culturally relevant felt needs materials.
6. Prepare culturally relevant visual aids.
7. Others?

E. ***Evaluating the Stage***

1. Evaluate the Preevangelism Stage formatively and summatively.
2. Publish relevant findings.
3. Revise the team Vision Statement and all strategies.
4. Identify routine activities that stifle personal growth and the development of nationals?
5. Others?

III. PREEVANGELISM Checklist

1. *Warfare strategy*
   Date begun ________ Date completed ________
2. *Language Objectives:*
   Level One
   Date begun ________ Date completed ________
   Level Two
   Date begun ________ Date completed ________
   Level Three
   Date begun ________ Date completed ________

Level Four
Date begun ________ Date completed ________

3. *Culture Objectives:*
Level One
Date begun ________ Date completed ________
Level Two
Date begun ________ Date completed ________
Level Three
Date begun ________ Date completed ________
Level Four
Date begun ________ Date completed ________

4. *Prayer times*
Date begun ________ Date completed ________
5. *Meet felt needs*
Date begun ________ Date completed ________
6. *Identify national believers*
Date begun ________ Date completed ________
7. *Identify decision-makers*
Date begun ________ Date completed ________
8. *Challenge worldview*
Date begun ________ Date completed ________
9. *Identify bridges and barriers to gospel*
Date begun ________ Date completed ________
10. *Discern learning styles*
Date begun ________ Date completed ________
11. *Identify evangelism time and place*
Date begun ________ Date completed ________
12. *Draft Phase I (evangelism stories)*
Date begun ________ Date completed ________
13. *Draft felt needs materials*
Felt need 1
Date begun ________ Date completed ________
Felt need 2
Date begun ________ Date completed ________
14. *Develop visual aids*
Date begun ________ Date completed ________
15. *Secure feedback*
Date begun ________ Date completed ________
16. *Recraft strategies*
Date begun ________ Date completed ________
17. *Develop relationships*
Date begun ________ Date completed ________
18. *Publish findings*
Date begun ________ Date completed ________
19. *Incarnate Christ*
Date begun ________ Date completed ________
20. *Develop relationships*
Date begun ________ Date completed ________

The Evangelism Stage Checklist (Learner, Evangelist Roles)

I. Some Key Questions

A. *Communicating A Holistic Message*

1. Are the people's felt needs being addressed?
2. What is the gospel?
3. What are the bridges and barriers to the reception of the gospel?
4. What redemptive analogies exist within the culture?
5. What cultural barriers should be challenged in the gospel presentation?
6. What key terms should be gathered? What key topics (myths)?
7. Where, when, how often, how long, to whom, should the gospel message be communicated?
8. Are decisions made individually? As a family? As a group?
9. How much background information should be presented so that the true meaning of the gospel will be comprehended?
10. How can the gospel message be presented so that the content also builds a platform for ongoing discipleship?
11. What does it mean to the target people to "pray this prayer"? Ask Jesus into your heart? Come forward? Repeat this phrase?
12. Are there other nationals that could assist in evangelism?
13. What is the social cost for a family to follow Christ?
14. How will you know if the gospel is comprehended?
15. How do you plan to address the spiritual forces?
16. Who could serve as your sponsor into a community?
17. Others?

B. *Utilizing Indigenous Learning Styles*

1. What teaching methodology will work best with these people?
2. What are five effective cultural illustrations for evangelizing?
3. Are radio broadcasts a possibility? Drama? Story? Other media?
4. What type of teaching aids should be produced?
5. What questions do people ask when they hear the gospel?
6. What strategies are other agencies using? How effective are they?
7. What strategies are nationals using? How effective are they?
8. Others?

C. *Developing A Holistic Curricula*

1. What questions do the audiences continue to raise?
2. What evangelistic materials currently exists? How effective are they?
3. Is the existing curricula reproducible by nationals on the lowest skill level?
4. Others?

D. *Evaluating the Stage*

1. How could the team have better prepared for the Evangelism Stage?

2. How does the team keep from routine activities that stifle personal growth and the development of nationals?
3. What records should be kept to preserve the advancement of the Kingdom of God among this people?
4. Others?

II. EVANGELISM Faith Objectives

A. *Communicating A Holistic Message*

1. Devise a strategy for spiritual warfare.
2. Continue to incarnate Christ.
3. Study the effectiveness of present evangelism approaches.
4. Locate a sponsor (person of peace).
5. Continue to address felt needs.
6. Present an adequate foundation for the gospel using the people's preferred learning style and illustrations.
7. Communicate the gospel to key decision-makers and their followers.
8. Include contradictions as well as conformities in your gospel presentation.
9. Establish a means of gaining reliable feedback.
10. List questions that the people raise so that repeated questions can be addressed in oral teaching and in the curricula.
11. Determine the outcome of the gospel presentation.
12. Pursue the natural flow of the gospel message.
13. Maintain records of new believers.
14. Determine how to equip new Christians without isolating non-Christians.
15. Build relationships with key members of the community.
16. Others?

B. *Utilizing Indigenous Learning Styles*

1. Analyze the socialization patterns for different age levels in the community.
2. Analyze discourse features from a broad spectrum of stories used in the community.
3. Discern the types of questions used in discourse.
4. Discern the purposes for the various types of meetings held within the community.
5. Others?

C. *Developing A Holistic Curricula*

1. Analyze questions raised by the audience during the Phase I presentation.
2. Revise Phase I draft.
3. Draft Phase II (for new believers).
4. Revise existing felt need materials and draft new ones.
5. Others?

D. *Evaluating the Stage*

1. Evaluate the Evangelism Stage formatively and summatively.
2. Publish relevant findings.
3. Revise the team Vision Statement and all strategies.
4. Identify routine activities that stifle personal growth and the development of nationals.
5. Others?

III. EVANGELISM Checklist

1. *Warfare strategy*
   Date begun _______ Date completed ______
2. *Locate sponsor*
   Date begun _______ Date completed ______
3. *Evaluate methods*
   Date begun _______ Date completed ______
4. *Meet felt needs*
   Date begun _______ Date completed ______
5. *Secure feedback*
   Date begun _______ Date completed ______
6. *Visual aids*
   Date begun _______ Date completed ______
7. *Teach Phase I (evangelism stories)*
   Date begun _______ Date completed ______
8. *Revise Phase I*
   Date begun _______ Date completed ______
9. *Identify new believers*
   Date begun _______ Date completed ______
10. *Draft Phase II (new believers)*
    Date begun _______ Date completed ______
11. *Recraft strategies*
    Date begun _______ Date completed ______
12. *Begin records for new believers*
    Date begun _______ Date completed ______
13. *Incarnate Christ*
    Date begun _______ Date completed ______
14. *Develop relationships*
    Date begun _______ Date completed ______

The Postevangelism Stage Checklist
(Learner, Evangelist, Teacher, Resident Advisor Roles)

I. Some Key Questions

A. *Equipping Believers*

1. What will a church look like among this people?
2. What are traditional meetings like? When are they held? Where? Why are they called? How long do they last? How often are they called? Who leads? Who participates? Who closes?
3. How far do they travel? How long do they stay? What can be expected in outreach?

4. What traditional behaviors should remain? Which should change? Which must cease?
5. What are five effective illustrations that can be used in teaching?
6. What type of teaching aids should be produced? By whom? How will it be funded? Distributed?
7. Are radio / TV broadcasts a possibility? Cassette tapes? Videos?
8. How can the message be contextualized?
9. What cultural barriers should be challenged in the message?
10. How do you plan to address spiritual forces?
11. What are the people's expectations about a place for religious purposes?
12. What theologies will the architecture and sanctuary express?
13. What will people say about the geographic location of the church in five years?
14. Others?

B. ***Equipping Equippers***

1. What is traditional leadership like? Traditional followership? How do they perpetuate these roles?
2. What is traditional discipline like? How do the leaders resolve conflict?
3. What role changes should team members be passing through?
4. What role changes should national leaders be passing through?
5. Is an association of churches needed? Mission agency (home and crosscultural)?
6. What should be included in the constitution?
7. Are the Christians being integrated functionally into the larger communities?
8. Can the churches survive economically?
9. Others?

C. ***Instituting Biblical Functional Substitutes***

1. How do the people use traditional prayer? Music?
2. Do the people use water ceremonially? How many should profess Christ before initiating baptism?
3. Do the people have formal / informal rituals that constitute belongingness? What stories accompany the rituals?
5. How do they use food and drink ceremonially? How will they interpret communion?
6. How do the people define giving?
7. How do they view the spirit world?
8. What do people do to protect themselves before embarking on a trip?
9. In what areas is syncretism present?
10. How will birth, marriage, initiation rights, and death be handled? What biblical functional substitutes are needed?
11. Others?

D. ***Developing and Disseminating Curricula***

1. What materials do the believers want published?
2. Who should be involved in the writing, production and

dissemination?
3. What types of visual aids will the target population find most meaningful?
4. What colors do they prefer?
5. Others?

E. *Evaluating the Stage*

1. How could the team have better prepared for the Postevangelism Stage?
2. How does the team keep from routine activities that stifle personal growth and the development of nationals?
3. What records should be kept to preserve the advancement of the Kingdom of God among this people?
4. Others?

II. POSTEVANGELISM Faith Objectives

A. *Equipping Believers*

1. Facilitate qualitative growth in worship.
2. Facilitate qualitative growth in instruction.
3. Facilitate qualitative growth in sociality.
4. Facilitate quantitative growth in evangelism and church planting.
5. Facilitate the believer's integration into the larger community.
6. Establish a means of gaining reliable feedback.
7. Build relationships with key members of the community.
8. Ascertain the use of facilities for religious purposes.
9. Others?

B. *Equipping Equippers*

1. Facilitate the immediate development of biblically qualified, indigenous leadership for local and itinerant roles.
2. Facilitate the development of a constitution.
3. Facilitate the planting and development of daughter and granddaughter churches.
4. Facilitate the development of an association of churches.
5. Facilitate the development of a mission agency.
6. Build relationships with key members of the community.
7. Others?

C. *Instituting Biblical Functional Substitutes*

1. Identify traditional ritual areas and accompanying stories.
2. Facilitate the introduction of biblical functional substitutes.
3. Others?

D. *Developing and Disseminating Curricula*

1. Facilitate the production and publication of culturally relevant curricula.
2. Facilitate the development of culturally relevant visual aids.
3. Facilitate the dissemination of published materials.

4. Others?

E. *Evaluating the Stage*

1. Evaluate the Postevangelism Stage formatively and summatively.
2. Publish relevant findings.
3. Revise the team Vision Statement and all strategies.
4. Identify routine activities that stifle personal growth and the development of nationals?
5. Others?

III. POSTEVANGELISM Checklist

1. *Warfare strategy*
   Date begun ________ Date completed ________
2. *Meet felt needs*
   Date begun ________ Date completed ________
3. *Secure feedback*
   Date begun ________ Date completed ________
4. *Constitution*
   Date begun ________ Date completed ________
5. *Christian integration*
   Date begun ________ Date completed ________
6. *Draft Phases II-IV*
   Date begun ________ Date completed ________
7. *Teach Phases II-IV*
   Date begun ________ Date completed ________
8. *Revise Phases II-IV*
   Date begun ________ Date completed ________
9. *Publish Phases I-IV*
   Date begun ________ Date completed ________
10. *Topical teaching Topic ...*
    Date begun ________ Date completed ________
    Topic ...
    Date begun ________ Date completed ________
    Topic ...
    Date begun ________ Date completed ________
11. *Book studies Book ...*
    Date begun ________ Date completed ________
    Book ...
    Date begun ________ Date completed ________
    Book ...
    Date begun ________ Date completed ________
12. *Disseminate curricula*
    Date begun ________ Date completed ________
13. *Biblical functional substitute Substitute 1*
    Date begun ________ Date completed ________
    Substitute 2
    Date begun ________ Date completed ________
    Substitute 3
    Date begun ________ Date completed ________
14. *Develop leaders Group 1*
    Date begun ________ Date completed ________

Group 2
Date begun ________ Date completed ________
Group 3
Date begun ________ Date completed ________

15. *Develop followers Group 1*
Date begun ________ Date completed ________
Group 2
Date begun ________ Date completed ________
Group 3
Date begun ________ Date completed ________
16. *Daughter churches Church 1*
Date begun ________ Date completed ________
Church 2
Date begun ________ Date completed ________
Church 3
Date begun ________ Date completed ________
17. *Association of churches*
Date begun ________ Date completed ________
18. *Mission agency*
Date begun ________ Date completed ________
19. *Recraft strategies*
Date begun ________ Date completed ________
20. *Publish findings*
Date begun ________ Date completed ________
21. *Incarnate Christ*
Date begun ________ Date completed ________
22. *Develop relationships*
Date begun ________ Date completed ________

The Phase-out Stage Checklist (Learner, Itinerant Advisor, Absent Advisor Roles)

I. Some Key Questions

A. Implementing Phase-out

1. How do team members know when their work is completed?
2. How should the team members withdraw from a church plant?
3. Are the spiritual needs of the second generation Christians being met?
4. Are the Christians being integrated functionally into the larger communities?
5. How does the team maintain relationships in absentia?
6. What other curricula should be produced?
7. What other part-time ministries should team members pursue?
8. What must be done to develop a mission agency?
9. How do you plan to address spiritual forces?
10. Others?

B. *Evaluating the Stage*

1. How could the team have better prepared for the Phase-out Stage?
2. How does the team keep from routine activities that stifle personal growth and the development of nationals?
3. What records should be kept to preserve the advancement of the Kingdom of God among this people?
4. Others?

II. PHASE-OUT Faith Objectives

A. *Implementing Phase-out*

1. Establish programmed absences for team members.
2. Facilitate the of integration of believers into the larger communities.
3. Facilitate the development of biblical qualified, indigenous leadership for permanent and itinerant roles.
4. Facilitate the development of multi-generational churches.
5. Facilitate the development of daughter churches.
6. Facilitate the development of a mission agency.
7. Facilitate the publication and distribution of relevant curricula.
8. Secure new part-time ministry.
9. Establish some means to maintain relationships in absentia.
10. Others?

B. *Evaluating the Stage*

1. Evaluate the Phase-out Stage formatively and summatively.
2. Publish relevant findings.
3. Revise the team Vision Statement and all strategies.
4. Identify routine activities that stifle personal growth and the development of nationals?
5. Others?

III. PHASE-OUT Checklist

1. *Warfare strategy*
   Date begun _______ Date completed _______
2. *Program absences*
   Date begun ______ Date completed _______
3. *Christian integration*
   Date begun ______ Date completed _______
4. *Generational needs*
   Date begun ______ Date completed _______
5. *Develop leaders Group 1*
   Date begun ______ Date completed _______
   Group 2
   Date begun ______ Date completed _______
   Group 3
   Date begun ______ Date completed _______

6. *Develop followers*
   Group 1
   Date begun ______ Date completed ______
   Group 2
   Date begun ______ Date completed ______
   Group 3
   Date begun ______ Date completed ______
7. *Daughter churches*
   Church 1
   Date begun ______ Date completed ______
   Church 2
   Date begun ______ Date completed ______
   Church 3
   Date begun ______ Date completed ______
   Church 4
   Date begun ______ Date completed ______
8. *Association of churches*
   Date begun ______ Date completed ______
9. *Mission agency*
   Date begun ______ Date completed ______
10. *Publish findings*
    Date begun ______ Date completed ______
11. *Secure new ministry*
    Date begun ______ Date completed ______
12. *Maintain relationships*
    Date begun ______ Date completed ______

1 See Rick Love's *Peacemaking* (1995) for some helpful materials.

Appendix G

Putting My Vision Into Action

My Name______________________________ Date____________

My Goal (Specifically stated with an action verb)	Projected Date of Achievement
______________________________	
______________________________	
______________________________	
______________________________	

Obstacles to overcome.
1.
2.
3.
4.
5.
6.
7.
8.
9.
10.

What I need to Know/Learn to accomplish the goal.
1.
2.
3.
4.
5.
6.
7.
8.
9.
10.

Who are the significant People that I need to involve?
1.
2.
3.
4.
5.
6.
7.
8.
9.

Appendix G

What is my Action Plan? (Specific steps to accomplish the Goal.)	Target Date	Projected Cost
1. ______	______	______
2. ______	______	______
3. ______	______	______
4. ______	______	______
5. ______	______	______
6. ______	______	______
7. ______	______	______
8. ______	______	______
9. ______	______	______
10______	______	______
Total Estimated Costs		

Key Results (Expected Benefits)
1. ______
2. ______
3. ______
4. ______
5. ______
6. ______
7. ______
8. ______
9. ______
10.

Faith/Prayer Targets--Specific things to pray for. (How God will need to intervene)	Date Answered
1. ______	______
2. ______	______
3. ______	______
4. ______	______
5. ______	______
6. ______	______
7. ______	______
8. ______	______
9. ______	______
10.	

Notes:

Appendix H

Distinguishing Types of Societies

Types of societies:	Postindustrial	Industrial	Peasant	Tribal
Universals:				
Material culture				
housing	comfort, privacy, individuality	uniform, pragmatic	protection, utility	protection
energy	nuclear, thermal,fiber optics multi-source	fossil fuel, water single source	fire human, animal, tools	fire huma n, animal, tools
travel	spatially international	spatially extended	spatially restricted	spatially extensive
Social organization				
family	private individualism	divided nuclear family	nuclear family a unit	extended family
children	limited by abortion, pill	desired, wage earners	desired, field workers	desired, social security
marriage	love	love	economics	economics
age	some esteem	little esteem	more esteem	great esteem
death	the end, reincarnation	lives on in heaven, hell	lives on in heaven, hell	lives on, has needs
Government				
officials	majority vote	majority vote	ascribed	achieved, ascribed
authority	decentralized	centralized	centralized	egalitarian
legitimacy	international, national law	national law	fuedual lord	tradition
sphere	global	national, city	local	local
control	state & federal laws, propaganda, warfare	state & federal laws, propaganda, warfare	shame, gossip, civil law, revolution	shame, gossip, sorcery tribal law, warfare
Economics				
land ownership	individual, government	some individual,	fuedal lord	gods, families
land use	recreation, privacy, sell	government resources	cultivation, domesticated animals	foraging,hunting
work sphere	office	factory	field	forest

Appendix H

Types of socities:	Postindustrial	Industrial	Peasant	Tribal
Universals:				
Economics, cont.				
economy base	labor, capital, energy, organizing information	labor, capital, energy	labor, land	labor, land
production purpose	profit exchange, self-fulfill- ment, improve environment,	profit exchange, surplus	surplus, consumption	consumpsion
product specialization	customized, small batch optimum	standardized, mass batch maximum	individualized minimum	individualized little
Socialization				
memory	museum, library, computer	museum, library	myths, legends, few books	myths, legends
type	formal, nonformal	formal, if time	apprenticeship,	informal, some formal
location	home, school	school	formal school, life	some school, life
cognitive style	abstract	abstract, concrete	concrete	concrete
synthesis	analysis	holistic	holistic	
teacher	specialist	specialist	elder	elder
subject	interdisciplinary	functional specialization	functional specialization	functional for life
duration	prescribed times, lifelong	prescribed times	prescribed times, lifelong	lifelong
Science and supernatural				
life perspective	pessimistic	optimistic	fatalistic	fatalistic
time	segmented, linear future oriented	segmented, linear future oriented	agriculture cycle present oriented	agriculture cycle past, present orient
change	good, rapid	good, continual	good, slow	dangerous
recreation	set times	set times	completion of activity	when needs met
values	pluralistic, change	standardized	standardized	unquestioned
religion	materialism, humanism "group conscience"	materialism secularism, individual	dichotomistic	holistic, benevolent and malevolent spirits
practicioners	professional, specialist maintenance of institution	professional, generalist maintenance of society	professional maintenance of instit	parttime maintenance of society

	THIRD WAVE	SECOND WAVE	FIRST WAVE
	1950	1750	

Appendix I

The Antipolo / Amduntug Annual Work Cycle

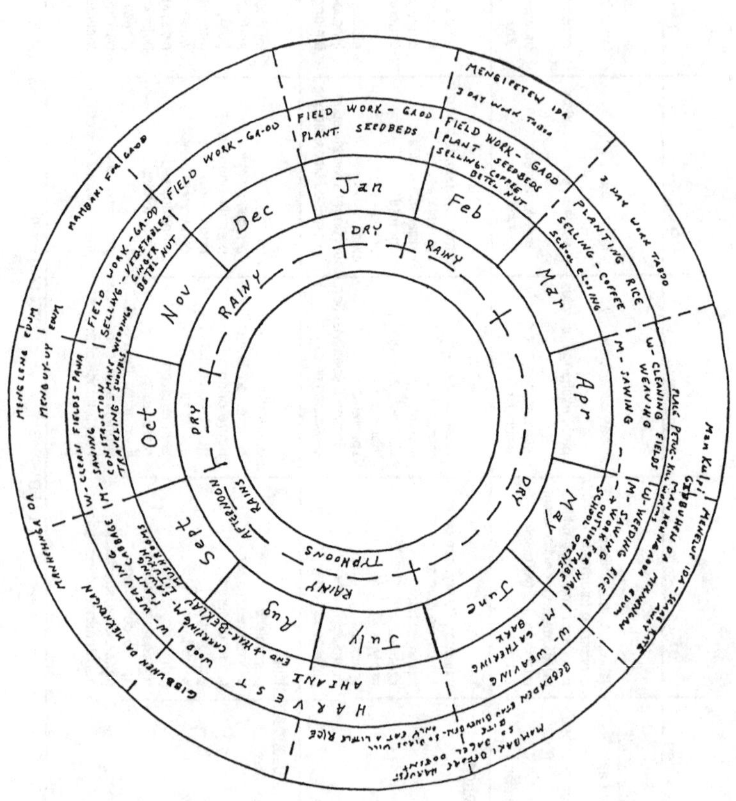

Appendix J

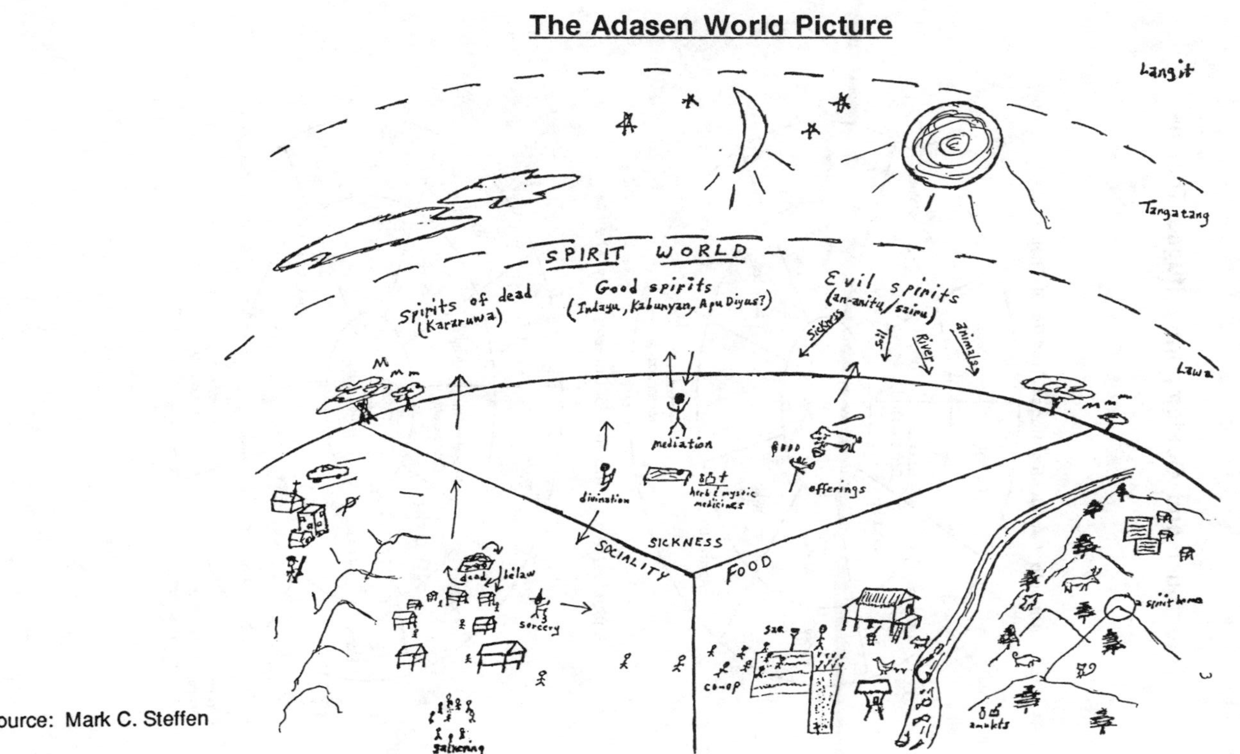

Source: Mark C. Steffen

Appendix K

Traditional and Contemporary Ifugao Themes

Antipolo / Amduntug Ifugao Traditional Themes

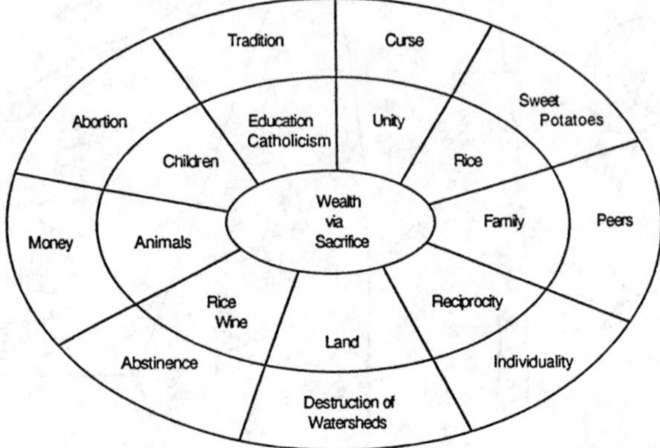

Antipolo / Amduntug Ifugao Contemporary Themes

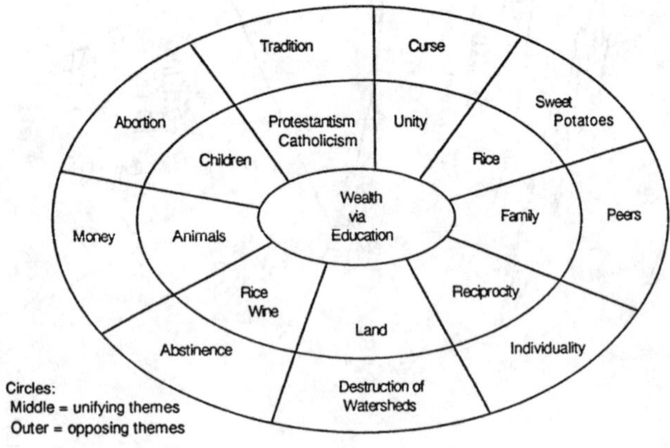

Appendix L

Socialization Among the Antipolo / Amduntug Ifugao

Socialization agent / Age	Parents	Children	Outsider / Insider					
			Traditional Religion	Catholicism	Protestantism	Councilmen	School	Peers
Prebirth	Centrality of children and religion	Soul - spirit						
2-6 years	Distancing	Confusion						
6-10 years	Patience	Responsibility						
10-15 years	Patience	Contributor to work force						
15 years and on	Respect / humor	Adult status						

Appendix M

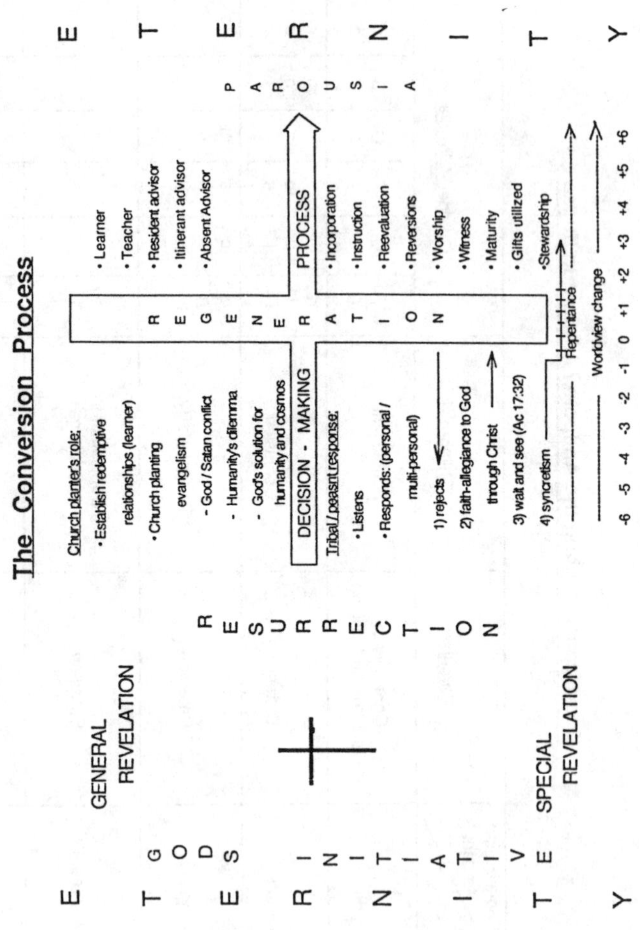

The Conversion Process
ETERNITY
GODS
INITIATIVE
GENERAL REVELATION
SPECIAL REVELATION
RESURRECTION
Church planter's role:
• Establish redemptive relationships (learner)
• Church planting evangelism
- God / Satan conflict
- Humanity's dilemma
- God's solution for humanity and cosmos
DECISION - MAKING
Tribal / peasnt response:
• Listens
• Responds: (personal / multi-personal)
1) rejects
2) faith-allegiance to God through Christ
3) wait and see (Ac 17:32)
4) syncretism
REGENERATION
• Learner
• Teacher
• Resident advisor
• Itinerant advisor
• Absent Advisor
PROCESS
• Incorporation
• Instruction
• Reevaluation
• Reversions
• Worship
• Witness
• Maturity
• Gifts utilized
• Stewardship
Repentance
Worldview change
-6 -5 -4 -3 -2 -1 0 +1 +2 +3 +4 +5 +6
PAROUSIA
ETERNITY

Appendix N

PHASE I OBJECTIVES

GENERAL OBJECTIVE:

Upon the completion of this phase the Ifugao should be able to comprehend a personal God who defeated Satan and provided a provisional substitute for humanity's salvation from sin through Jesus Christ, and appropriate this provision by faith.

SPECIFIC OBJECTIVES:

Word: Agree the Bible, God's Word, is superior to tradition for daily life and practice.

God: Acknowledge the God who created them is all-powerful in one's personal life, and over Satan and the demons.

Recognize God's holiness disallows their communion with him.

React positively to God's unconditional love in providing a substitute for their sin.

Satan: Identify Satan as the originator of all sin and the Father of all unsaved.

Access Satan's domination of the world system and its resulting affect upon them.

Desire to avoid God's impending judgment of Satan and all those related to him.

Humanity: Define their part in the great conflict now being waged between God and Satan.

Acknowledge their sin is the cause of their separation from God.

Appropriate Jesus Christ as God's provisional substitute for their salvation.

Rejoice in their new relationship with God through their mediator Jesus Christ.

World: Respect God's physical creation.

Appendix O

Chronological Teaching Evaluation Form

TEACHER: __________ AUDIENCE: __________
DATE: ______________ PHASE: __________
--

1. What level are you in language? _________ culture? ___________

2. How many times have you previously taught this phase crossculturally? _____

3. What religions are present in your area, including animism? ____________

4. Check your target audience:

mixed group _________ men's group ________ lady 's group __________
family _____________ individual _________ youth group __________
children ___________ other ____________

5. How many teaching sessions were needed to cover this phase? _________

6. What was the total length of time to cover this phase? __________

7. What was the average attendance per lesson? __________

8. What was the average time to cover a lesson? __________

9. How many stories were taught before the gospel was presented? _________

10. Which stories stood out to the audience? Why?

11. Which stories did not stand out to the audience? Why?

12. Which book studies stood out to the audience? Why?

13. Which book studies did not stand out to the audience? Why?

14. What do you consider the strengths of this phase?

15. What do you consider the weaknesses of this phase?

16. What suggestions would you make to improve this phase?

17. Who is involved in writing this phase?

18. How is / will this phase be distributed?

19. Have national teachers taught this phase? What are their commendations and criticisms? How have they changed it?

20. What was the reaction to any form of oral communication (song, drama, etc.) used along with this phase? Explain.